7

D1001139

Y

PATG 00- B9442

Introduction to Research and the Psychology of Music

Also by Edwin E. Gordon:

A Music Learning Theory for Newborn and Young Children

The Psychology of Music Teaching

Learning Sequences in Music: Skill, Content, and Patterns

Study Guide for Learning Sequences in Music

The Nature, Description, Measurement, and Evaluation of Music Aptitudes

Designing Objective Research in Music Education

Musical Aptitude Profile

Iowa Tests of Music Literacy

Primary Measures of Music Audiation

Intermediate Measures of Music Audiation

Advanced Measures of Music Audiation

Guiding Your Child's Music Development

Audie

Introduction to Research and The Psychology of Music

Edwin E. Gordon
Distinguished Professor in Residence
University of South Carolina

G-4855

GIA Publications, Inc.
Chicago

Library of Congress Cataloging-in-Publication Data

Gordon, Edwin, 1927–
  Introduction to research and the psychology of music / Edwin E. Gordon
  p. cm.
  Includes bibliographical references (p.) and index.
  ISBN 1-57999-016-9
  1. Musical ability. I. Title
ML3838.65 1998
  153.9′478—dc21   98-12260
                                                            CIP
                                                            MN

Introduction to Research and The Psychology of Music
by Edwin E. Gordon
Copyright © 1998 GIA Publications, Inc.
7404 S. Mason Ave., Chicago, IL 60638
International copyright secured
ISBN: 1-57999-016-9
Printed in U.S.A.

TABLE OF CONTENTS

FOREWORD

Great musical minds live and work in a wide world with narrow boundaries that are self-imposed and defined by aptitude. They do not seek that world, nor are they taught about it. They are born into it and they learn to give it and themselves refinement. As those minds mature in their work, they are sustained technically and philosophically by their environment. Without them we would have no musical culture. We are free to enter their world, to enjoy their art with them, and to learn from them. We should not expect that they strive to enter our world or understand us. Thus, it is our responsibility not to be intimidated by them, but to aid them in building and maintaining their world so that they will have the freedom to pursue their work and, in turn, reward us by enriching our world.

PREFACE

Though it does not seem long ago to me, I would not be surprised if you were an infant or were not even born when I published my first book in 1967. The book, *How Children Learn When They Learn Music*, was an outgrowth of my interest in music learning theory. Although few music educators at the time were concerned with the theory behind music learning, most were aware of its importance in practical application. My own curiosity was aroused primarily because after the *Musical Aptitude Profile (MAP)*, my first music aptitude test, was published by Houghton Mifflin in 1965, it was brought to my attention, much to my astonishment, that most, if not all, of the teachers who administered the battery did not know how to make use of the score results. Although instruction was provided in the MAP manual, it soon became apparent that teachers needed more information to help them understand the significance of the score results, and the publisher requested that I gather relevant facts based on research that could then be disseminated to teachers and administrators. That is how what began as a passing interest spurred my research into music aptitude, and this research has commanded my interest to this day, even into my retirement from routine teaching.

It was in 1969 that Prentice-Hall became aware of *How Children Learn When They Learn Music*, which I had been publishing myself, and suggested that it be given world-wide visibility through its company. The organization and title of the book were changed, and the initial printing of *The Psychology of Music Teaching* took place in 1971. The first part was *Musical Aptitude* and the second, *Musical Achievement*. Although the impetus for the book was music learning theory, the part on music aptitude received as much attention as the part on music achievement, and that still remains very much the case today.

As I continued my research in music learning theory and was able to expand extensively the knowledge base on the subject, I wrote another book devoted entirely to music learning theory. *Learning Sequences in Music: Skill, Content, and Patterns* was published by GIA in 1976, and I am currently working on the seventh revision along with the revision of a companion book, *A Music Learning Theory for Newborn and Young Children*, first published in 1990. In 1986 I wrote a separate book on music aptitude, *Musikalische Begabung: Beschaffenheit, Beschreibung, Messung und Bewertung* for the German publisher, Schott, and the following year it became available in English, published by GIA under the title *The Nature, Description, Measurement, and Evaluation of Music*

Aptitude. The need for a book in which music aptitude is the main topic was necessary because only one chapter of a summary nature is devoted to the subject in each of my two music learning theory books.

Not only have there been significant advances in music learning theory in the more than 25 years since 1971, but, relatively speaking, at least as much data have been gathered about music aptitude in the more than 10 years since 1986. Tests have been revised, some have gone out of print, and others have become available even for children of preschool age. More than that, the research on music aptitude and heretofore unrealized related subjects is fascinating as well as compelling and must be brought to the attention of all music educators. Undoubtedly it will have an enormous effect on how they teach music.

There has been a consistent demand for *The Psychology of Music Teaching* since its publication was discontinued in 1983. *Learning Sequences in Music: Skill, Content, and Patterns* was intended to fill the void, but even so, I am continually told, much to my satisfaction, that what is also desired is up-to-date information about music aptitude.

Thus, I have decided to revise the first part of *The Psychology of Music Teaching* and *The Nature, Description, Measurement, and Evaluation of Music Aptitudes* in entirety and combine them into one book. This should serve two important purposes: First, of course, as a presentation of the history and research on music aptitude and how music aptitude tests may be put to practical use in teaching, particularly in adapting instruction to students' individual musical differences. Second, as can be observed in the extensive bibliography, because the objective research base in music aptitude over the past 100 years carries forth a magnificent tradition and touches directly or indirectly on nearly every other aspect of what is typically included under the umbrella of the psychology of music, the book should be found to be valuable in raising compelling questions and suggesting further topics and valid experimental designs to young researchers as they embark on their discipline. I have not only attempted to bring closure to what the richness of the past has to offer, but have attempted to provide a foundation for contemporary and future scholars and researchers as well as to suggest practical purposes especially to those who, in the last few decades, have demonstrated a special interest in the psychology of acoustical phenomena. Moreover, given the temper of the times and the flurry of attention given to what is currently being referred to as criterion-referenced testing, authentic assessment, and alternative assessment, I hope the material in this book will promote a clear understanding and a renewed respect for classical procedures in psychological measurement and evaluation, particularly norms-referenced testing and associated concepts.

As I said in the preface of *The Psychology of Music Teaching,*

In 1931, James L. Mursell wrote in *The Psychology of School Music Teaching,* "There never was a time when music education more urgently needed the help that scientific psychology can give." It can be safely stated that almost forty years later, music educators' professional needs are not materially any less exigent.

Now more than sixty-five years have passed and, relatively speaking, only little has changed. I sincerely hope this book will be responsible to some degree for a change in the measure of the tide.

Edwin E. Gordon
Columbia, South Carolina 1997

CHAPTER 1

INTRODUCTION

Try to recall an incident that you, like most concert goers, have experienced on one or more occasions. You have just attended a school recital and were particularly interested in the performances of two students. Both students had studied with the same teacher for the same length of time, both demonstrated a similar level of technical skill on the same instrument, and both performed compositions of a similar level of difficulty. There were technical errors and lapses of memory in both performances. Still, you were of the opinion that one student had the potential to profit very much by continuing to study music, whereas the other lacked such potential and could profit only minimally by continuing to take lessons. How did you come to that conclusion? Though you may not be able to describe with precision what music aptitude is, your thoughts were based either consciously or unconsciously on what may be considered to be the comparative music aptitudes of the two students.

Moreover, as you listened to the performances of the two students, you were aware, in terms of music achievement, that to some extent one was superior to the other in rhythmic precision and tonal accuracy. That, too, is attributable to relative degrees of tonal aptitude and rhythm aptitude.

What seemed to make the one student outstanding, however, was his or her musical sensitivity, the ability to play with musical expression despite the occasional tonal or rhythm inconsistencies that are common to most young persons' performances. In this case, however, perhaps you also noticed that when such lapses in rhythm and pitch did occur, there was no hesitancy in the student's playing. The student continued to play as if to acknowledge that musical phrasing and expression were the essential ingredients of the performance. To the student, an improper musical solution would, itself, constitute the error. What made the circumstances more compelling is that what the student did came naturally, intuitively, because no one had ever coached the student on the proper way to correct those or other types of errors in performance.

As musicians and educators, whether we are aware of it or not, we are enormously affected by our own and our students' music aptitude. It interacts with all aspects of our professional development and pursuits. Although we know intuitively that it exists, we are at a loss to reify it, let alone describe it. Many persons dispense with the dilemma by simply adhering to the theory that music aptitude is a gift bestowed at birth on some persons and not on others. Such a theory is limited because not only does it ignore, among other factors, environmental influences, it relates only to the source of music aptitude. Moreover, it does not describe the nature of music aptitude, and as a result, it necessarily ignores the need to measure and evaluate students' music aptitude as a way to enhance our own teaching and our ability to advise and guide students honestly in their future studies.

Upon thoughtful reflection about the hypothetical recital you just recalled, it should become clear how important it is for musicians and educators to understand the source, description, measurement, and evaluation of music aptitude in order to make objective musical decisions concerning themselves as well as their students. With knowledge of each student's music aptitude, a teacher may encourage those with high music aptitude to study music. That there is much waste in human potential is substantiated by the fact that approximately half of the students with music aptitude above that of 80 percent of their peers do not receive any special music instruction in or out of school, and many do not even receive ordinary music instruction. Without appropriate instruction in music, no student with high music aptitude will achieve his or her potential. By accurately interpreting and using music aptitude test results, a teacher can also assist students with average and low music aptitudes to maximize their music achievement to the extent that their music aptitudes will allow and to guide them in forming realistic goals should they choose to study music. It is particularly important for parents to know if their child has low music aptitude. There will only be negative effects if parents have misguided hopes for such children and force them to practice when their potential and interests naturally lie elsewhere.

Perhaps even more important is that teachers and parents understand that music aptitude and music achievement are not the same. Music aptitude represents a student's potential to learn, whereas music achievement represents what a student has learned. When music aptitude and music achievement are mistakenly believed to be the same thing, students with high music aptitude who have not had the opportunity to study music, and so cannot demonstrate technical or music achievement, are usually judged to have low music aptitude. Thus, neither they, their teachers, nor their parents are encouraged to make special music instruction available. Also, when music aptitude and music achievement are believed to be the same, the pedagogical process of music education is less effective than it should be, because without specific knowledge of students' music aptitudes, a teacher is not able to offer precise instruction that takes musical differences among students into consideration. More specifically, not only do differences among students go unnoticed, but the musical strengths and weaknesses of individual students are not discovered.

Some musicians and educators ignore the difference between music aptitude and music achievement because they cannot find the appropriate language to define music aptitude. They deliberately use the words *gifted*, *talented*, and *musical*, none of which demarcates the difference between music aptitude and music achievement. In fact, many musicians and educators outside the United States persist in using the terms *musical ability* and *music intelligence*, which again cloud the distinction between music aptitude and music achievement. Music ability, after all, is born of a combination of the two.

Moreover, the majority of musicians and educators find it difficult to distinguish between various types of music aptitudes, such as tonal aptitude and rhythm aptitude, not to mention the several types of tonal aptitude and rhythm aptitude. It is only through the examination of the content of a valid music aptitude test that researchers themselves are able to gain an understanding of the description of music aptitude. The interaction between the content of a valid music aptitude test and the manner in which questions are asked in the test has, at least for the present time, become the essence of our understanding of music aptitude. Further, it is through the use of music aptitude tests that we can acquire indirect knowledge of the source of music aptitude.

There is an idea shared by some laypersons, musicians, and educators that tests are not to be trusted. That is unfortunate. Such an attitude is probably a result of the desire to believe that all persons are created equal, not realizing that it was equal opportunities and equal rights under the law that were guaranteed by the designers of our democracy, not equal potential to achieve. Certainly the Founding Fathers were aware that there are no two things, let alone two humans, that are exactly alike. Because test scores clearly underscore the fact that persons are not equal in their potential to achieve, aptitude being normally, not evenly, distributed, aptitude tests as well as achievement tests are often discredited by those who fear that the implications resulting from their use might be politically invidious.

Much of the continued adverse reaction toward tests and standardized testing is the result of a misunderstanding of the purposes and the use of test results, particularly in regard to intelligence tests, by some educators, scientists, sociologists, and politicians. The current craze of so-called alternative assessment and authentic assessment has tended somewhat to calm the public's alarm, and yet ironically, all this has little bearing on the validity and usefulness of a music aptitude test. In order for a student to take an academic intelligence test, the student must have at least a minimum of academic achievement. In other words, a student must have learned a language to understand and answer the questions that constitute an intelligence test. The same is not true for a valid music aptitude test. A student is able to take a music aptitude test, and in fact score quite high, without having had any formal music instruction. For that reason, a well-constructed music aptitude test is unbiased in terms of race, religion, and nationality and has no relation to actual language literacy. Therefore, a test of this kind can demonstrate a high degree of validity. Whatever one's philosophical persuasion, it must be granted that a valid music aptitude test is necessary for acquiring an understanding of the source and description of music aptitude

Of course, as I have explained, music aptitude tests have important practical as well as theoretical value. On the practical side, the results of a music aptitude test can be used to identify students who should be studying music, to diagnose students' individual strengths and weaknesses so that instruction can be adapted to their individual music needs, and to assist parents and teachers in making clear and unemotional decisions about the nature or degree of a student's participation in music. However, the results of a music aptitude test should never, under any circumstances, be used to prevent an enthusiastic student from studying music. All students, regardless of their comparative levels of music aptitude, can profit to at least some extent by engaging in music activities. A major benefit that should not be overlooked is that music aptitude test results can make parents and teachers aware of what students understand but are unable to put into words, and so help to protect students from the unreasonable demands of some parents and teachers.

CHAPTER 2

THE NATURE OF MUSIC APTITUDE

Throughout history, humans have been concerned with discovering their origin and destiny. It is no wonder then that we have also been consistently concerned with the nature of our special capacities. Music aptitude is one such capacity, and it certainly has not escaped examination by music educators and music psychologists. Although one might be curious about why for the past 75 years or more researchers have displayed more interest in music aptitude than in music achievement, it must be recognized that our understanding of the source, development, characteristics, and description of music aptitude should, and does, affect teaching procedures. It is for this reason that I believe a clarification of the nature of music aptitude is in order.

Think of music aptitude as a measure of a student's potential to learn music, and think of music achievement as a measure of what a student has already learned in music. Think of intuition as the underlying source of music aptitude, and think of insight as the underlying source of music achievement. Music aptitude is a hunger, whereas music achievement is the satisfaction of that hunger.

THE SOURCE OF MUSIC APTITUDE

Historically, the nature-nurture issue has probably had more direct influence on music education than any other single concept. Briefly, the concern in the early decades of this century was about whether music aptitude is innate or environmentally based. That is, if it could be shown that music aptitude is innate (supporting the nature theory), then it could be argued that the idea that students with little music aptitude should receive a music education in or out of school was suspect. Thus, music educators who believed that music aptitude is innate argued that only students with high music aptitude could profit from music instruction and so should be encouraged to engage in the study of music. Conversely, others argued that if it could be shown that music aptitude is influenced by the environment (supporting the nurture theory), then it would make sense to teach music to all students. A questionable but tacit assumption of many of those who subscribed to the nature theory was that music aptitude is a dichotomous trait—that is, that one is either born with it or without it. Because the nature-nurture controversy continues even to this day, it seems useful here to examine relevant philosophies and research findings.

European psychologists, many of whom were not musicians but were fascinated by what they called musical genius, began to investigate the enigma of "musicality" toward the turn of the last century. For unknown reasons, their work all but ceased early in the following century. Nonetheless, with regard to the source of music potential, they were instrumental in establishing the notion that music aptitude is inborn. To the best of my knowledge, they were so convinced of the nature position that they never even considered the possibility that environmental conditions might have contributed to the prowess of the musical geniuses they were observing. Men such as Carl Stumpf, Tom Hatherly Pear, Geza Révész, and Hans Rupp, by observing the accomplishments of musical prodigies, complemented one another's findings. Later investigators, and even some contemporary educators and researchers, also inferred the source of music aptitude through music achievement characteristics, but they attempted to do so in a more objective manner. V. Haecker and Theodor Ziehen, Hans Koch and Jan Alfred Mjøen, and Oswald Feis, using questionnaire and interview techniques, found that generally 1) if both parents are musical their children will very likely be musical, 2) if only one parent of the two is musical their children will usually be musical, and 3) if neither parent is very musical their children will be even less musical than they. It was also suggested that males as a group are more musical than females. Hazel Stanton came to similar conclusions as a result of working with 85 members of six families in which at least one member was a professional musician. The higher scores these family members earned on the *Seashore Measures of Musical Talent* when compared to those of individuals from less musical families gave rise to the supposition that innate potential is a more potent factor than environmental influences. In fact, Carl E. Seashore stated that "there is indication that the inheritance of musical capacities seems to follow Mendelian principles" (*The Psychology of Music*, 345). In a more recent study, which supports the role of heredity in music aptitude, Amram Scheinfeld investigated the backgrounds of 36 well-known instrumental musicians and 36 singers. For the former group, it was estimated that 17 mothers, 29 fathers, and about one third of the siblings were musical. For the latter group, 34 mothers, 13 fathers, and more than half of the siblings were found to be musical.

The results of some of these studies, however, indirectly suggest that innate qualities might not be the sole basis of music aptitude. The many exceptions to the rule, such as Toscanini, Rubenstein, Schnabel, and Gershwin, whose parents were found to be less musical than they, seem to bear out the environmental theory. Further, that the offspring of some musical parents were found to possess only limited musicality also favors the nurture theory. If, however, the nurture theory is correct, children with low music aptitude who hear music produced by their musical parents in the home should become musical, but if the nature and heredity theories are correct, musical parents should have given birth only to musical children. To resolve this apparent conflict, then, it might seem reasonable to conclude that music aptitude is a product of both innate potential and musical exposure.

We now know that if children, regardless of their high level of potential to learn music, are not exposed to music, their potential will not be adequately developed. It might even appear that they possess little music aptitude. Yet if one is born with a limited potential to learn music, it seems that no amount of exposure to music can raise that level of potential. If for no other reason, then, a good musical environment is essential if one is to be able to realize his or her maximum innate potential, whatever that level may be.

Despite the apparent possibility of this, the nature-nurture debate continued with intensity up to the 1940s. Although some continued to insist that music aptitude is solely a matter of heredity, others who adhered to the nature theory were divided about whether music aptitude is solely hereditary or somewhat environmentally based. Music aptitude, of course, can be transmitted through the genes without being strictly hereditary. That is, to be hereditary, whether one is born with a high or low level of music aptitude would be predictable on the basis of ancestry. Obviously, the data gathered about heredity has been inconclusive, and to fill the void, conflicting philosophical points of view have prevailed. Meanwhile, the possibility that the inheritance of music aptitude is latent or recessive, that is, that it occurs over several generations, has not been investigated.

Today, the Japanese music educator, Shinichi Suzuki, has been a major influence in shaping the argument. On the basis of his experience, he is of the opinion that the only superior quality any child can have at birth is the ability to adapt itself rapidly and with sensitivity to its environment. He goes on to suggest that should children not demonstrate the very best in music achievement, neither their personality nor their potential is at fault. Rather, their musical environment is lacking in quality. Perhaps the reason serious objective research has not been undertaken concerning the matter is that with the influence of this kind of thinking, the question of whether music aptitude is hereditary or not would make little difference in the current music education of young students. I believe, however, that the issue of whether music aptitude is innate, not whether it is hereditary, is of primary importance in developing realistic approaches to teaching music.

THE DEVELOPMENT OF MUSIC APTITUDE

Empirical knowledge tells us that persons are born with differing degrees of every aptitude, special or not. Thus, no two or more of us are born equal. Moreover, each person tends to excel in one or more pursuits but not in others. In a relatively early review of stability and change in human characteristics, Benjamin Bloom studied the extant research and found overwhelming evidence that indicates a child's intelligence level (potential) is well defined before he or she enters school. Bloom's conclusion was based on the high relation between scores earned on intelligence tests in the elementary grades and scores earned by those same individuals as young adults. At about the same time, Jerome Bruner and Jean Piaget, and earlier Maria Montessori, became convinced that preschool attendance would have a tremendously positive affect on the development of a child's ultimate level of intelligence.

Recent research completed by professionals who are not directly affiliated with music education offers compelling substantiation of the importance of the environment, while at the same time recognizing the role of nature and genetics, including music aptitude. As reported in *Newsweek,* February 19, 1996, and *Time,* February 3, 1997, numerous neurologists, pediatricians, biologists, and psychologists associated with universities and research institutes have come to believe that there are critical periods associated with surges of neurological connections and synapses that take place prenatally and during early childhood. They believe that cognition takes place in the outer shell of the brain, the cortex. The cortex consists of neurons that are interconnected by axons and dendrites, which are stimulated by syntactic activity. Nature provides the child with an overabundance of cells to make these connections, both before birth and at critical times after birth. Unless the cells are used for that purpose during these critical periods, they may be lost and never recaptured. As a result, possible peak times for a child's learning are diminished. For example, Torsten Wiesel and David Hubel discovered in 1960 that if a blindfold is placed over the eye of a kitten at birth and the cover is not removed until several weeks later, the animal will be blind in that eye for life. What the researchers seem to be saying is that unless cells are used to make neurological connections and synapses related to each of the senses at the appropriate times, the cells will atrophy or direct themselves to enhancing other senses, and the sense that is neglected will be limited throughout life. Thus, if a very young child has no opportunity to develop a music-listening vocabulary, the cells that would have been used to establish that hearing sense will be directed to another sense, perhaps the visual, and so the visual sense will be strengthened at the expense of the aural sense. Regardless of one's innate potential, no amount of compensatory education at a later time will be able to completely offset the handicap.

Though at one time it might not have seemed possible to settle the nature-nurture issue, recent continuing experimental research combined with systematic observation in music herald the beginning of that possibility, and it now appears that neither the nature theory nor the nurture theory by itself is correct. As I have explained, music aptitude is a product of both innate potential and early environmental experiences that contribute in unknown proportions to music aptitude. That is, whether innate potential or environmental experiences are more important, or if they are of equal importance, is not known. What seems to be the case is that regardless of the level of music aptitude children are born with, they must have favorable early informal and formal experiences in music in order to maintain that level of potential.[1] Further, unless they have favorable early informal and formal environmental experiences with music, that level of music aptitude will never fully be realized in achievement. It seems reasonable that regardless of how favorable children's early informal and informal experiences in music are, their music aptitude will never reach a level higher than that with which they were born. Although environmental influences cannot raise the innate level of children's music aptitude, favorable environmental influences are necessary if children are to maintain the level of music aptitude with which they were born. Unless children have favorable informal and formal environmental experiences, their level of innate music aptitude, be it high or low, will diminish, possibly decreasing to almost nothing. The higher the level of music aptitude children are born with, the more and the varied the early informal and formal experiences that are required if they are to maintain that level. The lower the level of music aptitude children are born with, the fewer the early informal and formal experiences that are required.

An explanation of the difference between developmental music aptitude and stabilized music aptitude is necessary to more fully understand
how nature and nurture interact in establishing music aptitude. Because
the level of music aptitude a child has at birth will change according to
the quality of the early informal and formal musical experiences he or she
receives, the music aptitude of children up to nine years of age is called
developmental music aptitude. Continuing research initiated more than
three decades ago substantiates the fact that music aptitude does not
continue to develop, either positively or negatively, after a person is
approximately nine years of age (Gordon, *A Three-Year Longitudinal
Study, 1967*). Because music aptitude becomes constant, that is, because
it crystallizes at approximately nine years of age or older, it is called
stabilized music aptitude.

The level of developmental music aptitude a student acquires by age
nine becomes stabilized and remains the same throughout life. That
should not be interpreted to mean that after age nine a person cannot
successfully be taught music. What it does mean is that persons can be
expected to reach in music achievement throughout their lives a level no
higher than that at which their potential to achieve has stabilized.
Unfortunately, the majority of us have not developed our music aptitude
to its highest possible level by age nine, and yet neither do we achieve in
music at as high a level as our stabilized limited music aptitude will allow.

It cannot be overemphasized that early informal guidance and formal
instruction in music, particularly from birth to eighteen months, from
eighteen months to three years of age, and then from three to nine years
of age, will prove to be of greater consequence than formal instruction in
music after age nine. The more appropriate early informal guidance and
formal instruction in music are and the younger children are when the
first informal guidance is offered to them, the higher the level at which
their music aptitude will most likely stabilize.

THE CHARACTERISTICS
OF MUSIC APTITUDE

There are several important characteristics of music aptitude. With
only slight differences, they are the same for developmental music aptitude and stabilized music aptitude. Throughout this chapter, music aptitude has been referred to in relative terms. That is, individuals are
described as having more or less music aptitude than others, but not as

having or not having music aptitude. There is ample evidence to support the position that music aptitude is normally distributed (Gordon, *Musical Aptitude Profile*, 1995). It is difficult to think of persons as unintelligent. Everyone we know is either more or less intelligent than someone else we know. Everyone has at least some music aptitude. From the examination of score distributions provided with proven music aptitude tests, it can be seen that a majority of persons (approximately 68 percent) have average music aptitude, fewer persons (approximately 28 percent) have either above or below average music aptitude, and only very few persons (approximately 4 percent) have exceptional or very little music aptitude. And, of course, there are gradations within these categories. For a test such as the *Musical Aptitude Profile (MAP)*, percentile rank norms are similar in variability for groups of students from different subcultures (Gordon, 1995). From the data derived from the national standardization of MAP, it was found that the scores of groups of students living in different geographical regions and attending schools of different sizes in urban and rural surroundings in the United States were quite similar in distribution. Data collected by Arthur Schoenoff and Vernon Sell, using translated versions of MAP after the national standardization program was completed, also indicate that score distributions are not materially different for American, European, and Asian students. While it is true that no music aptitude test is perfectly valid, evidence derived from the better-designed batteries verifies that among any group of students we teach, there are as many levels of music aptitude as a test author wishes to identify. Only by insisting that those students who score above a hypothetical point on a test possess music aptitude do we inadvertently support the educationally unsound "have or have not" theory.

Thus far I have discussed music aptitude as if there were only one general music aptitude. That can be misleading, because not only are there multiple intelligences, but music aptitude, itself, is multidimensional. During the prepublication research of MAP, more than 20 music aptitudes were discovered through factor analytical techniques. At least seven are of major importance to stabilized music aptitude and at least two are the basis of developmental music aptitude. Each student has different degrees of various music aptitudes, each of which is related to overall music aptitude, and students differ in these aptitudes both normatively (as compared to others) and idiographically (as compared to themselves). With the exception of average scores, it is rare for a student to have the same level of several dimensions of music aptitude, especially if a student scores extremely high or low in any of them. In that sense, nature has a way of compensating for one's weaknesses and for enhancing one's strengths. All music aptitudes are interrelated, and a substantial portion of each constitutes a unique aspect of overall music aptitude.

The final characteristic of music aptitude to be discussed is most important. In order to explain it, the verb *to audiate* had to be coined.[2] Audiation takes place when we assimilate *and comprehend* in our minds music that we have just heard performed or have heard performed sometime in the past. We also audiate when we assimilate and comprehend in our minds music that we may or may not have heard but are reading in notation or are composing or improvising. Aural perception takes place when we are actually hearing sound the moment it is being produced. We audiate actual sound only after we have aurally perceived it. In aural perception we are perceiving immediate sound events. In audiation, however, we are assimilating past or anticipated and predicted musical events. Compared to what is often called musical imagery, audiation is a more profound process. Musical imagery suggests a vivid or figurative picture of what the sound of music might represent. It does not require the assimilation and comprehension of the musical sound itself, as does audiation.

Audiation, as opposed to imitation, which is the first step in learning to make the best use of the potential for audiation, are often confused. The goal of imitation, sometimes called inner hearing, is a product, whereas audiation involves a process. It is possible, and unfortunately too often the case, for a musician to perform a piece of music by imitation without engaging in audiation. It is not possible to imitate and to audiate at the same time, however. What is audiated plays an important role later in how one learns and creates. What we audiate we never forget; it becomes a component of more complex audiation.

Like imitation, memory and recognition are part of the audiation process. Alone, however, they are not audiation. We can recognize a piece of music, even music performed with some incorrect pitches and durations, and still not be able to audiate it. We might be aware only of its melodic contour and rhythm. Many persons who recognize a song are unable to sing its resting tone, to identify and move to its fundamental beats, to hear its tonality and meter, or to specify the chord progression that underlies its melody.

You may audiate while you are listening to, recalling, performing, interpreting, creating or composing, improvising, reading, or writing music. Though it may seem contradictory that you can listen to music and at the same audiate that music, certainly you would agree that you automatically think about what is being said as you are listening to or participating in conversation. Listening to music with comprehension and listening to speech with comprehension involve a similar process.

The potential to audiate is a matter of music aptitude. Thus, audiation is the basis of music aptitude. The extent to which one intuitively audiates essential pitches and durations in music and organizes them subjectively or objectively is a measure of one's music aptitude. The level of developmental or stabilized music aptitude that one demonstrates is an indication of one's potential for learning how to audiate in a culturally accepted and more complex manner than mere intuition will allow. Audiation is also the medium by which one achieves in music. It is through structured and unstructured informal guidance in music that a child uses intuition to form the basis for learning how to audiate cognitively. It is through formal instruction in music that a child continues to learn how to audiate cognitively and learns the nature of the important characteristics of music that engender audiation.

There are eight types and six stages of audiation. Not all types include exactly the same stages, and although the stages are sequential, the types are not. Some of the types, however, serve as preparation for others. The eight types and six stages of audiation can be seen in the outline.

TYPES OF AUDIATION

Type 1	listening to	familiar or unfamiliar music
Type 2	reading	familiar or unfamiliar music
Type 3	writing	familiar or unfamiliar music from dictation
Type 4	recalling and performing	familiar music from memory
Type 5	recalling and writing	familiar music from memory or in silence
Type 6	creating and improvising	unfamiliar music while performing
Type 7	creating and improvising	unfamiliar music while reading
Type 8	creating and improvising	unfamiliar music while writing

The six stages of audiation and the mental process that takes place within each stage can only be theorized. Logic and reason suggest, however, that when learning conditions for a given type of audiation are ideal, all relevant stages are included in one form or another and interact in a complex circular sequence of mental activity. Moving forward and backward in this complex circular sequence prepares us for the type of audiation activity required in the other stages, so that after the first stage of audiation is initiated and the ideal audiation process continues, from two to six stages of audiation seem to occur concurrently. When one or more of the relevant stages is omitted in the audiation process, however, the stages cease to be sequential, and learning becomes less than optimum. Though it is an oversimplification, we can say that stages 1 and 2 of audiation define developmental music aptitude and that stages 1, 2, and 3 define stabilized music aptitude.

STAGES OF AUDIATION

Stage 1   momentary retention

Stage 2   imitating and audiating tonal patterns and rhythm patterns and recognizing and identifying a tonal center and macrobeats

Stage 3   establishing objective or subjective tonality and meter

Stage 4   retaining in audiation tonal patterns and rhythm patterns that have been organized

Stage 5   recalling tonal patterns and rhythm patterns organized and audiated in other pieces of music

Stage 6   anticipating and predicting tonal patterns and rhythm patterns

Serious music educators must be concerned with how best to assist students in learning music and in making the most of their music aptitudes. Being aware that music aptitude is a matter of both innate potential and early environmental influences, that it comprises more than one dimension, and that every student we teach can be expected to have at least some potential to achieve in music that will stabilize after he or she reaches nine years of age can help us to attain that goal. In order to understand how students learn when they learn music, however, it is essential that we become knowledgeable about the nature and scope of music aptitude and the role it plays in the learning process. Without such understanding, it is not possible to teach to students' individual musical differences in a professional manner, because students learn most and with greatest efficiency when instruction is adapted to their individual musical needs, whether the students are in preschool, engaged in general music, or are members of performance groups.

In our efforts to distinguish between music aptitude and music achievement, we will learn the specific degrees to which music aptitude is related to other important human traits such as general intelligence and academic achievement. We will discover that the relation between music aptitude and music achievement is quite similar to the relation between music aptitude and academic achievement, and that the relation between music aptitude and music achievement is considerably less than that between intellectual aptitude and academic achievement. This, of course, suggests that many students are not achieving in music in accordance with their musical potential. We should not be surprised to learn, then, that the music aptitude of 20 percent of students who are members of music performance groups falls in the lowest third of the population at large, and that only 40 percent of this select group rank in the upper quarter (Gordon, *Musical Aptitude Profile,* 1995). The implications of such findings should provide significant motivation to teachers and administrators to investigate the value of music aptitude tests and the teaching procedures they might point to.

---

1 For detailed information about appropriate early childhood music instruction, read *A Music Learning Theory for Newborn and Young Children* by Edwin E. Gordon (Chicago: GIA, 1997).

---

2 For a comprehensive description and explanation of audiation, read chapter 1 of *Music Sequences in Music: Skill, Content, and Patterns* by Edwin E. Gordon (Chicago: GIA, 1997).

CHAPTER 3

THE DESCRIPTION OF STABILIZED MUSIC APTITUDE

Because few students may participate in a recital, a member of the audience might lament that there are not more students in the school who have music aptitude. Such a view, of course, erroneously implies that music aptitude is demonstrated by performance, and that music aptitude and music achievement are synonymous.

In general, technical ability may be considered to be part of music achievement. However, though one may develop technical ability in singing or in playing the piano, for example, none of these tasks is necessarily contingent on music aptitude. The piano and the singing voice are only media through which one can express music aptitude, whether at a high or low level, just as the speaking voice is a medium through which one can express intelligence. Possessing good technical facility does not necessarily mean that one has corresponding music aptitude. Specifically, music aptitude is the basis for a performer's musical understanding, and it paves the way for musical expression in the performer's use of technical skill to interpret music. Not all persons develop technical skill commensurate with their music aptitude, however, even when they are given the opportunity to do so.

What then is music aptitude? We cannot define aptitude with any more certainty than psychologists can define intelligence. We can, however, study subjective opinions and objective ideas in an attempt to explore the matter to the fullest extent possible. In this way we can describe in an educated fashion the factors that determine music aptitude, which, as I have suggested, is the foundation for music achievement. With such insight we will be better prepared to understand the degree of music achievement that may be reasonably expected from each one of us and from our students and children.

Early researchers did not make a distinction between stabilized and developmental music aptitudes. Nevertheless, we now know that the nature theory is more closely associated with stabilized music aptitude than is the nurture theory, and that both the nature and the nurture theories have relevance to developmental music aptitude. A case might be made for crediting early researchers with understanding that not only is there more than one dimension of music aptitude, but there are different types of music aptitude. However, because current objective evidence indicates that music aptitude is ultimately a product of innate potential and environmental influences, and because the nature and nurture theories of the past were thought of as contradictory and not as interacting on a continuum, that case would be difficult to defend. What is abundantly clear, however, is that early researchers thought of music aptitude as being fixed, stabilized at birth. Carl E. Seashore, for example, expressed a commonly held belief in regard to the "sense of pitch" when he wrote "The physiological limit for hearing does not improve with training" (*Psychology of Music*, 58).

Because early researchers used the term music aptitude to mean "crystallized" music aptitude, all of their research and writing applies only to stabilized music aptitude. Thus, to maintain the historical perspective, a description of stabilized music aptitude is presented below, before the description of developmental music aptitude.

SUBJECTIVE OPINIONS

Any discussion about the description of stabilized music aptitude must begin with inchoate subjective opinions. Subjective opinions, unlike objective theories, are those that are not supported by data resulting from experiments and investigations. In general, subjective opinions about the description of music aptitude were held by those who also had subjective views about the nature of music aptitude, specifically about its source and some of its characteristics. Subjective opinions generally preceded or evolved concurrently with objective theories, and these subjective opinions invariably confused music aptitude with music achievement. The need for objectivity became increasingly apparent primarily as a result of the increasing awareness of this confusion and its consequences.

In an effort to describe music aptitude, some authorities simply posed opinions about what they believed are the attributes that separate the accomplished musician from the average person. Paul C. Squires, Philip

E. Vernon, and Bella Gross and Robert H. Seashore, in their retrospective analyses of composers' abilities, attributed success to overall "toil and sweat," intelligence, and the use of imagery to perceive musical sound. Imagery is what I think of more precisely as audiation in the cognition of music.

Introspective analyses of the processes involved in creating music were conducted by musicians as well as psychologists. The two groups came to similar conclusions. Henry Cowell, a composer, and Evelyn Benham, a psychologist, agreed with each other and with the positions of others when they suggested that musical imagery is an important dimension of the musical mind. Geza Révész and Carl Stumpf further concluded that musical imagery is a vital part of the personality of the musician. And Carl E. Seashore stated that "Perhaps the most outstanding mark of the musical mind is auditory imagery" (*The Psychology of Music*, 161).

Révész and Stumpf also reported other attributes that they found to be indicative of the "musically gifted." Révész, working with the Hungarian musical prodigy Erwin Nyiregyhazy, concluded that the ability to recognize and to name chords and intervals and the ability to transpose, improvise, and compose music are basic attributes of musicianship. Stumpf found that the young genius Pepito Areola, who ostensibly had a high level of musical potential, demonstrated timbre discrimination, was facile in using dissonant chords, could improvise melodies that went beyond the ordinary tonalities of major and minor, and had perfect pitch.

Although the distinction between music aptitude and music achievement was invariably ignored or misunderstood by psychologists and musicians who were forming subjective ideas of their own about music aptitude, and although none of the psychologists or musicians made a distinction between developmental and stabilized music aptitudes, a singular concept emerged in their writings. This was that musical imagery, or aural imagery, is the most important aspect, if not the basis, of music aptitude, or what they commonly referred to as musicality, musical talent, and musical giftedness. The terms "musical imagery" and "aural imagery," which were used synonymously, prophesy the significance of audiation, particularly the types and stages of audiation. And it is important to remember that skill in improvisation was not ignored in their thinking.

OBJECTIVE THEORIES

To be sure, there was not unanimity in the conclusions drawn by those who theorized about music aptitude on the basis of objective evidence. As different persons engaged in research, however, there was a general similarity in the conclusions they reached. There were those, such as Robert Lundin in America and John Booth Davies in England, who, besides offering their own description of music aptitude, suggested the design for the development of a music aptitude test, although none was ever published bearing their names. Others in this country, such as Jacob Kwalwasser, published or simply offered suggestions for the design of a music aptitude test and then engaged in research to support their positions, while colleagues, notably Lowell Tilson, authored music aptitude tests without previous confirming research.

The disagreements among and between American and European researchers were enormous and, to some extent, responsible for the delay in the acquisition of valid scholarly information. For example, music psychologists, such as Paul Farnsworth, James L. Mursell, Robert Lundin, and Harry Lowery, disagreed about how music aptitude might best be described. The source of the problem was that Europeans strongly insisted that research into the matter be based on "Gestalt theory," whereas Americans were persistent in their belief that the "atomistic theory" would be the more valid one. This means that the British, for example, adhered to the idea that music aptitude is a unitary, or all-inclusive, trait (which they believed had a great deal in common with general intelligence), and that therefore the component parts (if indeed they agreed that there were parts at all) of music aptitude should be considered in totality. Americans, on the other hand, went to extremes to describe mutually exclusive aspects of music aptitude (all of which, by definition, had to be related to overall music aptitude). The Americans were quick to admit, however, that when these aspects were combined, an overall description of music aptitude would be a natural consequence. This theoretical split between continents has all but vanished over the years so that now eclecticism has become the rule.

When the researchers happened to agree with one another on specific factors with regard to music aptitude, they appeared unaware of that fact or did not care to call attention to it. But although their undertakings were not generally planned in a cooperative or scholarly manner, their findings were largely systematic. That is, the landmarks in the research are obvious. Further, the transitions from one landmark to another are strikingly logical. It is those structural turning points that are emphasized throughout this book. Less convincing and compelling points of view may be found in a variety of sources, in journal articles as well as in books.

As I have implied, it became evident to all seriously concerned participants in the pursuit of a reasonable description of music aptitude that it would have to be music aptitude tests, objectively validated, that would provide the answers they were seeking. Because that direction of inquiry still holds the most promise, it is necessary that we examine the content of tests that offer at least some degree of objectivity in support of their design and of the results they provide. The landmark tests will, of course, be accorded primary attention.

THE EARLY YEARS

Seashore

In 1919, Carl E. Seashore, an American, was the first to publish a standardized battery of music aptitude tests. It was called the *Seashore Measures of Musical Talent.* The tests were based on approximately 20 years of research into the characteristics and description of music aptitude. With assistance from students, and particularly his colleagues Joseph Saetveit and Don Lewis, Seashore's research continued, and in 1939 the battery was revised and renamed the *Seashore Measures of Musical Talents.* By adding the "s" to the word "talent," Seashore emphasized his disagreement with those who contended that there was only one overall music aptitude. In the 1919 and 1939 editions, there were two series, A and B, the only difference between the two being that the content, not the design, of B was more difficult. The Columbia Graphophone Company produced three 78 rpm records for the 1919 version, and the RCA Manufacturing Company reproduced them in a 1939 version. The test manual for the revision was published by the University of Iowa. Though the tests remained unchanged, in 1957 one 33-1/3 rpm record of Series A of the 1939 version, published at that time in conjunction with a test manual by the Psychological Corporation, replaced the 78 rpm records. Series B was discontinued without explanation. Seashore's research into the description of music aptitude culminated in the test battery, but it is the tests themselves that are our main concern here. It will soon become apparent, however, that it is almost impossible to fully separate a description of music aptitude from the method that is used to measure music aptitude. In fact, it might be said that the method itself necessarily constitutes the description.

Seashore distinguished between the psychological aspects of sound, which he called pitch, loudness, time, and timbre, and the corresponding physiological aspects of sound, which he called frequency, amplitude, duration, and form. He reasoned that the physiological aspects are the bases of the psychological aspects, and that unless one had the acuity to understand the physiological, one would be unable to comprehend the psychological. Thus, for Seashore, music aptitude was best described by what can be observed objectively in the sound wave. He went on to say, however, that the four physiological sensory capacities and their psychological counterparts, the sense of tone quality, the sense of volume, the sense of rhythm, and the sense of consonance, are best understood when they come together and function as "complex forms." Seashore declared that to derive a comprehensive description of music aptitude, these complex forms must be considered without singling out their elemental components, the physiological and psychological underpinnings.

Although Seashore believed in the importance of stressing the complex forms of music aptitude, his research focused on the acoustical (the physiological and psychological) aspects of music aptitude. Evidently Seashore believed that in order to understand the complex, one must first understand the simple, and he left it to others to investigate the more elaborate structure of music aptitude. Nonetheless, Seashore gave direction to the research of those in generations to follow by making the need obvious. Without his keen mind and intellectual curiosity to identify important ideas in conjunction with his fundamental research to serve as an impetus and a guide, I believe our understanding of music aptitude would not have progressed to the extent it has.

The basis of Seashore's description of music aptitude can be understood by examining his research into the simple psychological aspects of pitch, loudness, time, timbre, and consonance. And, although Seashore does not categorize them as either elemental or complex forms, his research into tonal memory and rhythm must be given commensurate consideration, because they, along with pitch, are the most widely acknowledged components of music aptitude that have come to be associated with the Seashore legacy.

For Seashore, the sense of pitch is simply the ability to discriminate between two pitches. The more pitch aptitude one has, the finer the discriminations between pitches one should be able to make. Specifically, Seashore believed that to demonstrate pitch aptitude, one had to be able to determine if the second of a pair of pitches is higher or lower than the first. It was important that the tones representing the pitches be pure and lacking in overtones and harmonics, and that all acoustical properties other than pitch be held constant. Thus, the tones to be compared could not be produced using an actual musical instrument. An electronic beat-frequency oscillator, which at the time had just replaced resonators and tuning forks, was used to produce the tones. The two tones in the pair were performed at approximately 500 cycles, each had a duration of 0.6 of a second, and the pitches differed from each other by only 2 to 17 cycles.

Seashore described the sense of loudness as the ability to determine if the second of a pair of tones is stronger or weaker than the first. Again, to be assured of pure tones with the degree of loudness as the only variable under scrutiny, the same apparatus for measuring pitch discrimination was used for measuring loudness discrimination. The tones were held constant at 440 cycles, and they varied in loudness by as little as 0.5 to 4.0 decibels.

To measure the sense of time, Seashore again used the beat-frequency oscillator for producing pairs of pure tones. The frequency of the tones was, as before, held constant at 440 cycles, and the differences in duration between them ranged from .05 to .30 of a second. The capacity to discriminate time was determined by the ability to know whether the second of the pair of tones was longer or shorter than the first.

Timbre discrimination was measured by the capacity to determine whether the second of two tones produced with a special generator sounded the same as or different from the first. Each tone consisted of a fundamental component with a frequency of 180 cycles and its first five overtones. The timbre of the tones was varied by reciprocal alterations, ranging from 0.7 to 10.0, in the intensities of the third and fourth harmonics.

Seashore considered the sense of consonance to be an important component of music aptitude. He experienced difficulty, however, in measuring that capacity. The directions for responding to stimuli could not be made clear, and subjects who participated in the research made preferential rather than objective judgments. Seashore reasoned that to demonstrate a sense of consonance, one had to be able to perceive which of a pair of dyads had more "smoothness, purity, and blending." Based on Constantine F. Malmberg's research, the order of merit of two simultaneously sounding tones on a consonance-dissonance scale that Seashore identified were, from highest to lowest, the octave, perfect fifth, major sixth, major third, perfect fourth, minor sixth, minor third, diminished fifth, minor seventh, major second, major seventh, and minor second. Interestingly, it was found that whether the tones were selected from the tempered or untempered scales and performed using a resonator, piano, or pipe organ had no affect on the judgments (preferences) reported by the subjects.

The five components of music aptitude that Seashore postulated were observable in the sound wave. That was not the case for the two capacities, tonal memory and rhythm, the latter being included in the 1939 revision of the battery. Not only did Seashore not discuss their allusive quality in the sound wave, he did not refer to either as a category of elemental or complex forms. Nonetheless, he considered the two to be as important as the other five capacities in contributing to the description and measurement of music aptitude.

Seashore proposed that to demonstrate tonal memory, one had to be able to determine by number which single pitch in a series of three, four, or five is different when the series is heard twice. Christian Paul Heinlein, however, offered evidence that suggested this might not be the case, because he discovered that persons known to be "musical" apprehend a series of pitches as a totality and find it disturbing to have to concentrate on individual pitches. Seashore, nevertheless, disregarded such criticism and declared only that it is important that the pitches in either series have no syntactical relation to one another, because, as he stated, if they did, what would be measured would be more indicative of music achievement than of music aptitude. Thus, because of the "atonal" or neutral nature of the series, the measures could be used to undertake valid research with all persons, regardless of their race, religion, or nationality. In a word, the series of pitches would not be indigenous to any particular culture and so would be culture-free. The eighteen tempered chromatic steps upward from middle "C" performed on an electric organ served as the stimuli, with tempo and intensity carefully controlled. No explanation was offered about why pitches 100 cycles apart (chromatic steps) were used in the tonal memory subtest, whereas much finer differences were incorporated into the pitch discrimination subtest.

Rhythm patterns served as the stimuli in Seashore's rhythm subtest. One had to be able to determine whether two rhythm patterns consisting of five, six, or seven durations sounded the same or different. A beat-frequency oscillator set at 500 cycles was used to perform the rhythm patterns, and the tempo was held constant at 92 quarter-notes per minute. According to the short accompanying test manual for the 1957 version of the test battery, "The first ten items contain patterns of 5 notes in 2/4 time; the next ten, patterns of 6 notes in 3/4 time; and the last ten, patterns of 7 notes in 4/4 time." Because the patterns had no melody and no accented beats, all patterns were aurally perceived by most subjects in duple meter, regardless of the intention of the test author or the way the patterns were notated. Further, because even as Seashore suggested, humans subjectively organize for themselves series of objectively produced sounds into patterns, such as the ticking of a clock or the sound of moving train wheels, this tends to reinforce the idea that the rhythm subtest may not be culture-free either. It is curious, meanwhile, that to demonstrate the capacity of tonal memory, one had to count the sequential position and be acutely aware of individual pitches in a tonal pattern, whereas to demonstrate the capacity of rhythm (actually rhythm memory), one had only to compare one complete pattern to another in terms of sameness and difference. Seashore never addressed why this should have been the case, although over time it has become a very important issue. Perhaps even more problematic is that although Seashore made sure it was understood that pitches had to be musically unrelated in the tonal memory subtest in order not to confuse tonal achievement with tonal aptitude, he did not make clear how it was possible that rhythm aptitude would not be confused with rhythm achievement if meter were subjectively established by the listener in the rhythm subtest.

Although the sense of consonance played a formidable role in Seashore's early deliberations about music aptitude, he later took the position that the sense of timbre was the more important factor of the two in the description of music aptitude. Moreover, although initially he was of the opinion that the sense of time was fundamental to music aptitude, he soon came to the conclusion that it was not sufficient in itself and that a rhythm component was essential for fully acquiring an understanding of music aptitude.

Because Seashore was a great pioneer, the first researcher to give sustained scholarly attention to the nature and description of music aptitude, he had many critics in the United States, Canada, and abroad. That he changed some of his positions was undoubtedly due more to the views of his adversaries than to his advocates. Christian Paul Heinlein, on the basis of his own research, published two studies in 1928 in which he criticized Seashore's philosophical and experimental methodology and conclusions. James L. Mursell, coming from mainly a philosophical orientation, disagreed with Seashore's validation procedures and his interpretation of data. The objections in England by Harry Lowery and James Mainwaring, for example, were even greater.

It was difficult for Seashore's critics to understand how the discrimination of pitches less than a semitone apart, and particularly those that differ only nine cents of the one hundred cents in a semitone, had a significant relation to music aptitude. Though it might aid in tuning an instrument, they reasoned that pitch discrimination would seem to offer little in helping a musician learn how to adjust intonation in ensemble performance. Moreover, Seashore's antagonists did not agree that time discrimination could contribute in any significant manner to rhythmic understanding, that loudness discrimination had any relevance to expressive understanding, or that timbre discrimination could in any way be connected with the sense or production of tone quality. These theorists took the position that the capacities to discriminate between tones in terms of pitch, time, loudness, and timbre are measures more of acoustical acuity than of music aptitude. Specifically, they believed that one's ability to make generalizations about a series of musically unrelated pitches would have little if any value for predicting how well one can develop a sense of tonal syntax in music.

These concerns, as well as others, led to the Gestalt-atomistic controversy. The essence of the argument by the critics was that music aptitude cannot be divided into component parts, and that even if it could, the whole would be different from, if not greater than, the sum of its parts. Seashore maintained the position that indeed music aptitude does comprise several different capacities, and that in order to gain a precise understanding of the totality of music aptitude and to fully describe it, each of the component parts of music aptitude must be considered independently of every other and studied in that manner. For example, on the basis of the near-zero correlations among all of his subtests, Seashore insisted that pitch and tonal memory, on the one hand, and time and rhythm, on the other, are distinctly different types of capacities from each other. To reaffirm his position, Seashore refused to develop norms for a composite score on his test battery, believing that the value of describing and measuring the component parts of music aptitude would be obscured by the acknowledgment of an all-inclusive total score.

The Gestalt-atomistic controversy went further, however. Seashore's critics believed that in order to arrive at a true description of music aptitude, tests must include musical rather than acoustical content, and that the medium through which the music is performed must be that of one or more musical instruments. Seashore protested against this view, maintaining that just as an artist must possess visual acuity, that without the acoustical capabilities that his tests measure, a musician would not adequately be able to comprehend music itself. There was no question in Seashore's mind but that the physiological forms the basis for the psychological in fusing elemental capacities into a complex musical whole. He did admit, however, that "it does not follow that goodness in these capacities alone will make a good artist" (*Seashore Measures of Musical Talents,* 7). He also admitted that success in music was also dependent on factors that his tests did not measure, perhaps personality traits, motor ability, and the quality of music instruction. Such an admission prompted some to observe that the Seashore tests have negative validity, and that because they can be used to indicate only what cannot be included in a description of music aptitude, they serve little purpose in identifying what should be included in that description.

Other of Seashore's concepts that came under attack had to do with the manner in which he distinguished between music aptitude and music achievement. As I have explained, only when measuring timbre and rhythm did Seashore ask whether what was to be compared was the same or different, and thus he argued that the tests required absolutely no musical achievement on the part of the subjects being tested. The critics had little quarrel with that. What disturbed them, however, was that in the case of the pitch test, one had to know the difference between higher and lower, and that knowledge of those words required music achievement. They explained that those words are abstractions, only to be understood in terms of the placement of notes on the staff, and it could not be denied that music literacy, specifically reading, is an integral aspect of music achievement. While it can be said that familiarity with the difference between stronger and weaker and longer and shorter does not depend on music achievement, using those words in association with the sound of music might require knowledge beyond that which one might have if one had no exposure to music instruction of any kind. With regard to tonal memory, it was the British, in particular, who observed that to count and remember the ordinal number of a pitch that was changed in a series of three or more pitches, one necessarily had to have acquired some degree of academic achievement, not to mention a substantial degree of intelligence. To that extent, they claimed, Seashore was unwittingly concurring with the view that music aptitude and intelligence are very closely related.

The absence of preference measures in Seashore's thinking loomed large among the Europeans. Those who held to the Gestalt position were particularly unyielding in their view that musical preference was the *sine qua non* of music aptitude. That alone, some believed, would best distinguish among those with high, average, and low music aptitudes. Seashore found himself in a difficult position, because neither the sense of consonance nor the sense of timbre was designed to yield preferential responses. Yet, even Seashore acknowledged that his measure of the sense of consonance was problematic, because those whose music aptitude he intended to measure based their responses on their preferences. After all, is it possible to expect that being told to react to smoothness, purity, and blending would not result in a preference rather than in objectivity? Still, for all intents and purposes, Seashore was not among those who could be called upon to defend the importance of musical preference to music aptitude.

There was also a problem associated with Seashore's technique for measuring rhythm aptitude. He used very short durations, of always the same length, excluding any sustained tones. Thus, the difference between silence (rests) and duration in terms of intended note lengths had to be imposed subjectively by the listener. That listeners did just that compounded the problem of normal illusion, an acoustical phenomenon that permeated all of Seashore's measures. For example, high pitches subjectively sound louder than low pitches. Thus, even though it was thought that pitch was the only variable being measured in the pitch subtest, a listener with a poor sense of pitch and a good sense of loudness could nonetheless score high on the pitch subtest simply because of the association of the normal illusion of loudness with the higher pitch in a pair. There is also the normal illusion that a pitch is lower than it actually is if it is long or rich in overtones, and this too would affect the validity of the time and timbre subtests. The fact that in Seashore's tests normal illusion could not be avoided gave justification and impetus to the Gestalt theory of music aptitude.

All of the aforementioned criticisms aside, some researchers questioned Seashore's assumptions, not on the basis of the musical content and techniques he used, but rather on his steadfast conviction that music aptitude could not be improved with practice and training. They believed that by contradicting Seashore's conviction in this matter, they might shed light on the credibility of his description of music aptitude. Researchers on both sides, such as Edward H. Cameron, Alexander A. Capurso, Earle Connette, James Mainwaring, James Martin, Robert H. Seashore, Franklin O. Smith, and Elizabeth Taylor, conducted numerous studies to determine if Seashore's assertion would or would not be corroborated objectively. A classic study and perhaps the best known, one which Seashore's son, Robert, with the encouragement of his father, helped design, is Ruth Wyatt's. Though the experimental designs of many of the studies would not measure up to today's standards and the findings were often contradictory, most probably because such an array of inappropriate as well as appropriate criteria were used to investigate the validity of the tests, the consensus was that scores on the tests, particularly the measure of one's sense of pitch, could indeed be improved with practice and training. Unfortunately, the researchers made no distinction between the nature of practice as opposed to the nature of training, nor was it apparent that they were aware that when different types of practice and different types of training are examined, conflicting results should be expected. Moreover, they relied on statistical significance alone, giving no attention whatsoever to practical significance, when they compared the scores of students who received practice and training to those who did not.

Nevertheless, Seashore's critics declared that his tests were measuring music achievement and that, therefore, the results were irrelevant to the description of music aptitude. In his own defense, Seashore explained that the instruction provided in the experiments had raised students' cognitive scores and not their physiological scores, and that physiological results would be obtained if students were tested individually in a laboratory, whereas cognitive results are naturally obtained when students are tested in a group in a large room with inadequate supervision. He also contended that a rise in cognitive scores is only temporary, and that if students were retested some time later, it would be discovered that the initial increases in their scores would disappear. Given present understanding of research techniques, there is good reason to believe that Seashore was correct. Unfortunately, none of the groups was ever retested.

Meanwhile, there were those who believed that the 1919 *Seashore Measures of Musical Talent* was a music achievement test because the B series was purposely designed to be more difficult than the A series. That may seem logical at first, but upon reflection it is not reasonable. Because one test is designed differently and may be more difficult than another, it does not necessarily follow that both are achievement tests, or that the easier one is an aptitude test and the other is an achievement test. As will be explained later, different levels of complexity of musical content, as well as procedures for performing that content, are necessary to measure the developmental music aptitudes of students who have had varying amounts of exposure to music, and this does not jeopardize the validity of the tests as measures of music aptitude.

Of primary importance to music psychologists who are familiar with the concept of audiation is that Seashore was concerned with only the first stage of audiation in the description, and ultimately the measurement, of music aptitude. Whether Seashore made that decision deliberately is open to debate. Recognition of the types and stages of audiation is recent (the word "audiation" was coined some 20 years after Seashore's death), and it is unknown from his writings whether Seashore went beyond the general concept of imagery to give consideration to the possibility of the existence of stages, if not types, of audiation that we progress through when we learn music. Nonetheless, Seashore obviously believed that music aptitude is best described by how well one can retain and compare in aftersound the immediate aural impressions made by tones that were heard seconds before. Because the two tones used to measure the sense of pitch, loudness, time, and timbre and the series of three to five tones used to measure tonal memory are without musical syntax, audiation at the second and higher stages was not measured. As I have explained, developmental music aptitude includes the first and second stages of audiation, and stabilized music aptitude includes the first, second, and third stages. That only the first stage is considered in Seashore's research indicates that although in his description of music aptitude he speaks of the importance of both the musical and the acoustical aspects, in his measurement of music aptitude, the results of which were to be used to support his position, he measures only the acoustical aspects.

It is true that the series of tones, which are essentially rhythm patterns, in the rhythm test are syntactical. It would be an exaggeration, however, to say that even that one subtest of the six in the revised battery describes and is a valid measure of music aptitude, because all of the patterns are audiated in the same meter. Again, even though the rhythm subtest may be the most indicative of music aptitude when compared to the other subtests, Seashore considered the sense of time, not rhythm, to be basic to music aptitude, primarily because it can be observed in the sound wave.

Regardless of how one may respond to Seashore's description of music aptitude, the general validity of his objective tests intended to support his views must be examined. Unless the validity of the tests can be demonstrated, agreement or disagreement over the accuracy of his description of music aptitude becomes a moot question. If it can be shown that the tests have validity, his description of music aptitude would appear to have validity, but if no validity can be found, it is almost certain that his description of music aptitude is inadequate.

The reliability of the tests will be considered first, because this, as well as some other factors, is an indirect, if not a preliminary, indication of the validity of the tests. Unless results on a test are consistent, they cannot be valid. Seashore reported the reliability for each of his subtests in the 1939 revision in the test manual that accompanied the 1957 edition. For 300 students approximately 10 and 11 years old in grades 5 and 6, the Spearman-Brown corrected odds-evens internal consistency reliabilities range from .69 for the timbre subtest to .84 for the tonal memory subtest. The remaining four subtest reliabilities ranged from .73 to .79. For 300 students approximately 12 and 13 years old in grades 7 and 8, the Spearman-Brown corrected odds-evens internal consistency reliabilities ranged from .69 for the rhythm subtest to .87 for the tonal memory subtest. The remaining four subtest reliabilities ranged from .75 to .80. The Spearman-Brown corrected odds-evens internal consistency reliabilities for senior high school students, college students, and adults together go no higher than .88 for any of the subtests.

It is unfortunate that the reliability coefficients were calculated for two or more grade or age levels combined, because the resultant coefficients become spuriously high when heterogeneity is artificially increased without objective justification. The more variability in a group, the higher the reliability that can be expected. Thus, though the reliabilities for separate grades and ages are not reported by the test author, it can be reasonably assumed that they are lower than those for the combined grade and age groups.

The relationships among most of the subtests were found to be low. That finding led Seashore to maintain that each subtest was measuring one of the factorially pure music capacities he had described. It should be noted, however, that a correlation between any two measures is limited by the low reliability of even one of the measures and to a greater extent by the low reliability of both.

Seashore, disregarding the diverse composition of the groups he used in gathering norms, not only portrayed the reliabilities of his test as high, but he pronounced the tests valid as a result of those reliabilities. He took the liberty of interpreting the internal consistency reliability coefficients as "internal validity" coefficients. To Seashore, internal validity meant internal consistency. His circular reasoning was that because the two halves of each subtest were highly related, they were measuring the same capacity. In other words, no external criterion of validity was needed because each half of the subtest validated the other. Yet the problem remained: Seashore had no evidence that either half of the subtest related to a criterion representing music aptitude.

The reliabilities reported by Seashore are high enough to indicate that his subtests could demonstrate experimental validity, but the validity of a test may only be inferred, not proved, from reliability data. Nonetheless, he claimed that all of the subtests "have been validated for what they purport to measure. When we have measured the sense of pitch, that is, pitch discrimination, in the laboratory with high reliability and we know that pitch was isolated from all other factors, no scientist will question but that we have measured the sense of pitch" (*Seashore Measures of Musical Talents,* 7). Seashore summarized his position by stating that attempts to validate his subtests by correlating them with "fallible external criterion measures such as judgments of omnibus musical behaviors were inappropriate" (7).

I can empathize with Seashore's frustration in identifying an external valid criterion measure. Just as the magnitude of the correlation between two tests is dependent on the reliability of both tests in question, so, too, is the magnitude of the correlation between a test and a validity criterion dependent on the reliability of both factors. From personal experience, I have observed that students' performances as well as teachers' judgments of their students' musicianship are inadequate indicators of the students'

music aptitude. Further, even a heterogeneous group of subjects is generally so lacking in variability in music achievement that it is impossible to
expect them to provide useful responses. For example, because audiation
cannot be directly observed, the most acceptable indirect criterion that
might be used to validate a music aptitude test would be samples of
students' improvisations. Yet few persons in our society are able to improvise even at the most elementary level.

Validity, particularly of an aptitude test, is understood best through
longitudinal predictive studies. Though a predictive test is not necessarily an aptitude test (although a valid aptitude test must be a predictive
test), customarily the validity of an aptitude test is determined through its
predictive validity. Longitudinal predictive validity studies are rare
because they are more expensive and time consuming than concurrent or
criterion-related validity studies.

A longitudinal predictive study undertaken by Hazel Stanton for the
Seashore battery (commonly referred to as the Eastman Study, because
data were collected from students at the Eastman School of Music over a
period of 10 years) was given a poor reception by reviewers, because
Stanton designed her study in an unorthodox manner and then reported
her results in a way that deprived readers of some of the most important
findings. To predict success in music, she took the composite score of all
five Seashore subtests included in the first edition (pitch, loudness, time,
tonal memory, and consonance) and combined them with other criteria,
including teachers' ratings, scores on an entrance audition, numerical
values for past music achievement and academic achievement, and intelligence test scores. By combining those scores, the power of the Seashore
tests themselves to predict the subjects' rate of graduation from the
conservatory was obscured.

The following are the specific details of the design of the Stanton
study. In 1925, 164 freshman entered the Eastman School of Music. Upon
admission, each of the students was labeled "safe," "probable,"
"possible," "doubtful," or "discouraged" in terms of a prediction as to
whether the student would graduate from the school in 1929, within the
normal four-year period. Students were put into one of those five categories on the basis of the combined criteria described above, which
Stanton referred to as the "cumulative key." Although other criteria of
success were examined, such as scholarships, honors, and recital appear-
ances, graduation from the school was given primary consideration. It
was found that 60 percent of students in the "safe" group, 42 percent in
the "probable" group, 33 percent in the "possible" group, 23 percent in
the "doubtful" group, and 17 percent in the "discouraged" group graduat-
ed in 1929. It can only be assumed that the percentages for all of the

Seashore subtests alone in predicting success in music would have been even less accurate, although simple biserial correlations between the total scores on the Seashore battery and graduation would have been helpful in evaluating the validity of Seashore's description of music aptitude. Even if those coefficients proved to be low, however, it would have been understandable, because there are many extra-musical factors involved in determining whether or not one graduates from school, financial resources being not least among them. Nonetheless, specific information pertaining to the study has probably long since been destroyed.

Seashore gave musicians and educators a broad basis for their initial thinking about the nature and measurement, as well as the description of, music aptitude, although the realm of his contributions has generally been relegated to subjectivity and not considered in terms of the objectivity he championed. Some of his students and others he influenced indirectly duplicated his work, while others went beyond it. Among his more progressive students was Jacob Kwalwasser. In 1931, he and Peter Dykema published the *Kwalwasser-Dykema Music Tests*, which may have stimulated Seashore's interest in revising his test battery. Meanwhile, research by Herbert Wing, in England, gave support to the idea that music preference plays a formidable role in the description of music aptitude.

Kwalwasser

As I have indicated, in 1930, midway between the publication of the first and second editions of the Seashore battery, Kwalwasser developed and together with Dykema published the *Kwalwasser-Dykema Music Tests*, commonly referred to as the K-D tests. There is a great deal of similarity between the two test batteries. Possibly because the ultimate level of attainment of *musically trained students* is best predicted by past achievement, Kwalwasser, unlike Seashore, included music achievement measures in his battery. Obviously, he was more interested in the practical aspects of his work than in the search for a viable description of music aptitude. Six of the ten subtests that constitute the K-D battery were developed to measure the same factors found in the Seashore battery, although they were designed and titled differently. To that extent, Kwalwasser's description of music aptitude was similar to that of Seashore's. In contrast to Seashore, however, Kwalwasser employed actual orchestral instruments and the Duo-Art Reproducing Piano as stimuli for some of the subtests. And although he used pairs of tones for discriminatory purposes in other subtests, he did provide for syntactical musical relationships among tones in the *Tonal Memory* subtest. As a result of these and other relatively small differences, such as greater extremes between tones in the *Pitch Discrimination* subtest, the K-D battery was considered to represent a different concept in its approach to music aptitude and, in addition, it developed the reputation of being "easier" than the Seashore battery. It is now known that tests either measure the aptitude of individuals in a specified group with precision or they cease to be valid for that purpose. However, this not to say that special tests cannot be developed to discriminate more precisely among students within a restricted music aptitude level.

With particular regard to the description of music aptitude, the six subtests comparable to the Seashore battery are *Tonal Memory, Pitch Discrimination, Intensity Discrimination, Time Discrimination, Rhythm Discrimination,* and *Quality Discrimination* (quality meaning timbre). *Melodic Taste* and *Tonal Movement* were the preference measures. For the former subtest, the subject is asked to indicate which of two endings provides the best tonal termination of a short melody. Although in practice, rhythm is an integral part of melody, the subtest of *Melodic Taste* is not specifically constructed to allow rhythm to influence preferential responses. The subtest of *Tonal Movement* measures the ability to judge the tendency of the final tone in a succession of tones to proceed to a point of rest. Kwalwasser's two achievement subtests are *Rhythm Imagery* and *Pitch Imagery.* For both of those subtests, the subject is asked to indicate whether what he or she hears is notated on an answer sheet.

From an analysis of the K-D tests, it can seen that the psychological constructs of the battery offer a broader description of music aptitude than that offered by Seashore and his colleagues. Not only is that attested to by the presence of musical preference and music achievement measures, but the use of actual musical instruments as stimuli certainly makes apparent the nature of some major disagreements with Seashore. Whether there is significant merit to justify these differences is doubtful in my mind. Moreover, in comparative studies of the Seashore and K-D batteries, both Paul Farnsworth and Paul Whitley found subtests bearing the same title to have no common base, but they did declare Seashore's measures superior from a point of reliability.

Although Seashore was maligned for including acoustical acuity in his description of music aptitude, at least it can be said that he was consistent in his belief that it was necessary to keep measures of music aptitude pure to facilitate research, and so he did not contaminate them with extraneous factors in an attempt to improve their predictive validity. Whatever the benefits, he was not prone to compromise, particularly for political or commercial reasons.

In further defense of Seashore it should be recognized that for the *Tonal Movement* subtest, the correct answers to questions are limited largely to the recognition of whether the final pitch of a series corresponds to traditional, but narrow, standards. This can also be said for Seashore and his consonance subtest. By unilaterally deciding what are the correct answers to questions, however, Kwalwasser does not engender much confidence in anyone seeking objective substantiation of his description of music aptitude. The same criticism applies to the *Melodic Taste* subtest. Here, one cannot help but wonder about the validity of the findings, because of Kwalwasser's suggestion that if there is not enough time to repeat the short *Melodic Taste* subtest, scores should be multiplied by two before converting them to percentile ranks. The monotonic effect of simply doubling scores rather than administering a test a second time would not increase its reliability, and certainly it would not affect its validity.

It is apparent that Kwalwasser never questioned whether the music aptitude of children younger than eight years old could be measured. He must have concurred with Seashore that either music aptitude stabilizes at age eight or nine or that children younger than that are incapable of understanding the directions for taking a music aptitude test. Whereas Seashore provided norms for different age groups, combined as they were, Kwalwasser offered combined norms for children as young as eight through professional musicians 40 years old. He explained that music achievement, implying chronological age, had no appreciable effect on K-D test results.

It has always been common knowledge that achievement tests are more useful than aptitude tests for predicting future achievement. In the case of academic work where all students in a given grade are given instruction in reading, for example, we can expect reading achievement to satisfactorily forecast skill in reading at higher grades. In the case of music, however, only a small percentage of students in a school are given special instruction in music and, therefore, it is neither realistic nor fair to use current music achievement as the basis for prophesying students' future skill in musical endeavors. The large percentage of students who are ill-equipped to demonstrate performance skill or even to respond to questions that require knowledge about music are at a disadvantage. We know that there are students with high music aptitude who demonstrate only a low level of music achievement. That is why, unlike the case for academic intelligence tests, music aptitude tests are a necessity.

Thus, as already explained, even if music achievement tests are found to be highly predictive of the degree of a musician's further musical accomplishment, they still have little, if any, relevance to our attempt to describe music aptitude. It is not axiomatic that a test that has predictive validity is necessarily an aptitude test. For example, strength of hand might prove to be an excellent predictor of success in playing the string bass but, strictly speaking, this physical ability cannot be construed to be an aptitude for music.

In 1953 Kwalwasser authored another music aptitude test, the *Kwalwasser Music Talent Test.* Unlike the earlier test, only four discrimination factors are measured and electronic equipment, a pitch oscillator, is used exclusively as the source of stimuli. It should be emphasized that he excluded preference measures. To the extent that Kwalwasser drastically altered what he considered to be the description of music aptitude is alarming, particularly because no information is provided in the accompanying test manual or elsewhere to explain why or how this change came about. It is obvious that his disagreements with Seashore about what should be measured and how it should be measured had been resolved, that is, that he determined that the totality of what he considered to be music aptitude paralleled Seashore's constructs, though his ultimate conclusion did not take into account all of Seashore's factors. Kwalwasser acknowledged the importance of only pitch, time, rhythm, and loudness, but, like Seashore, he did provide two forms of the test that differed only in the difficulty of the content.

Kwalwasser directed test administrators to explain to subjects taking the test that they would hear two series of three tones. When the second series was heard, it would include a pitch, time, loudness, or rhythm change. The subjects were to mark on an answer sheet which type of change they heard in the 40 or 50 series performed, depending on which form of the test was being administered.

To illustrate the move of Kwalwasser's thinking in Seashore's direction, I will paraphrase Kwalwasser's words on method found in the manual for the *Kwalwasser Music Talent Test:* In pitch, controlled differences range from 5 to 70 cents; in time, the tempo changes from 40 percent to 5 percent of the standard metronomic marking of 90 to the quarter note; in loudness, the variation falls between 10 to 2 decibles from the standard; and in rhythm, organizational changes in duration vary from easily recognizable differences at the beginning to progressively more difficult patterns at the end.

Whether Seashore was encouraged and gained more confidence in his description of music aptitude by Kwalwasser's more mature declarations was not made public. Although Seashore could claim superficial support, there were underlying issues that suggested the opposite. Kwalwasser's time factor was actually a tempo factor, having nothing in common with

Seashore's time subtest, and although there were no obvious components of music achievement in the test, they were actually indigenous. For example, to understand the four option responses of pitch, time, loudness, and rhythm, and to be able to remember what the first series of tones sounded like while listening for all of the variables and deciding which to concentrate on, certainly requires some memorization. We know that whereas memory is associated with music aptitude, memorization is a distinct form of music achievement. Also, while Kwalwasser did offer separate scores as well as a total score for the K-D test, he did not consider the four parts of his new test to be subtests, therefore offering only a total score for all parts combined. That would be more in keeping with Gestalt principles than Seashore would have been comfortable with.

It should not go unsaid that Kwalwasser was particularly proud of the new test because it took only 10 minutes to administer. Did he really believe that an adequate measure of all of the facets of music aptitude could take so little time, or was he more interested in pleasing impatient and imprudent adversaries?

As I explained, the extent of the stability (reliability) and the interrelationship (correlation) of subtest scores included in a test battery bear on, and ultimately affect, the validity of the description of music aptitude it represents and, of course, bear on the validity of the battery itself. Neither reliability nor intercorrelation data are reported in either of the Kwalwasser manuals. Therefore, although Kwalwasser in his first test offers scores for 10 separate factors of music aptitude, we cannot be sure of the extent to which they actually exist, nor can we be sure of the degree to which they comprise a single unitary trait. Furthermore, in neither test manual does the author offer evidence of experimental validity, even for the total score.

Before moving on, I would like to make clear that although I have organized headings in this chapter chronologically, not all theories about the scope and description of music aptitude and the corresponding tests that resulted are presented in strict historical order. That is, because some authors, such as Kwalwasser, offer different points of view and produced supporting tests years apart, and because at times topological organization in terms of philosophy seem to be more appropriate and logical than an absolute chronological one, I have taken the liberty of making some small adjustments in the next two sections.

THE MIDDLE YEARS

Tilson

In 1941, shortly after the appearance of the first Seashore revision, the *Tilson-Gretsch Musical Aptitude Tests* were published. Lowell Tilson (Gretsch was the sponsoring instrument manufacturer) included only four parts in his test: *Pitch, Intensity, Time,* and *Memory*. The psychological constructs of these parts, in terms of content and the recorded sound-producing equipment, are almost exactly the same as corresponding subtests in the Seashore battery. Tilson's logic was that by including only four parts rather than six subtests in his test while still demonstrating results comparable to the Seashore battery, his test would be more attractive, because it would require less time to administer. Evidently, contrary to Seashore's contention, Tilson did not believe that rhythm and timbre represent important dimensions of music aptitude.

Tilson, unlike Seashore, provided criterion-referenced validity and norms for only the total test score, that is, for all parts combined. Whether norms for only the total test score were offered because of the unreliability of the individual parts or because Tilson was more attuned to the European point of view, in terms of Gestalt principles, is unknown. Both Seashore and Tilson used heterogeneous groups for deriving reliability estimates for their respective measures. Seashore, in his revised version, combined the test results of fourth and fifth grade students, sixth through eighth grade students, and those of high school freshman through college seniors. Tilson combined the scores of students in nine grades, four through twelve. Nonetheless, based on a sample of 767 young children through adults, Tilson found only scant test-retest reliabilities. These were .59 for *Pitch,* .44 for *Intensity,* .48 for *Time,* .72 for *Memory,* and .83 for the entire test. The practice of ignoring the effect of test reliability on test validity seemed at that time to be an accepted procedure, and as will be seen, Raleigh Drake, even a decade or so later, followed the same course when he reported chronological age norms based on two and three-year intervals from ages seven through twenty-two.

There is only one validity study of the Tilson test reported in the test manual, presumably for all students combined. Students were categorized into four groups based on their levels of performance talent, and their scores on the test were compared with the others in each of the assigned groups. Even when chronological age was ignored in the determination of the performance skills that were evaluated, it was found that although 92 percent of students in the lowest quartile were given grades by their teachers below the median, 33 percent of students in the highest quartile were also graded below the median. On the basis of these results, Tilson nonetheless concluded in his very short manual that "if the director of the high school band, orchestra, glee club, or chorus would enter the pupils with highest scores on this test into his organizations, it would seem fair to predict that most of them would develop into good performers." It is obvious that Tilson was more preoccupied with the prediction of success than with gaining insight into the description of music aptitude as the basis of success.

It is known that, generally, the more heterogeneous a group, the higher the test reliability will be for that group. But the fact remains that no matter how high a reliability coefficient is, it is of limited value if it is not relevant to the specific group for which the test is intended to be used. For example, if a test were administered to fifth grade students in order to measure their music aptitudes, we would need to know the stability of scores for those fifth grade students as a group, and we would need to disallow factors other than music aptitude which would be sure to affect test reliability, especially broad chronological age. All that can be revealed by a multigrade reliability coefficient is that the individual grade coefficients would probably not be any higher and would most likely be lower.

Gaston

A few years after the Tilson test became available, E. Thayer Gaston published the *Test of Musicality*. Though its content duplicates that of earlier as well as later versions of tests authored by Jacob Kwalwasser, Raleigh Drake, Herbert Wing, and others, it is unique in its construction. The piano is the stimulus for the entire test, which includes four recorded parts, totaling 40 questions, and there is no pretense of making these parts serve as individual subtests. Thus, neither separate scores, reliabilities, nor norms are offered for the parts. Instead, data are reported only for the total score.

As in the Wing *Pitch Change* subtest, a pitch and then a chord are played in part one and the subject indicates whether that pitch is in the chord. Part two resembles one of the Kwalwasser-Dykema achievement tests, where the subject must decide if what is seen in notation is heard on the record. If there is a difference, the nature of the difference, tonal or rhythm, must be identified. The Kwalwasser-Dykema *Tonal Movement* subtest is the model for part three, and part four is designed similarly to the Drake *Musical Memory* test, where a melody is played and then repeated, and the listener must decide if the two are the same, if there was a note (pitch) change, or if there was a rhythm change.

The split-halves reliabilities reported by Gaston are impressive, but they are for combined grades: .88 for grades 4 through 6, .88 for grades 7 through 9, and .90 for grades 10 through 12. In contrast, validity information is unclear, particularly because statistical probabilities are noted rather than correlation coefficients, and to decipher their meaning is next to impossible. To gather evidence of the validity of the *Test of Musicality*, Gaston asked teachers to evaluate the "musical personality" of each student from 1 to 5 and then he compared those ratings to scores on the test. Using a Chi-Square analysis, an association was found between the two variables, leading Gaston to conclude in his brief manual that "the musicality test is a valid test and measures what it purports to measure."

We are left to infer for ourselves what the results of Gaston's criterion-related validity study has to do with the description of music aptitude. Subjectively, however, while it does seem obvious that Gaston's opinions differ widely from Seashore's, by paraphrasing the tests of Kwalwasser, Drake, and Wing, he nonetheless gives tacit support to their beliefs that, among other things, Gestalt principles are compelling and that past achievement in music should not be overlooked when drawing conclusions about the nature of music aptitude. Further, that separate norms are reported for boys and girls makes the Gaston test reminiscent of achievement tests in general, and because results from a teacher's personal inventory for each student contributes in no small way to the students' ranking in terms of music aptitude suggests that he believed that extra-musical factors are also influential.

Drake

In 1932, Raleigh Drake described four tests of music aptitude that were soon to be available to the public. The tests measured melodic memory; interval discrimination; pitch memory; and "feeling" for key center, phrasing, and rhythmic balance. For this reason we might conclude that Drake believed that both auditory acuity and musical expressiveness were important components of music aptitude. In 1954, however, when the *Drake Musical Aptitude Tests* were published, only the idea of the melodic memory test (later titled *Musical Memory*)was carried over from the earlier battery. The other of the two tests that constituted the new battery was called *Rhythm*. Thus, the notion that acoustical phenomena have any important role in the description of pitch or melodic aptitude seems to have been abandoned.

The piano is used as the recorded stimulus in Drake's memory test and all questions involve coherent syntactical melodic phrases. Drake emphasized this by calling the test *Musical Memory*, rather than, in contrast to Seashore's parallel subtest, tonal memory. For Drake's test, a short musical phrase is heard once and then seven renditions of it follow. Each may sound the same as the original phrase; each may, as stated in the recorded directions, be in another key; each may have some notes (pitches) changed; or each may have a time (rhythm) change. The task is to indicate the nature of the rendition. To be familiar with the concept of modulation and to know the difference between "time" and "note," the test taker should have had some formal music instruction. Because of this, it can be assumed that Drake, like Kwalwasser and Gaston, considered music achievement to be a factor in the description of music aptitude. After all, although he calls the test an aptitude test, he couples it with achievement in at least some small measure. Moreover, both tonal and rhythm responses are required in the same test, and recent research suggests that while it is not only acceptable, but preferable, for older students who are, of course, in the stabilized stage of music aptitude to hear melodic passages and to make determinations about either a tonal or rhythm change, it cannot be expected that young children, those in the developmental stage of music aptitude, are able to cope with such demands. Whether this is a result of cognitive development or of music achievement, and what differential impact this might have on the description of music aptitude, raises some interesting speculations that require serious research.

The underlying constructs of the newer *Rhythm* test seem to have little in common with the established constructs of the memory test. The first part of the *Rhythm* test involves clicks. Four clicks of the metronome are counted out on the recording and then there is silence. The subject is to keep counting quietly at the established tempo until told to stop, and the number at which the student arrives is the student's answer. The second part of the test is similar to the first except that interference from clicks performed at a different tempo is heard in place of the silence provided in the first part.

Undoubtedly, the ability to maintain a consistent tempo, except when purposely altered for expressive reasons, is important to musical performance. But in musical practice, tempo interacts with rhythm, meter, and melody. Drake was certainly aware of this when he designed the memory test, and so one cannot help but wonder if the *Rhythm* test might be superfluous. If one cannot audiate a consistent tempo, how would one determine if a rhythm change has or has not taken place? Is it possible that consistency of tempo has an all-important separate role in describing music aptitude, one that has little or no bearing on any other dimension of music aptitude, including meter and rhythm? Perhaps because Drake comes to the psychology of music as a psychologist, as did most before him, including Seashore, and not as a formally educated musician, his attention is focused more on test content than on consequential musical factors. Obviously, yet another important research project is in order if we are to continue to pursue a greater understanding of music aptitude.

Only tests of high reliability are capable of exhibiting substantial correlations with one another. Both Drake tests demonstrate high test-retest reliability, as they should, considering that they are based on the combined results of students of widely different chronological ages. Nevertheless, this makes the reported low correlations between them noteworthy, and that forces us not to dismiss the constructs underlying Drake's tests. When we consider the dichotomy in the design and content of the two tests, we should expect the tests to measure different traits, but it would be more instructive if we had some empirical evidence that both test scores are related to musical capacities and that each trait contributes to overall music aptitude. Drake does not offer such information in terms of diagnostic validity. Rather, he reports criterion-related validity for each of the tests based only on teachers' ratings of the same criterion of "expression in playing and the rapidity of learning" (*Drake Musical Aptitude Tests,* 17), and the validity coefficients run from very low to extraordinarily high, each in association with rather small groups of students. What Drake seems to be suggesting is that although music aptitude is unidimensional, and not multidimensional, different tasks are nevertheless required to reveal the totality of music aptitude. Who can say with certainty that oblique approaches to the measurement of music aptitude are inappropriate for ultimately describing music aptitude? Complications in designing a study to investigate that question are enormous, but the results could offer unanticipated and exciting insights.

Two distinct characteristics of both of Drake's tests should be emphasized: 1) Drake provides two forms of each test, differing in difficulty, and 2) norms are offered for both nonmusic students (third grade through college seniors) and music students (fifth grade through college seniors). Music students, as defined by Drake, are those who have had five or more years of musical training. Theoretically, music students, their musical education notwithstanding, should not score higher than nonmusic students on a music aptitude test, only on a music achievement test. However, music students as a group, depending on the test under consideration, may score higher simply because it is an established fact that students with superior music aptitude more often elect to study music than do students with lower music aptitude.

There is one study that I completed in 1961(*A Study to Determine the Effects of Practice and Training*) that bears on the nature of Drake's tests and deserves attention, because it supports Drake's belief that his tests are representative of music aptitude and not of music achievement. It has to do with the effects of training on the *Musical Memory* and *Rhythm* scores. It was found that even when students are given the opportunity over a period of a semester to become familiar with the words Drake uses in the recorded directions for taking his tests and to respond to original melodies and series of clicks similar to those found on the tests, the students' scores did not increase significantly upon retesting.

Jack Heller and John Farrell agree with Drake that both of his tests rely to some degree on music achievement, and that this means their content and construction should not weigh heavily in our description of music aptitude, yet Drake tells us in his test manual that scores on the Drake *Rhythm* test correlate from .02 to .11 with scores on the Seashore *Rhythm* subtest, from .00 to .14 with scores on a test of art ability, and from -.07 to .10 with scores on a general intelligence test. The only information reported, found in Drake's manual, for the *Musical Memory* test is that scores on it correlate from .05 to .28 with scores on a general intelligence test. This convinced Drake that by deriving data that tell us what his tests are not measuring (inverse or indirect validity), his tests are measuring music aptitude. Without direct validity data at our command as well, however, we cannot be sure whether that indeed is or is not the case.

Wing

Herbert Wing was the first after Seashore to develop major innovations in music aptitude testing. An Englishman, he was undoubtedly influenced in establishing psychological constructs for his test by other English authorities such as Cyril Burt, Philip E. Vernon, James Mainwaring, Harry Lowery, and Boris Semeonoff. The *Wing Standardized Tests of Musical Intelligence* (1958) include seven subtests. The first three are nonpreference tests—*Chord Analysis, Pitch Change,* and *Memory* —and measure tonal concepts. The remaining four subtests—*Rhythmic Accent, Harmony, Intensity,* and *Phrasing* are preferential in nature. None should be confused with Kwalwasser's *Tonal Movement* subtest which was, in hindsight, comparatively superficial, because the answers determined to be the correct ones for the Kwalwasser subtest were completely arbitrary.

Whereas a nonpreference test has correct answers that are meant to be objective, a preference test requires subjective responses from the listener, and the preferred answers, in the case of the Wing subtests, were established on the basis of the way renown composers actually composed their music, not on theoretically derived rules, as is the case with Kwalwasser's subtest. With regard to the *Musical Aptitude Profile,* even more advanced methods have been researched for establishing what should be considered an appropriate preferential response.

The Wing test differs from Seashore's test in two important respects: For each of Wing's subtests, a musical instrument, the piano, is used as the recorded performance medium, and, thus, the content of each question is actual music, not acoustical sounds. In the *Chord* subtest, the listener indicates how many pitches are heard in each chord, and in the *Pitch* subtest, the listener indicates whether the second of a pair of chords is different from the first, and if it is, whether the difference is a result of a pitch moving up or down. In the *Memory* subtest, a series of tonally related pitches is heard. Each series has distinct rhythm, although this is not relevant to the correct answer. When the series is repeated, the listener is directed to count and to indicate which pitch, if any, was altered. In all four preference subtests, familiar melodies are performed either as they were originally written by what Wing considered master composers or in "mutilated" fashion. The type of change corresponds to the specific subtest being heard. That is, there are either rhythmic, accent, intensity, or phrasing alterations. The listener is to decide if the performances are the same or different, and if they are different, which of the two renditions sounds better. In Wing's thinking, the performance of the music as originally composed was always the better performance, but it might be surprising to discover that when listening to the recordings, the unintended answer is sometimes the better of the two.

The following historical perspective should be of assistance in our deliberations about music aptitude. Three years before the 1939 revision of the *Seashore Measures of Musical Talents* became available, Herbert Wing completed his masters thesis, *Tests of Musical Ability,* at the University of London. In 1941, Wing's doctoral thesis, *Tests of Musical Ability and Appreciation,* evolved into the first edition of the *Standardized Tests of Musical Intelligence,* published in 1958. Wing, a psychologist, wrote and engaged in research about music aptitude long before he compiled his final tests. Much of that work is contained in a monograph, *Tests of Musical Ability and Appreciation,* which was first published as an article in the *British Journal of Educational Psychology, Monograph Supplement* and later reproduced by University Press. His commitment to the importance of musical preference in the description and measurement of music aptitude was profoundly influenced as much by the work of Kate Hevner and her colleagues at the University of

Oregon as by his own countrymen. Hevner, in the *Oregon Musical Discrimination Tests,* devised measures in which an excerpt from a piece of music belonging to the standard repertoire was paired with a distorted version of the same piece. The listener is asked to determine which of the two performances is better and whether the alteration was melodic, rhythmic, or harmonic. It is important to note that Hevner did not refer to her test as one of music aptitude but rather as one of music appreciation. Be that as it may, John McLeish, in a factor analytic study of the Seashore, Wing, and Hevner tests conducted in England, found that, regardless of the intent of the authors and their beliefs, all three tests were essentially measuring the same common factor. That should not be surprising when one understands that the statistical procedure that McLeish employed is designed to give rise to a general factor. If McLeish had gone further and had rotated the factors, as most Americans do, the chances are that he would have garnered more fruitful results.

Wing not only believed that music aptitude is a general attribute that includes music preference, but also insisted that music aptitude must be described and measured in terms of musical stimuli. He explained that musical stimuli have two components: the sound source and the content of the sound. Whereas Seashore measured music aptitude using an electronic instrument as the sound source and used musically unrelated pitches as the content of the sound (except, of course, in the case of durations and rhythm), Wing measured music aptitude using a piano as the sound source and musically related pitches as the content of the sound. Moreover, Wing cited evidence from factor analytic studies that strongly suggests that general intelligence is an essential component of music aptitude, which may in part account for the use of the word *intelligence* in the title of his tests. Wing's idea that music aptitude embraced music preference, that it could be understood only as a totality in conjunction with general intelligence, and that it was dependent on music syntax generated by a musical instrument certainly established him as a Gestalist. The British went as far as to refer to Wing's description of music aptitude as an "omnibus theory," and giving it the label of "judicious musical," whereas what they considered Seashore's "atomistic theory," they labeled "mechanical acoustical." Juliane Ribke, in more recent research, continues indirectly to support the European approach in that she believes that being able to distinguish between excerpts that are or are not variations of a melody is basic to musicianship.

Although Wing believed that music aptitude is a general factor that cannot be separated into parts, he nevertheless, as I have already explained, described music aptitude as comprising three nonpreferential components and four preferential components. It is also apparent that he, like Seashore, considered pitch discrimination and tonal memory to be important to music aptitude, differences in how these should be measured notwithstanding. Wing referred to pitch discrimination as chord analysis and pitch change and to tonal memory simply as memory. Because a melody, by definition, incorporates rhythm, what he called memory is what he more accurately referred to as musical memory in other writings. As heretofore described, Seashore believed that if one has tonal memory, this is most precisely determined by how well one interacts with a series of musically unrelated pitches that are all of the same length, that is, that are without rhythm. This points to another important distinction between Gestalt and atomistic approaches. Wing contended that not only should a sound source be a musical instrument and the composition of the sound consist of musically related pitches, but that music aptitude is best described in terms of melody, because rhythm is a natural, if not a subordinate, concomitant. It is inconceivable to a music psychologist of strict Gestalt conviction, such as Wing, not to describe music aptitude in terms of combined musical elements. Thus, for Wing, there was no question but that pitches must be discriminated between in a musical context, within a chord, in order to identify how many pitches are perceived and the direction of their change.

Though it might seem inconsequential and insignificant to some, in this connection it is important not to overlook the fact that Wing attempted to move away from music achievement in his measurement of music aptitude by refraining from using the words *higher* and *lower*, as Seashore did, and by substituting *up* and *down* in the *Pitch Change* subtest. Nonetheless, the problem remains about whether music appreciation, being coterminous with the preference tests, relates more to a description of music achievement or more to music aptitude. Actually, the preference tests might be more properly titled recognition tests, because listeners who have previously heard the music that constitutes content for the test questions might attempt to determine which rendition of a performance was written by the original composer and is therefore more consistent with traditional interpretation, rather than to determine which of the two performances is more sensitively performed. That a listener is not familiar with a piece of music as a result of a lack of formal instruction, and so might prefer an altered version of that music, does not necessarily signal less than high music aptitude. Some aspects of the music of any famous composer may indeed stand improvements.

In a discussion of the reliability of the last revision of his test, Wing reports a split-halves coefficient, Spearman-Brown corrected, of .90 for older students and .70 for younger students (*Standardized Tests of Musical Intelligence*, 1958). Impressive as the higher one may be, it must be remembered that the coefficients are for the total test score and for heterogeneous students representing wide differences in age. Wing states that "groups of non-volunteers gave lower figures...[as] did children" (4). It should be further noted that although Wing offered norms by chronological age from eight to seventeen and older and separately for scores on the combined nonpreference tests and the total test, reliability data are again given only for all students combined and all subtests combined, and no information concerning the intercorrelations among the subtests is reported. Given this, Wing's description of music aptitude must be seriously questioned. As we know, the longer a test is, the more reliable it usually is, and so it would be most surprising if the reliability of a total test were not considerably higher than any one of the subtests that it includes. Jack Heller offers objective evidence specifically about the Wing subtests to corroborate that point. Wing summarized the reliability of his test more than twenty years after its publication by stating, "Thus, if only on grounds of reliability, high aptitude scores are satisfactory, but low aptitude scores should be regarded with reservation" (*Tests of Musical Ability and Appreciation,* 87), supporting Seashore's discredited assertion that music aptitude is dichotomous. Nevertheless, Wing offers norms to distinguish among the 90 percent of students he identifies as having less than high music aptitude.

In addition to the concerns based on objective data about Wing's description of music aptitude, there are subjective matters. Test reliability, of course, is increased when guessing is controlled by increasing the number of option responses for the test questions. For the *Chord Analysis* subtest, the answer sheet indicates that as many as five pitches may be heard in each chord in a test question, but there are never more than four pitches actually sounded. Ironically, although reliability is bolstered in such a case, validity suffers. For the *Memory* subtest, the answer sheet indicates that from eight to ten pitches may be heard in a melody in some test questions, but there are never more than seven. That, along with the fact that listeners are directed to choose "same" as the correct answer if two melodies sound the same, though, in fact, no pair of melodies are ever the same, also artificially inflates reliability. Such psychometric techniques suggest that Wing was aware of the low reliabilities of the subtests, and that his reporting of a reliability coefficient for the total test, combined age groups notwithstanding, was predicated on more than simply Gestalt theory.

Wing, like Seashore, was convinced that a person with high music aptitude is capable of knowing the ordinal number of a pitch that is changed in a series of pitches, though in Wing's opinion the pitches had to be musically related, but Seashore contended that it would be even more indicative of music aptitude if the pitches were not musically related and so were culture-free. Either way, the ability to determine the ordinal number of the changed pitch within a series is characteristic of general intelligence, particularly when the pitches are of different lengths, as in a melody where rhythm influences note length. Thus, it would not be unreasonable to assume that Seashore's *Tonal Memory* subtest, as well as Wing's *Memory* subtest, are possibly more related to general intelligence or to academic achievement than to music aptitude, and perhaps this is why the results of Wing's test form a common factor with scores on a general intelligence test, leading him to believe that music aptitude and intelligence are inseparable.

Unfortunately, there have been no longitudinal predictive validity studies conducted concerning Wing's test. Wing, however, did report the results of two criterion-related validity studies (*Standardized Tests of Musical Intelligence*). As I mentioned before, criterion-related validity is a poor substitute for longitudinal predictive validity, because in such studies an explanation of the relation between test scores and criterion scores, such as some form of achievement in music, must be inferred. Because the relation is of a concurrent nature, that is, because the test scores and the criterion scores are obtained within close proximity in time, one does not know for sure whether high music aptitude scores are responsible for high music achievement scores or whether high music achievement scores are responsible for high music aptitude scores. For that reason, criterion-related validity is classically referred to as concurrent validity. In a longitudinal predictive validity study, a music aptitude test is administered before music instruction is begun, and the measurement and evaluation of music achievement is undertaken after instruction has taken place. Thus, if there is a longitudinal relation found between music aptitude and music achievement scores, there can be little doubt that high music aptitude is responsible for high music achievement.

In Wing's first study, all seven subtests were administered to 333 boys from 14 to 16 years old who had begun taking lessons on a musical instrument. On the basis of their total test scores, the boys were divided into three groups: above average (the upper 30 percent), average (the middle 40 percent), and below average (the lower 30 percent). Wing reports that 98 percent in the above-average group, 73 percent in the average group, and 60 percent in the below-average group continued their lessons on a musical instrument. In the second study, all seven subtests were administered to 223 junior musicians in the Royal Marines School of Music, so the subjects were considerably older than those for whom the tests were primarily designed. Nonetheless, the musicians were then graded in music achievement by their instructors as above average, average, and below average. Wing found that there was a positive and significant correlation between these gradings and the test results. He did not, however, report the magnitude of the validity coefficient.

Why, if one designs a music aptitude test, is it common practice to validate it against a criterion of music achievement rather than a criterion of music aptitude? The straightforward answer is simple: Because no one knows with certainty what music aptitude is, only that it exists, and so the use of music achievement data is the only feasible option available. It certainly makes sense, however, to believe that if one possesses a high degree of music aptitude and is given an opportunity to make use of it, one should excel in music achievement. Thus, until a direct definition of music aptitude can be deduced (which is one of the goals this book is striving toward), the indirect approach must be pursued. It is because of this very delicate situation that longitudinal predictive validity studies, and not criterion-related validity studies, represent the only course to follow if we ever hope to arrive at a valid description of music aptitude.

Stages 1 and 2 of audiation are associated with developmental music aptitude, and stages 1, 2, and 3 of audiation are associated with stabilized music aptitude. At stages 1, 2, and 3, audiation is activated through music aptitude in conjunction with music achievement acquired in, at the least, an informal manner. At stages 4 and 5, audiation is activated through music aptitude in conjunction with music achievement acquired in a formal manner. That is, to function at these stages of audiation, formal music achievement is a necessity. Because in the preference subtests Wing employs familiar music, stages 4 and 5, in addition to stages 1, 2, and 3, of audiation would assist a listener in making appropriate responses to the test questions. Thus, as a result of evoking stage 4 of audiation, which requires the recall of music, and stage 5, which requires the ability to anticipate what will be heard next in familiar music and to predict what will be heard next in unfamiliar music, it would seem that the Wing subtests inadvertently declare themselves as music achievement tests. Nevertheless, Wing improved upon Seashore's work in describing music aptitude, because he understood and brought to the fore the realization that stage 3 of audiation is an integral part of stabilized music aptitude.

Wing's major contributions to the understanding and description of music aptitude may be summarized as follows: He recognized the importance of music preference to music aptitude; he brought attention to the idea that music memory is an integral part of music aptitude and that it involves the interaction of tonal and rhythmic elements; and he substantiated the idea that in order to investigate what might be included in the definition and description of music aptitude, musical instruments and questions that involve actual music are fundamental to the process.

Bentley

By and large, music aptitude tests have been designed for use beginning with students in grade four who are approximately nine years old. Although Drake provided norms for seven-year-olds and Wing for eight-year-olds, Arnold Bentley's more recent test is designed for children as young as seven years old who are in grade two. The *Measures of Musical Ability* (1966) comprises four recorded parts: pitch discrimination, rhythm memory, tonal memory, and chord analysis. The last two parts are constructed similarly to the Wing *Memory* and *Chord Analysis* subtests, and the pitch discrimination part corresponds to the Wing *Pitch Change* subtest, except that in the Bentley measure, single tones are used rather than chords. The rhythm memory part is similar to the tonal memory part except, of course, that it deals with rhythm patterns. As in the Seashore test, an oscillator is the stimulus for the pitch discrimination part, but for the remaining three parts, an organ is used, even for the rhythm part, which has no melodic component.

Bentley cites statistically nonsignificant relations among the four parts of the test, but he neglects to discuss the reliability or validity of the separate parts, disregarding the fact that low reliabilities for any two factors is sure to result in a low intercorrelation between them. Further, as with Lowell Tilson, he reports criterion-related validity findings based on the performance of older students at the college level as well as professionals, even though the test was specifically designed for use with very young children. As for the Wing test, only total score norms are made available on a five-category scale, and Bentley makes no pretense of being able to provide percentile ranks.

Suffice it say that the Bentley test combines both Gestalt and atomistic principles in its construction without an obvious rationale. About the only clue we have to what Bentley might have been thinking is that he supported Wing's ideas and attempted to make his test directions more accessible than Wing's to young children. Because Bentley's test offers no innovations or new insights into our understanding of music aptitude, we can only assume from the content of his test that he preferred a noncontroversial approach and, consequently, supported eclecticism in his description and measurement of music aptitude. Obviously, Bentley believed that the description of music aptitude is not materially different for younger and older children, only that it is necessary to take care to make the test directions comprehensible to all. We shall discover that this is not necessarily the case.

Before moving ahead to an examination of more up-to-date music aptitude tests and their implications for establishing a firmer description of music aptitude, I would like to make reference to some transitional information that bears on two philosophical points of view that did not culminate in published tests of music aptitude, and on one that did but did not receive wide recognition.

Harvey Whistler and Louis Thorpe published the *Musical Aptitude Test* in 1950. One of the main reasons the test did not have great appeal is that the content of the questions was not recorded and, therefore, had to be performed at the keyboard. Given all the inherent problems associated with such a process, it is no wonder that it was even published at all. Aside from whether the content is or is not correctly performed, to obtain consistency in performance by one person, let alone groups of persons with different orientations and backgrounds, would seem impossible. Thus, the statistical data reported in the test manual leave much to be desired, because they cannot be interpreted with confidence from one occasion to the next.

The Whistler-Thorpe test includes five parts: *Rhythm Recognition, Pitch Recognition, Melody Recognition, Pitch Discrimination,* and *Advanced Rhythm Recognition.* It is the *Pitch Recognition* part that offers us the possibility of including a new dimension in our formulation of the description of music aptitude. In that part a pitch is performed and a short series of pitches follow that are referred to as a melody, but they do not really qualify as such because all of the pitches are to be performed with equal length. The subject is asked to indicate how many times that pitch was heard in the melody. No specific data of score results are offered, but I believe the approach embraces a unique concept that merits further attention through systematic research.

Kai Karma in Finland and John Booth Davies in England, both psychologists, have postulated descriptions of music aptitude that have led them to consider novel and divergent ideas about the measurement of music aptitude that have not, to the present, found their way into the form of formal published tests. Both are extremely critical of all past attempts at measuring music aptitude and each feels that he has discovered an acceptable method for doing so. Davies's skepticism about past attempts to measure music aptitude is almost abusive. What the two seem to agree upon is that, as Karma suggests in his article *Musical Aptitude as the Ability to Structure Acoustic Material,* a valid test of music aptitude should "be objective and free from the effects of culture and training, and, on the other hand, would measure the basic understanding of the general holistic properties of music" (28). How Karma believes this is possible is explained below in terms of his experimental test.

A sequence is formed by three renditions of simple structures of pitch, intensity, duration, and time. The repetitions follow one another without pauses or other indications of where one ends and the other begins. The subject's task is to determine if the isolated structure heard later is simply the same or different from the consecutively repeated structure. The listener is not asked to identify which of the four elements might have been different. Karma's constructs are reminiscent of Seashore's, the philosophy of the two men fundamentally attempting to eschew culture and, as a necessary result, relying on acoustical perception rather than musical cognition and audiation. To that extent, both approaches might claim to have negative validity, that is, unless a subject scores high on the test, he or she could not become a good musician, but if a subject should score high, the test results would not particularly be useful in determining objectively whether he or she has the potential to become a good musician.

Davies's solution is even more succinct: "To sum up, it is possible, therefore, to test musically relevant capacities without using musical material; the use of non-musical material does not confine one to testing simple sensory processes" (*Psychology of Music,* 140). Specifically, Davies believes in the use of "sweep-frequency tones" for measuring music aptitude. He would expose the listener to a pitch and then ask if that pitch were contained in the acoustical frequency sweep. I hope Davies would agree that if such a measure were found to have predictive validity, he would nevertheless be hard pressed to defend the notion that it contributes in any way to a description of overall music aptitude. Although all aptitude tests are predictive tests, not all predictive tests are aptitude tests.

Putting the three methodologies on a continuum, Whister-Thorpe's would be most musical; Davies's the least; and Karma's somewhere in between. Nonetheless, they form a succession that suggests a point of view that was not part of previous thinking, and it would be difficult to summarily dismiss them. Collectively their approach has something to say, but the message remains unclear.

CURRENT TRENDS

Thus far, we have seen that if it can be shown that a test is valid, that is, when scores on a test with music content that is presented in a musical manner accurately predict success in musical endeavors, it would make sense that what is being measured is indicative of music aptitude. Still, we have been considering only what might be called functional aspects of music aptitude rather than the more important and compelling structural base of music aptitude. Theories, whether they are subjective or claim to be objective but have little supporting research, particularly in the form of measurement, are problematic. It is with this concern in mind that the remainder of this and the next few chapters are written. Even though more recent music aptitude tests will be examined, however, my primary intention will be to move closer to a creditable and more trustworthy definition of the structural substance of music aptitude.

Musical Aptitude Profile

The *Musical Aptitude Profile* (Gordon, 1995), referred to as MAP, has been described as an eclectic test in regard to the atomistic and omnibus theories, because while both nonpreference and preference subtests constitute the battery, and the test questions consist of specially composed music performed by professional musicians, the battery does, nevertheless, provide for the evaluation of seven postulated factors of music aptitude. The musical dimensions measured by the battery are classified into three total tests: *Tonal Imagery, Rhythm Imagery,* and *Musical Sensitivity.* Two subtests are provided for each of the nonpreference total tests, *Tonal Imagery* and *Rhythm Imagery.* They are *Melody* and *Harmony* for the former and *Tempo* and *Meter* for the latter. The preference total test, *Musical Sensitivity,* comprises three subtests: *Phrasing, Balance,* and *Style.* The entire test is recorded.

In the *Melody* and *Harmony* subtests, the listener is asked to compare a "musical answer" to a short but complete musical statement. The violin is the stimulus for the former test, and both the violin and cello, in duet, are used for the latter. The musical answer contains more tones than the original phrase, and the listener is to determine if the answer is similar to the original (if it is, it is a tonal variation) or different from the original (not a tonal variation). When in doubt about the correct answer, the listener is directed to use the "in-doubt" response on the answer sheet. The upper part of the musical restatement for the questions in the *Harmony* subtest, which is actually of a contrapuntal nature, is always the same. The embellishment takes place only in the lower part.

Both *Tonal Imagery* subtests incorporate a variety of keyalities, major and minor tonalities, and multitonal/multikeyal music. Usual duple, triple, and combined meters and a variety of tempos and rhythmic permutations, such as syncopation and anacruses, are used. Although particular attention is given to a musically expressive performance and all test questions incorporate rhythm as an integral part, the listener is called upon to make decisions only about the tonal elements of the music.

For the *Tempo* subtest, the tempo of the ending of the restatement is performed faster than, slower than, or exactly the same (re-recorded) as the ending of the original statement, the tonal aspects, of course, being the same in both the statement and the restatement. If the ending of the restatement is performed either faster or slower than the statement, the listener indicates that the two are different; if the endings are performed at the same tempo, the listener indicates that they are the same; and if the listener is unsure about the correct answer, the "in-doubt" response is marked. For the *Meter* subtest, the listener indicates whether the meter of the two statements is exactly the same or different, and if the listener is unsure, again the "in doubt" response is marked. Usual and unusual meters, various tempos, and different rhythmic nuances are employed in both subtests. The expressive and tonal elements of the questions in the rhythm subtests are as comprehensive as those found in the tonal subtests. In keeping with the design of the battery, for the two rhythm subtests, listeners are asked to make only rhythmic decisions. The violin is the medium of performance.

The *Musical Sensitivity* subtests require the listener to decide which rendition of a specially composed, and thus unfamiliar, melody makes the better musical sense. In the *Phrasing* subtest, the same melody is performed a second time with different musical expression, and the listener is asked to make a judgment about which version sounds better. In the *Balance* subtest, the endings of the two melodies are different, and the listener is asked to judge which melody has the better ending. In the *Style* subtest, the melody is performed a second time in a different tempo, and the listener is asked to decide which tempo best complements the melody. The violin and cello are used as performance media for all three subtests. Although the listener reacts to dynamics, tempo, tone quality, intonation, and tonal and rhythmic contour and style, the only answer that is required is 1, 2, or "in doubt."

The foregoing description of the seven subtests should support the idea that the psychological constructs underlying the *Musical Aptitude Profile* are significantly different from those used in previous tests. For example, the *Tonal Imagery* subtests go beyond measuring aural discrimination of isolated pairs of pitches or the ability to determine specifically which pitch in a restated series is changed. They are instead concerned with tonal and rhythmic syntax. The *Rhythm Imagery* subtests also embody unique psychological constructs. That is, rather than using nonmelodic rhythm patterns or metronomic clicks, the *Tempo* subtest allows for tempo to be influenced by, and to interact with, melodic rhythm as well as with expressive elements typically found in music.

Likewise, the *Meter* subtest has similar characteristics, except that in this measure, meter must be interpreted in conjunction with a variety of tempos. It is interesting to note that this battery, unlike the Seashore measures, does not contain any type of time discrimination test.

The *Musical Sensitivity* preference subtests reflect some ideas used by earlier test developers. For example, the *Phrasing* subtest is similar to the Wing subtest of the same name, but it consists of originally composed music that elicits judgment rather than recognition responses. Furthermore, using string instruments as the medium of presentation allows for flexibility in intonation and dynamics as they interact with tempo and tone quality. The *Balance* subtest has some commonality with the Kwalwasser *Melodic Taste* subtest, although the former is designed to provide for both tonal and rhythm elements to complement musical form. There is no prototype for the *Style* subtest, which acknowledges that tempo plays a formidable role in musical form and phrasing.

National norms and reliability coefficients are provided for scores on each of the seven subtests, the three total tests, and the composite test, separately for grades 4 through 12. The fact that there are low intercorrelations among subtests comprising different total tests and only somewhat higher intercorrelations among subtests included in the same total test indirectly indicates overall validity for the battery. Interestingly, the highest relation between measures was found between the nonpreference *Meter* subtest and the preference *Balance* subtest. That the seven music aptitudes represented in the battery are related to specific musical attributes and that the composite test score is related to overall musical understanding has been suggested by independent investigators, such as Leon Fosha, James Froseth, Warren Hatfield, Doris Norton, and Stanley Schleuter and Lois Schleuter. My own prepublication and post publication research pertaining to the *Musical Aptitude Profile* found in the test manual, *Implications for the Use of the Musical Aptitude Profile with College and University Freshman Music Students* (1967), *The Contribution of Each Musical Aptitude Profile Subtest to the Overall Validity of the Battery* (1968), and *An Investigation of the Intercorrelation Among Musical Aptitude Profile and Seashore Measures of Musical Talents Subtests* (1969), for example, also suggest this. A unique aspect of MAP is its demonstrated predictive validity. In a two-year longitudinal predictive validity study, *Taking Into Account Musical Aptitude Differences Among Beginning Instrumental Music Students,* pretraining music aptitude scores predicted the success of elementary school students in beginning instrumental music instruction with unusually high precision (Gordon, 1970). Also, after two years of typical instruction, it was found that students' scores were not increased significantly, and that in fact some student's scores remained almost the same or decreased.

Probably the most significant difference been the Seashore and Wing methodologies and resultant conclusions, on the one hand, and my further research (as evidenced in the *Musical Aptitude Profile),* on the other, is in regard to memorization (which both refer to as memory) and recall. Whereas Seashore and Wing believed that memorization is part of music aptitude, I have taken the position that memorization is a factor indicative of music achievement. One must achieve to be able to memorize what one hears, but one can recall what was heard without formal instruction. In order to memorize music, one must be able to recall music, but it is not necessary for one to memorize music in order to recall it. When familiar music is used as content in a music aptitude test, that problem is exacerbated.

The difference between recall and memorization notwithstanding, audiation takes place in both the recall and memorization of music. The first three stages of audiation are associated with recall, whereas the fourth stage of audiation requires at the very least some memorization of music. Thus, when stage four of audiation becomes a concomitant part of the description and measurement of music aptitude, music achievement necessarily supersedes music aptitude.

In addition to tonal memory and rhythm memory, Seashore included pitch discrimination and time discrimination in his description of music aptitude. Because he found negligible relations between his measures of pitch discrimination and tonal memory and between his measures of time discrimination and rhythm memory, he considered discrimination to be an important component of music aptitude. I uncovered some revealing and contrary information, however. Students who demonstrate a high level of pitch discrimination do not necessarily score high on the MAP *Tonal Imagery* subtests, but students who do score high on the MAP *Tonal Imagery* subtests necessarily have a high level of pitch discrimination. Similarly, students who demonstrate a high level of time discrimination do not necessarily score high on the MAP *Rhythm Imagery* subtests, but students who do score high on the MAP *Rhythm Imagery* subtests necessarily have a high level of time discrimination (*An Investigation of the Intercorrelation Among Musical Aptitude Profile and Seashore Measures of Musical Talents Subtests, 1969*). Barring persons who are profoundly deaf or unsighted, it would seem that acoustical acuity, in isolation, is as unrelated to music aptitude as visual acuity is to art aptitude.

As I mentioned before, Wing emphasized tonal skills in his description of and measurement of music aptitude. All three of his nonpreference measures deal only with tonal elements. Rhythm is of no consequence, even in his *Memory* subtest, and only one of his four preference subtests relates to rhythm, and in that case it deals only with accents. In prepublication studies of the *Musical Aptitude Profile*, I learned that rhythm aptitude is the foundation of music aptitude. Thus, when one demonstrates a high tonal aptitude but shows a low rhythm aptitude, high overall music achievement may not be an expected outcome. The reverse, however, is not true. When rhythm aptitude is high and tonal aptitude is at least at the 60th percentile, high overall music achievement is realistically attainable. Thus, the high relation found between the MAP *Meter* and *Balance* subtests must not be overlooked.

Advanced Measures of Music Audiation

Compared to the *Musical Aptitude Profile*, where diagnosis of students' musical strengths and weaknesses is one of its primary purposes, the *Advanced Measures of Music Audiation* (Gordon, 1989), referred to as AMMA, is relatively short. Also, whereas MAP is a stabilized music aptitude test designed for students in grades four through twelve, AMMA may be used with students in grades seven and higher, with college and university students, and with laypersons and music professionals alike. As for any valid music aptitude test, no formal music background is necessary in order to score high on AMMA.

A series of short recorded melodies in a variety of tonalities and meters, performed on a synthesizer, constitute the test. The listener indicates whether the statement and restatement of each short melody sound the same, whether they sound different because of one or more tonal changes, or whether they sound different because of one or more rhythm changes. There is only one correct answer for each question. Although AMMA incorporates only one test, the results yield separate tonal and rhythm scores in addition to a total score.

Reliabilities, which range in the .80s, are reported for each of the three scores, and norms are available for music and nonmusic majors in junior and senior high school and for adults. Interestingly, the differences between mean scores within groups for students of different chronological ages in junior and senior high school and for adults are negligible and inconsistent. Various types of validity studies, including a one-year longitudinal predictive study, concurrent studies, and practice and training studies have, in general, substantiated the test as one of music aptitude (Gordon, *Predictive Validity Study of AMMA* , 1990). There is one doctoral study by Stephen Estrella, however, that, based on the issues of practice and training, sheds some doubt on the validity of the test as one of music aptitude and suggests that it may be a music achievement test.

As I explained with regard to the Seashore test, if it can be shown that results on a so-called music aptitude test are not impervious to subjects' practice and musical training, the validity of the test is called into question. To examine the concern in an intelligent manner, however, it must be understood that there are two relevant types of training and one of practice. The first type of training consists of typical instruction, and the other is designed to make the listener comfortable and familiar with the sort of musical content that is found on the test. Practice, on the other hand, is a matter of repeatedly administering a similarly designed test with musical content paraphrased from the original test. It is understandable why some persons might believe that an increase in test scores as a result of either type of training might impinge on the validity of a test measuring music aptitude, but it should not be surprising that intensive practice of the type described increases test scores, thus invalidating a valid test for proper use. Astonishingly, though, it has been found that such practice does not always result in an increase in test scores, and when increases are discovered, though they may portray statistical significance, they usually have no practical significance whatsoever.

In the one study (Estrella) with conclusions that do not necessarily substantiate AMMA as a music aptitude test, practice in taking the test was given over an extended period of time. The results of the study, however, are not clear because of the untenable design (a control group was used unnecessarily, thus clouding the outcome of the statistical analysis) and, therefore, the results are reported ambiguously.

There are several subjective reasons for believing that AMMA is a music aptitude test and not a music achievement test. First, the capabilities measured in the test are not formally taught to students. Second, because it uses original material, a listener could not have achieved familiarity with the music that constitutes the test questions. Third, although because of formal or informal music instruction some listeners may have theoretical knowledge of the words *tonal* and *rhythm,* other students will quickly acquire an understanding of the words when listening to the practice exercises. Fourth, there is not enough silent time between the performance of the two renditions to allow a listener to even attempt to memorize the first one in the pair for comparative purposes.

Before suggesting a reasonable description of music aptitude as we conclude this chapter, a few words about the relations among the various music aptitude tests might be helpful, in spite of their apparent differences, as a way to gain perspective when considering the validity of the more recent tests. I have already explained that, in correlation studies, Paul Farnsworth and Mary Whitley found that, except for the tonal memory measures, subtests of the same name in the Seashore and K-D batteries have little in common, and Drake had reason to believe that his and Seashore's rhythm subtests were not measuring the same capabilities. In my comparative analysis of the Seashore and MAP batteries, it was found that the composite scores of the two batteries correlate much lower with each other than the MAP composite score correlates with an objective longitudinal criterion of music achievement.

There are also factor analytic studies that bear on the matter. Raleigh Drake, using subtests from various batteries, concluded that tonal memory, pitch discrimination, rhythm memory, and tonal movement, along with general intelligence, can be considered in combination as a general factor of music aptitude. Wing, like Cyril Burt before him and Philip E. Vernon after him, found evidence of not only a general factor, which includes intelligence, but also of two group factors, the first comprising tonal elements ("analytic") and the other musical preference ("synthetic") as depicted from his battery alone. It will be remembered that John McLeish's analysis of the Wing and Seashore batteries uncovered a general factor in which tonal elements play an important role. Both Bruce Faulds and Erik Franklin, the former working principally with the Seashore subtests and specifically designed nonmusical acoustical tests, and the latter with these and the Wing subtests, supported the British hypothesis that music aptitude has two main divisions, "mechanical acoustic and judicious musical." Charles Manzer and Samuel Morowitz, using only K-D subtests, found two group factors. The two imagery subtests combined into a "musical training factor" and the eight remaining subtests formed a "sensory factor." Dealing primarily with thirty-two audio-acoustical tests, J. E. Karlin identified as many as eight group factors, the three most important being pitch discrimination, memory for isolated elements, and memory for series of pitches. Like Karlin, Libbie Bower found no general factor but rather three group factors. Her factors, which greatly overlapped but were different from Karlin's, included 1) tonal memory, pitch and rhythm discrimination, and melodic preference, 2) loudness and time, and 3) tonal memory and rhythm discrimination.

CONCLUSIONS

Given that music aptitude is a product of innate capabilities that must be nourished through environmental influences beginning at an early age, it is the understanding of what those environmental influences are that offers us significant insight into the description of music aptitude. We can never be sure, of course, that our conclusions about music aptitude will be correct, but there is ample objective evidence, gathered primarily as a result of the examination of the content of music aptitude tests and the extent to which those tests have been appropriately deemed to have validity, to make our judgments more than simply arbitrary or personally satisfying.

There appear to be three main components of stabilized music aptitude: tonal, rhythm, and aesthetic expressive-interpretive. Empirical evidence indicates that the tonal dimension is one of tonal audiation: we hear, recall, understand, anticipate, and predict what is absorbed as tonal elements in music as we phase through, in a circular, not linear, manner, the first three stages of audiation. Although there have been liberal references to imagery found in the various descriptions of music aptitude, it is actually audiation that is the essence. The same may be said of rhythm audiation as the essence of the rhythm dimension, although the rhythm dimension is even more far reaching than the tonal dimension. Rhythm, fundamentally meter and tempo, seems to be the basis of music aptitude, because it provides the foundation for the cohesion of pitches and, perhaps more important, for style and expressiveness in music. The counting and memorization of and the discrimination among isolated pitches and durations in terms of up or down, skip or step, higher or lower, longer or shorter, louder or softer, richer or duller, or ordinal position, either in or apart from a musical context, certainly involve perception, but not necessarily musical understanding. Such mechanical-acoustical feats or acts of intelligence are necessary for one to demonstrate music aptitude, but it is misleading to believe that they, themselves, represent music aptitude. Music aptitude is an awareness of melodic contour and syntactical pitch and durational relationships that give rise to either a subjective or objective sense of tonality and meter. It is giving intuitive meaning to sound that is indicative of music aptitude and taking formal meaning from sound that is characteristic of music achievement.

Although rhythm is basic to music aptitude, it appears that it is the expressive aesthetic-interpretive dimension of stabilized music aptitude, not the recognition of music, that amalgamates the tonal and rhythm dimensions of music aptitude and, in turn, gives rise to comprehensive music aptitude. Because the content of the MAP *Musical Sensitivity* subtests plays such an important role in our eventual determination of the description of music aptitude, a word about how the subtests were objectively validated is in order. To begin, test questions were composed by the author and then recorded by professional musicians. At any given time, from five to fifteen recorded questions were personally administered or sent to ten academic and professional musicians at random from a pool of more than twenty. Performers, conductors, composers, and arrangers, all involved in classical, popular, and commercial music, were included in the group. Unless the answers of at least nine of the ten musicians agreed for a test question, and not necessarily with the test author or the recording musicians, changes in the notation were made, then re-recorded, and subjected again to the same process, or the questions were discarded. That lengthy procedure was followed until the desired number of test questions was developed to insure acceptable test reliabilities. Next, the remaining questions were administered to students in elementary schools in various locations. Unless a question demonstrated a satisfactory item difficulty level (at least .58) and an item discrimination level (at least .20) for students of all ages, the question was discarded. More than seven hundred questions were composed and recorded in order to develop the ninety that are included in the three preference subtests. Finally, the longitudinal predictive validity of the entire battery was investigated and a validity coefficient of .75 was found, indicating that approximately 55 percent of the reason or reasons students are successful in school music is associated with their composite scores on the *Musical Aptitude Profile,* and that the three preference subtests contributed significantly to that finding.

In a word, it is the impressions that we subjectively or objectively audiate and associate with the sound of music that allows us to make musical inferences and judgments, thus stimulating relevant musical thought rather than thought about music. That process, though it manifests itself somewhat differently for those in the developmental and stabilized stages of music aptitude, is music aptitude.

CHAPTER 4

THE DESCRIPTION OF DEVELOPMENTAL MUSIC APTITUDE

As long ago as when Carl E. Seashore first engaged in research, it was understood that the younger a child is when the child's music aptitude is measured and followed by appropriate music instruction, the more the child will be able to achieve in music. When a child's music aptitude is measured using a battery of subtests, the child's musical strengths and weaknesses become obvious. Given that diagnostic information, the teacher and parents may adapt informal guidance and formal instruction in music to meet the individual musical needs of the child. Thus, before research findings indicated that there are two types of music aptitude, developmental and stabilized, investigations were undertaken to determine if the same music aptitude tests could be used with students of all ages, including those younger than age nine. Most test authors believed tests would yield most practical results when used with students nine years old and older. Wing, who believed that one music aptitude test is appropriate for all, offered norms for students as young as eight.

Because most investigators were of the opinion that the administrative procedures, test directions, or both, for existing tests were too lengthy and complex for young children to understand, they developed modified versions of available tests of music aptitude (we now know that all of them were tests of stabilized music aptitude) for use with students younger than those for whom the tests were originally intended. It was reasoned that if administration procedures and test directions could be simplified and made to require less time, young children would have less difficulty in responding to the musical content of the test questions.

As I already explained, in 1966 Arnold Bentley devised a test in four parts, *Pitch Discrimination, Tonal Memory, Rhythmic Memory,* and

Chord Analysis, to measure the music "ability" of seven-year-old through fourteen-year-old students. With the exception of the addition of the rhythm part and the absence of preference tests, the psychological constructs and design of the Bentley tests parallel those of Wing's. In keeping with his belief that the musical content as well as the test directions for young children must be kept simple, the musical content and directions in Bentley test are not as difficult as those included in the corresponding Wing subtests.

In neither the case of Wing nor Bentley is the reliability of the measures substantial enough to suggest that there is merit in either of their approaches. Bentley extracted a reliability coefficient of .84 for only the total test score using a heterogeneous group of students from approximately ten to twelve years of age (*Musical Ability in Children*), completely ignoring the primary purpose of his test, and test validity was not even taken into consideration. Although a test may be reliable or valid for a group of students of one age, it may be entirely inappropriate for a younger or older group. As with Bentley, Wing never reported, and probably did not investigate, the reliability or validity of his test when used only with children younger than nine years old.

As reported in the test manual, during the development of the *Musical Aptitude Profile,* I administered the two subtests, *Meter* and *Phrasing,* later to be included in the final version of the battery, to approximately 150 children in kindergarten through third grade in Ottumwa, Iowa. The children were identified by their music teachers and supervisor as having attained the highest levels of music achievement among all children from five to eight years old who were enrolled in all elementary schools in the city. The investigation was designed to aid in establishing the validity of the subtests. It was reasoned that if young children with little or no formal instruction in music could attain high scores, that would indicate that the subtests are indeed measures of music aptitude and not of music achievement. The secondary purpose of the investigation, which is of main concern here, was to determine whether children from five to eight years old could understand the test directions and if they were capable of making the same types of responses to the same music content as are students nine years of age and older. A parent was assigned to assist a child other than his or her own in marking the child's verbal response to each test question. No additional help was offered. When necessary, additional time was allotted by stopping the test recording after the music for each question was heard so parents could mark the answer sheets. Thus, the test procedure took one hour rather than the typical fifteen minutes for each subtest.

The overall validity of MAP was enhanced by the data. It was clear from the means and score ranges that formal music achievement is not necessary to score high on either subtest. The mean on the *Meter* subtest for the kindergarten children was the same as that for a musically hetero-geneous group of sixth grade students, and the mean on the *Phrasing* subtest for the kindergarten children was only three-tenths of a point lower than that for a musically heterogeneous group of fourth grade students. The means for children in grades one, two, and three were comparably high. Nonetheless, on the basis of the overall evidence it was concluded that using either of the subtests in the *Musical Aptitude Profile* with children younger than nine would be inappropriate. Because a few musically select young children experienced some difficulty in under-standing the test directions, experienced difficulty in keeping pace with the recorded directions, became confused with how the answer sheets were being marked, and made mistakes in what to listen for in the questions, it follows that invalid results may be expected for many of less-musical children of the same age who comprise as much as 80 percent of the school population. For a music aptitude test to be accept-able, it must yield valid results for all students, those with low and aver-age music aptitude as well as those with high music aptitude.

Harrington

In an attempt to modify the procedures for administering MAP so that the subtests might be used to measure and diagnose the music aptitudes of children younger than nine, Charles Harrington wrote simplified direc-tions, renamed the subtests, and designed a color-coded answer sheet. Children who were not able to read could follow the different colors on the answer sheet in order to mark their answers to the test questions. Harrington found that musically heterogeneous kindergarten and first grade children could not understand the simplified versions of the battery, nor could they deal with the complexity of sounds heard in the test ques-tions. Further, he discovered that only three subtests, *Melody, Tempo,* and *Phrasing,* accorded reasonably high reliabilities, from .68 to .88, and this only for second and third grade students. Even children of seven and eight years old expressed difficulty in understanding what to listen for in the remaining four subtests in the battery. Harrington's recommendation was that until appropriate tests can be written, the description and measure-ment of the music aptitude of children under nine years old should not be attempted.

Simons

As part of a project to evaluate the comparative music-listening skills of groups of children in kindergarten through grade three, Gene Simons developed a music achievement test, *Simons Measurements of Music Listening Skills,* observing in the test manual that there was a "scarcity of published tests of musical achievement for young children" (1). Though his measures are designed to measure music achievement and not music aptitude, they are relevant to the present discussion, if for no other reason than that they may serve in pointing out the necessary distinction between the music content of music achievement and music aptitude tests, indirectly suggesting a description of music aptitude applicable to young children.

There are nine very short parts to the test, each including only five questions, and each part is recorded with directions and practice exercises. A violin, piano, drum, and reasonator bells are used as stimuli. In the *Melodic Direction* part, children are asked to decide whether the direction of the melody is "up, down, or straight"; in the *Steps/Jumps* part, they decide whether the melody is "stepping or jumping"; in the first *Harmony* part, they decide whether the sound they hear includes one or more bells; in the second *Harmony* part, they count and decide which one of four chords does not sound the same as the others; in the *Meter* part, they identify the meter as either "1-2" or "1-2-3"; in the *Tonal Patterns* part, they identify two melodies as sounding the same or different; in the *Rhythm Patterns* part, they identify two rhythm patterns as sounding the same or different; in the *Dynamics* part, they decide whether a melody becomes "louder, softer, or remains at the same level"; and in the *Tempo* part, they decide whether a melody becomes "faster, slower, or stays at the same speed." Given what we already know about the nature of music aptitude of older children, it is apparent that the Simons test is an agglomeration of music aptitude and music achievement, perhaps more correctly considered an ability test, and offers no new insights into the description of music aptitude, even for young children.

Simons offers no reliability or validity information because, he claims, such statistical data are inappropriate for group criterion-referenced mastery tests, particularly when the parts may be used individually or in any combination. As the concluding statement in the test manual reads, "This test is designed to measure music achievement of *groups* of children...as an aid to program evaluation and revision....The low range in which all kindergarten scores lie indicates that this test is unsuitable for most kindergarten children." (4)

Zenatti

After studying for a number of years the responses to music of 7000 young children, Arlette Zenatti recorded the *Tests Musicaux Pour Jeunes Enfants*. Those five measures of "musicality" were developed for children as young as four years of age and as old as seven years, eleven months. Because Zenatti wanted to learn how young children think about music (which might offer some information about the description of music aptitude for young children), and because of her desire to assist psychologists in the treatment of pathological conditions in young children, she designed the measures to be administered in a play situation suitable for young children on an individual basis. Just what Zenatti concluded about how young children think about music was not reported with the publication of the test. Nonetheless, the designs of some of the measures are unique and deserve our attention.

Rosamund Shuter-Dyson and Clive Gabriel, in their account of Zenatti's work, report a test-retest reliability of .84. Unfortunately, that is for the total test score based on a heterogeneous group of 136 children ranging in age from almost four and a half to eight years old, and the reliability of the quality of children's music performances is more a matter of the reliability of the test administrator making the judgments than of the test itself. In the *Tests De Réproduction Rhythmique*, after tapping rhythm patterns that were tapped by the tester as practice, the child taps rhythm patterns that were played on the piano by the tester, thus demonstrating skill in music achievement. In the *Tests de Jugement Esthétique D'Eléments Harmoniques, Mélodiques, et Rhythmiques*, the child indicates a preference for the first or second of a pair of examples for each musical dimension. The preferences are based on consonant and dissonant harmonies, tonal or multitonal melodies, and simple or varied rhythms. Each example is performed twice and, interestingly, the child's score is determined by the consistency of the child's choice and not on the choice the child makes. Thus, the measure is not actually one of aesthetic preference, but one of consistency of judgment. In *Forme A* of the *Tests De Discrimination De Modifications Harmoniques, Mélodiques, et Rhythmiques*, the child indicates 1) whether the first or second of two chords is different from or the same as the two original chords that were heard, 2) whether the first or second of two pitches is different from or the same as the two original pitches that were heard, and 3) whether the first or second of two rhythm patterns is different from or the same as the two original rhythm patterns that were heard. In *Forme B* of the *Tests De Discrimination De Modifications Harmoniques, et Mélodiques,*

Rhythmiques, the child indicates 1) whether the first or second set of two chords is different from or the same as the two original sets of chords that were heard, 2) whether the first or second set of two pitches is different from or the same as the two original sets of pitches that were heard, and 3) whether the first or second sets of two rhythm patterns is different from or the same as the two original sets of rhythm patterns that were heard. The content of both forms is more acoustical than musical in nature, but because it puts less emphasis on memorization, the easier *Forme A* may be considered better related to music aptitude than *Forme B.* In the *Tests D'Identification Harmonique, Mélodique, Rhythmique, et Par Aprentissage Discriminatif,* the child is taught to associate two harmonized melodies with pictures of different animals. When the melody that has been associated with a dog is heard, the child is expected to point to the picture of a dog, and when the melody that has been associated with a horse is heard, the child is expected to point to the picture of a horse. The child's score is determined on the basis of the speed as well as of the accuracy of his or her responses. It would seem that the Zenatti test does achieve its main purpose in gathering information about the general psychological inclinations of children but, even taking into consideration aspects of the originality of its design, it offers little about children's music aptitudes.

My research into the description and measurement of developmental music aptitude began with three experimental investigations over a period of eight years (*Toward the Development of a Taxonomy,* 1974; *Tonal and Rhythm Patterns,* 1976; and *A Factor Analytic Description,* 1978). It focused on the categorization and determination of the comparative difficulty of audiating tonal patterns in the same and different tonalities, such as major and harmonic minor, and rhythm patterns in the same and different meters. Only those patterns that children found easy to audiate were used as content in the next stage of the research, which included the direct measurement of the tonal and rhythm aptitudes of young children. The results gathered from testing more than 10,000 young children who participated in the series of investigations revealed interesting facts about unique aspects of the measurement and description of music aptitude of young children. Before discussing these, I will give a brief overview of how the research was undertaken.

Large groups of stratified random samples of students of various ages across the country were asked to listen to recorded tonal patterns and rhythm patterns and to indicate whether each pair in a series of patterns they heard sound the same or different. If the patterns in a pair were the same, and if most students in the group were aware that they were, the pattern was considered easy to audiate; if the patterns in a pair were the same, but approximately half the students were unaware that they were, the pattern was considered moderately difficult to audiate; and if the patterns in a pair were the same, but only a few students in the group were aware of this, the pattern was considered difficult to audiate. No analysis was undertaken for pairs of patterns that were different. Surprisingly, it was found that the difficulty levels of the patterns had virtually no relation to the frequency with which the patterns are found in standard music literature.

Perhaps the most important discovery was that the music aptitude of children younger than nine is developmental, that is, that the younger children are, the more sensitive their levels of music aptitude are to environmental influences as they move toward and away from their birth levels (Gordon, *The Manifestation of Developmental Music Aptitude*, 1981). Music aptitude does not stabilize until approximately age nine. Other very important revelations bear on the nature of what children younger than age nine respond to musically and the way those responses are best elicited.

Children in the developmental stage of music aptitude can concentrate on only one dimension of music at one time. It might be said that they respond to music in atomistic terms, not in Gestalt terms. For example, they can make reliable decisions about a tonal pattern they are listening to only if that tonal pattern is not in a rhythm context. All pitches in the tonal pattern must be of equal length. Children at this age can also make reliable decisions about a rhythm pattern that they are listening to, but only if that rhythm pattern is not in a tonal context. Though all durations in the rhythm pattern can be stylistic and expressive, they must be of the same pitch. Only two dimensions of developmental music aptitude, tonal and rhythm, have thus far been identified, and they are nonpreferential. The separate parts of rhythm, such as tempo and meter, and the separate parts of tonal, such as melody and harmony, seem not to be discernible to young children.

When young children are asked to tell whether the same melodic pattern performed twice has the same or different tone quality (timbre), almost all are able to answer the question correctly if the differences are exaggerated. When the difference is even slightly less than pronounced, almost none are able to answer the question correctly, and reliability approaches zero. And, as with tone quality, when young children are asked to tell whether the same melodic pattern performed twice has the same or different dynamic level, almost all are able to answer the question correctly if the difference is exaggerated. To be sure that the children were not experiencing difficulty in responding to questions about tone quality and dynamics as a result of hearing melodic patterns (patterns combining tonal and rhythm dimensions), they were asked to make the same judgments when hearing tonal patterns or rhythm patterns. The results were the same, making the reliability of their responses not significantly different from zero.

Further, only two nonpreference, and no preference, dimensions of developmental music aptitude were identified. Regardless of the manner in which questions were asked or the nature of the content of the questions, young children were incapable of making reliable judgments pertaining to their music preferences. That is to say, music preference did not present itself as a dimension of developmental music aptitude. It is possible, of course, that an appropriate method of measuring music preferences of young children has not yet been discovered. Moreover, it may be that young children's aptitude for preferences, like that for other dimensions of music, such as harmony, are latent. There is promising ongoing research relating to young children's understanding of harmonic patterns that is presented in chapter 10. Nonetheless, I should explain that when I observe young children in their spontaneous musical play, they rarely give any evidence of expressive response to music. Young children would rather perform and listen to music than to explain the music itself. They are more interested in how music is constructed, as can be observed in their participatory performance, than in how different pieces of music affect their emotions. Evelyn Moorhead and Donald Pond came to similar conclusions more than fifty years ago.

Though it may seem an insignificant matter, it was discovered after considerable research that young children in the developmental music aptitude stage find it difficult to organize rhythm patterns that they have just heard, unless they are given assistance in determining the placement of macrobeats in the patterns in order to define the tempo of each pattern. To ask a young child to listen to and compare two rhythm patterns and then to indicate whether the two sound the same or different is not sufficient to yield a reliable response. Either the tempo must be established before the rhythm patterns are heard or the tempo must be outlined as the patterns are being heard. It was discovered that to establish the tempo using soft underlying clicks produced simultaneously with the performance of a pattern on the test recording is the more satisfactory of the two approaches.

It quickly became apparent to me and my colleagues that young children do not develop the second stage of audiation in terms of rhythm patterns as rapidly as they do in terms of tonal patterns. Such a deficiency can be observed even in students who have recently entered the stabilized stage of rhythm aptitude. Thus, although clicks are not necessary to establish tempo as rhythm patterns are being heard by students in the stabilized stage of music aptitude, durations that would have coincided with clicks if they had been present must be accented. That principle was followed in the construction of the *Rhythm Imagery-Tempo* subtest of the *Musical Aptitude Profile.*

An unanticipated finding was that young children in the developmental music aptitude stage lose the focus of their concentration when a musical instrument is used as the stimulus when they are asked to compare two tonal patterns or two rhythm patterns. They seem to attend more to the musical instrument than to the music content they are hearing and to the questions they are being asked to answer. That is true for keyboard, bell-type, percussion, woodwind, brass, and string instruments. Such a finding offers additional evidence to suggest that developmental music aptitude is more related to atomistic than to Gestalt thought. For that reason, Seashore, even though he was concerned with stabilized music aptitude, might have been predisposed to using an electronic instrument as the stimulus in his research and test development. Ruby Friend's research lends credence to that assumption. In terms of reliability and construct validity, it soon became obvious to me in my research with young children that a synthesizer was the best instrument to use, because young children do not react positively or negatively to the sound and it does not command their full attention. The synthesizer also proved to be superior to a simple electronic acoustical instrument when testing children's sensitivity to rhythm. That is so because the synthesizer can provide for the duration of a beat as well as for the attack of the beat itself.

Extensive studies I also conducted were undertaken to learn more about the way young children in the developmental music aptitude stage process musical sound (*The Manifestation of Developmental Music Aptitude,* 1981, and *The Importance of Being Able to Audiate,* 1986). As in some of my previous research, I asked young children to compare a pair of tonal patterns or a pair of rhythm patterns and to decide whether they sound the same or different. The patterns covered a wide range of difficulty. I found that young children are more preoccupied with the perception, perhaps the conception, of sameness and difference than with the music content of the music they are listening to. When the results of their responses to a series of forty tonal patterns and forty rhythm patterns were factor analyzed separately, or when the eighty pairs were combined, it was discovered that the patterns generated only two group factors, and these were associated with whether the correct answer to a question was same or different, that is, they constituted sameness and difference factors. Contrary to expectation, the tonal patterns did not cluster, for example, into factors according to tonality, keyality, length, melodic direction, intervalic descriptions, or range. Nor did the rhythm patterns cluster into factors according to meter, length, rests, ties, upbeats, syncopation, or long or short durations. Sameness and difference were of more consequence than the music content.

Why young children should depend more heavily on and take their cues from sameness and difference, rather than from the characteristics of music content, for making differentiations has not yet been explained. There is evidence to suggest, however, that such behavior is in keeping with the developmental music aptitude stage. For both tonal pattern and rhythm pattern comparisons, pairs for which the correct answer is "same" were judged correctly by young children more often than pairs for which the correct answer is "different." In support of the validity of the importance of knowing difference is the fact that when studying only the twenty pairs of patterns with "different" as the correct answer, the total score reliability was almost as high as when all forty pairs of patterns with either "same" or "different" as the correct answer were analyzed.

Perhaps the ability to function at the second stage of audiation is not so crucial when there is repetition in what is being audiated. It might be much the same as when young children are becoming acculturated to language and subjectivity is more the rule than objectivity in thinking and audiating. Even when young children are specifically guided in listening to music content, they nevertheless attend to sameness and difference. Moreover, it is known that explanations about making judgments of same and different offered in addition to those already given in the recorded directions for the *Primary Measures of Music Audiation* make only little difference in young children's scores on the test. Suffice it to say that although chronological age is a factor in determining whether one is in the developmental or the stabilized music aptitude stage, it would seem possible to be engaging in preparatory audiation or in audiation itself when one is the developmental or the stabilized music aptitude stage.

Primary and Intermediate
Measures of Music Audiation

The importance of the use of categorical perception and audiation of tonal patterns and rhythm patterns to derive musical meaning in terms of subjective and/or objective keyalities, tonalities, tempos, and meters is the basis of the rationale of the *Primary Measures of Music Audiation* (Gordon, 1979) and the *Intermediate Measures of Music Audiation* (Gordon, 1982). Isolated tones or durations are syntactically assimilated into tonal patterns and into rhythm patterns. The *Primary Measures of*

Music Audiation (PMMA) and the *Intermediate Measures of Music Audiation* (IMMA) are similarly designed, but the former includes patterns easy to audiate and the latter difficult patterns to audiate. Both consist of two subtests, *Tonal* and *Rhythm,* yielding a tonal, a rhythm, and a composite score. The child is asked to decide whether two tonal patterns or rhythm patterns sound the same or different. Although the test questions are performed in a musical manner using a synthesizer, the tonal subtests are without rhythm and the rhythm subtests are without variable pitch. What must be emphasized is that there is only enough controlled silent time between the performances of the two patterns in a pair to provide the child with audiation time, but not enough time to allow the child to attempt to memorize the first pattern in the pair for comparative purposes.

The tonal patterns in the *Primary Measures of Music Audiation,* which are from two to five pitches in length and with an emphasis on major tonality, are performed at the same tempo and are in the same keyality. At least one pattern of the pair in each tonal question includes the tonic. The tonal patterns in the *Intermediate Measures of Music Audiation,* all of which are three pitches in length with an emphasis on harmonic minor tonality, are also performed at the same tempo and in the same keyality. In some tonal questions, neither pattern of the pair includes the tonic. As a result of subjectively or objectively audiating a resting tone, the listener is guided in inferring syntax for each tonal pattern primarily in terms of keyality and occasionally, but not necessarily, in terms of tonality. Keyality seems to be the mainstay of developmental music aptitude and tonality the mainstay of stabilized music aptitude. As music aptitude moves from the developmental stage to the stabilized stage, children begin to make decisions based on a sense of tonality. The higher a child's tonal aptitude, the sooner the child begins to make those decisions.

The rhythm patterns in both PMMA and IMMA include macrobeats that may or may not be systematic in number and length, because relative note values remain constant between, as well as within, meters. Underlying macrobeat clicks are performed at a relatively low dynamic level compared to the patterns themselves. Unlike the PMMA *Rhythm* subtest, the majority of questions in the IMMA *Rhythm* subtest rely on patterns in the same meter, thus contributing to the increased difficulty of making comparisons between the two patterns that constitute a question. As a result of responding to macrobeats, the listener is guided in audiating and inferring syntax for each rhythm pattern primarily in terms of tempo and occasionally, but not necessarily, in terms of meter. As music aptitude moves from the developmental stage to the stabilized stage, children begin to make decisions based on a sense of meter. The higher a child's rhythm aptitude, the sooner the child begins to make those decisions.

Each of the forty questions in the *Tonal* and *Rhythm* subtests of PMMA and IMMA is identified on the recording by the name of an object, such as a car or a spoon. After the name of the object is announced, the child hears the word *first*, followed by the first pattern of the pair, and then the word *second*, followed by the second pattern of the pair. There are five seconds between questions to allow the child to audiate and mark the answer on the answer sheet. If the two patterns in the pair sound the same, the child draws a circle around the box showing two faces that look the same located under the picture of the object named on the recording. If the two patterns in the pair sound different, the child draws a circle around the box showing two faces that look different located under the picture of the object named on the recording.

All of the questions in the *Tonal* subtest are in the keyality of C, that is, the tonic of each pattern is C. The tonic is established immediately in the practice exercises. Due to the pitches offered, the melodic contour, or both, differences may occur at the beginning, middle, or end of the second pattern of the pair. With regard to the *Rhythm* subtests, all usual and unusual meters are included in the test questions.

The *Primary Measures of Music Audiation,* the *Intermediate Measures of Music Audiation,* and the *Advanced Measures of Music Audiation* (Gordon, 1989) all include the word *audiation* in their titles. Yet, the results of empirical research insist that there need to be significant differences in the design of the three tests, primarily because PMMA and IMMA are for children in the developmental music aptitude stage, whereas the *Advanced Measures of Music Audiation* (AMMA), like MAP, is for students in the stabilized music aptitude stage. How this information bears on music aptitude it not altogether clear. What is evident is that one definition and description of music aptitude is not suitable for persons of all chronological ages, at least not in terms of how music aptitude is best measured, evaluated, and ultimately interpreted.

For whatever the reasons, to derive valid results with young children from three to nine years old requires that recorded test content include separate tonal patterns and separate rhythm patterns, not melodic patterns. Moreover, pitch center, keyality, tonality, and/or meter should not be established on the recording, allowing each to be audiated and inferred by the listener in either a subjective or objective manner. This type of music aptitude test construction is representative of PMMA and

IMMA.

MAP, on the other hand, is a test of stabilized music aptitude. It was found that to achieve valid results for students in the fourth through twelfth grades, tonal patterns and rhythm patterns are not appropriate. Students must listen to melodies, that is, to both tonal and rhythm elements combined, in the recorded test content. However, although both tonal and rhythm dimensions are being performed, the student is required to make decisions about only tonal aspects or only rhythm aspects of the music. AMMA, another test of stabilized music aptitude, suitable for those in junior and senior high school through adulthood, including laypersons as well as nonprofessional and professional musicians, also combines tonal and rhythm dimensions, but the listener must be attentive to both tonal and rhythm changes in the recorded musical test content. It seems likely that the different processes required for responding to MAP and AMMA is largely a matter that relates to differences in chronological age for persons within the stabilized music aptitude stage. In both MAP and AMMA, keyality, tonality, tempo, and/or meter are defined for the listener on the recording because, of course, they are inherent in the melodies that represent the test content.

Audie

Audie (Gordon, 1989), a developmental music aptitude test for children three and four years old, is actually a game that takes between five and ten minutes to play. Audie is a character that talks and sings short songs, including one special short song. The object of the game is to say "yes" when Audie sings his special song and "no" when Audie sings another song. A parent or teacher marks the answer sheet according to the child's response. There are recorded directions and practice exercises for each of the two subtests, *Tonal* and *Rhythm,* and each subtest includes ten questions.

Oddly, unlike other developmental music aptitude tests, the child listens to the different tonal patterns in a rhythm context and to different rhythm patterns in a tonal context, but in the *Tonal* subtest, if Audie does not sing his special song, it is because a pitch was changed in the melodic pattern while the rhythm component has stayed the same. In the *Rhythm* subtest, if Audie does not sing his special song, it is because a duration was changed in the melodic pattern while the tonal component stayed the same.

In the development of the test, particularly regarding its reliability, which is rather high (in the .80s for the two subtests combined) considering its brevity, it was soon discovered that the options "same" and "different" could not be used. The majority of young children would answer "same" to all questions, because the voice performing the patterns, of course, always sounded the same. The children's attention was not on the music. Thus, by changing the option responses to "yes" and "no," their attention was directed to the music. It would reasonably seem that this issue would have no relevance to the description of music aptitude, but one can never be sure. As a matter of fact, in further research since the publication of PMMA and IMMA, it has been discovered that reliability increases when the option responses "same" and "not same" are used in place of the more traditional "same" and "different." Perhaps at a very young age, there is a relation between music aptitude and general intelligence, or between music aptitude and, still as yet, some unknown factor.

CHAPTER 5

MUSIC APTITUDE AND OTHER FACTORS

An understanding of the relation of music aptitude to psychological and physical characteristics and to environmental background can further contribute to our understanding of music aptitude. While it would seem that objective evidence should make such relations obvious, it must be kept in mind that objectivity is dependent on the validity of the music aptitude tests used to elicit the evidence as well as on the reliability of the nonmusical factors being examined.

To insure that the following overall survey does not inadvertently overlook possible important issues, the relation of valid stabilized music aptitude scores, specifically those derived from the *Musical Aptitude Profile*, and the relation of valid developmental music aptitude scores, specifically those derived from the *Primary Measures of Music Audiation* and the *Intermediate Measures of Music Audiation*, to other factors, will be studied separately.

STABILIZED MUSIC APTITUDE

The standardization of MAP involved the selection of a representative sample of students in the United States in accordance with sampling techniques similar to those used in the development of other professionally designed test batteries. In this way, the random sample of students who participated in the standardization program was stratified according to school geographical location, school size, the rural or urban setting of the school, and the socio-economic status of a school system. An analysis of the test results showed no discernible differences in score distributions in terms of those four factors. That is to say, the proportion of students at all stabilized music aptitude levels was found to be similar for groups of students regardless of significant nonmusical factors associated with their school.

To consider environmental factors that might be expected to affect stabilized music aptitude, two highly specialized studies of socioeconomic status were conducted. In the first (Gordon, 1965), MAP results of junior high school disadvantaged students were compared to those of heterogeneous students. Students in the former group were technically classified as "educationally deprived" under the provision of the Elementary and Secondary School Act, Title 1. The differences in MAP mean scores found between this group and the corresponding group that participated in the standardization program were also negligible, and the standard deviations, which give evidence of the variability of test scores, did not differ in any meaningful way. The second study (Gordon, 1967), was designed to investigate the predictive validity of MAP, and it provided evidence that the correlation between the composite MAP score and the occupation of the head of the household is positive, but low, and is significantly lower than that between students' levels of music achievement and this same MAP score. Furthermore, the corresponding coefficients representing the relation of stabilized music aptitude and music achievement scores to the college attendance of parents were, as expected, almost identical to those for occupation. Another factor, parents' interest in the music achievement of their children, can be inferred by the presence of a piano and recording equipment in the home and the degree to which children are encouraged to listen to music, live or recorded. All of these variables, including the extent to which parents supervise home music practice, are correlated with music aptitude scores to a significantly smaller degree than is parents' occupational and educational status. Further, the parents' occupational and educational status correlates significantly higher with music achievement measures than with MAP scores. From the evidence presented, it appears that although our level of music aptitude is affected by early childhood environmental influences, stabilized music aptitude is not conditioned by socio-economics. Students with great musical potential can be found as readily in deprived areas as in more privileged neighborhoods and, conversely, students with limited musical potential are as numerous in affluent environs as in ghettos.

Perhaps the most comprehensive investigation ever undertaken to gather information about stabilized music aptitude was a five-year longitudinal study of the musical achievement of disadvantaged students (Gordon, *Fifth-Year and Final Results of a Five-Year Longitudinal Study*, 1975). MAP was administered to all fifth and sixth grade students in four disadvantaged elementary schools and three other schools with a more general population in Des Moines, Iowa. Then, every student, regardless of his or her MAP scores, who volunteered to take instrumental music lessons and to participate in band activities for a five-year period, was lent a new brass or woodwind instrument free of charge. A substantial effort was made to allow students to study the instrument of their choice. The available instruments were divided equally, according to type, between the two groups of schools, and the students were taught music as a curricular subject twice a week, in groups and individually, by the regular music teachers in the school district.

Although there were 82 disadvantaged students and 96 more advantaged students participating at the onset of the study, because some students moved and as a result of other unforeseen but compelling factors, only 28 disadvantaged and 35 of the more advantaged students completed five-years of instruction. The music achievement criteria used to assess the students' consisted of scores students received on appropriate levels of the *Iowa Tests of Music Literacy* and on ratings given to students by outside professional judges who listened to three recorded etudes performed by the students. One etude was prepared with teacher help, another was prepared without teacher help, and a third was sight-read. The students were tested at the end of each year of the study, and the differences in mean scores between the two groups on all criteria were compared and examined for statistical significance.

Based on the accumulated evidence, it was concluded that if given appropriate compensatory instruction over a period of years, students who attend disadvantaged schools, although initially deficient, can ultimately surpass in music achievement students who attend more advantaged schools, and that is true for both music performance skills and cognitive music skills. Specifically, because music aptitude is similarly distributed in both types of schools, environmental factors will be found to be irrelevant to students' music achievement when all students receive suitable instruction. Moreover, groups of disadvantaged students who possess below-average stabilized music aptitude can ultimately attain standards in music achievement similar to those demonstrated by other groups of students who possess above-average music stabilized aptitude. However, overall, students with above-average stabilized music aptitude, regardless of their cultural background, can achieve more successfully in musical endeavors than those with below-average stabilized music aptitude.

The relation of stabilized music aptitude scores to the amount and type of music instruction students received was investigated in conjunction with the standardization of the MAP battery. It was found that participants in school music performance organizations score higher as a group on MAP than do nonparticipants, and although, as a group, members of choral organizations score higher on MAP than do nonparticipants, members display only slightly less music aptitude than do instrumental music students. However, the lack of participation in a school music performance organization is not a limiting factor in demonstrating high-level music aptitude scores, nor does membership in a school music performance organization assure the demonstration of high-level music aptitude scores. These facts, outlined in the test manual, are specifically identified in the Sandusky prestandardization study of MAP, but they become even clearer through a comparison of the standard score-percentile norms provided in the MAP manual. It is interesting to note in this study that music aptitude score distributions of students who perform on keyboard, percussion, brass, woodwind, and string instruments are highly similar.

Data from the Sandusky study also indicate that approximately 40 percent of students who have had little or no formal music instruction score at the 80th percentile and above on the MAP composite score. A similar percentage of students who have had extensive musical instruction score at the 20th percentile and below on the composite MAP score. Evidently, whether we consider the general socio-economic factor or the more restricted musical status factor as an indicator of environmental background, we must acknowledge that stabilized music aptitude is not contingent on favorable social circumstances. Thus, music educators must be challenged by the suggested findings that no matter what group of students we are associated with, we can identify individuals with high-level stabilized music aptitudes that we must assist in developing and a proportionate number of students with lower stabilized music aptitude levels we must assist by adapting instruction to compensate for specific musical deficiencies.

As suggested by Catherine Cox and Hazel Stanton, performing musicians, music educators, and the lay public generally concur with the idea that musicians as a group, like other professionals, enjoy a high level of general intelligence. These findings notwithstanding, music psychologists are divided in their opinion. When test scores are used as criteria of music aptitude, investigators maintain that the relation between stabilized music aptitude and academic intelligence is positive but low. European researchers, who employ subjective criteria as evidence of music aptitude, generally report rather high relations. H. Schüssler, V. Haecker and Theodor Ziehen, and Richard Miller for example, found the relation between intelligence and music aptitude, even though it was inferred from music performance skill, to be noteworthy. Paul Farnsworth, James Albert Highsmith, Leta Hollingsworth, Sylvia Bienstock, and Charles

Lehman, on the other hand, found, at best, only a limited relation between intelligence and stabilized music aptitude test scores. The latter two even give credence to the belief that, low as it is, the correlation between intelligence and music achievement is higher than that between intelligence and stabilized music aptitude. Henry Cowell and Ray Moore tend to support that position. Paul Farnsworth cites evidence of the musical prowess of some savants. Research carried out by Carl E. Seashore and G. Mount, Jacob Kwalwasser, and Raleigh Drake, as well as my own research (*Musical Aptitude Profile*) provides data that further suggest that there is no more than 10 to 20 percent in common between scores on tests of stabilized music aptitude and general intelligence tests, regardless of the type of intelligence test (verbal or nonverbal) used as a criterion.

While it might be gratifying to the musician's ego if the foregoing information were interpreted to support the notion that all intelligent persons are not necessarily musical but that all musical persons are intelligent, we would best temper our approval by bearing in mind that creative persons are not necessarily highly intelligent. That is, like intelligence and music aptitude, the correlation between measures of intelligence and creativity, not necessarily musical creativity, has not been found to be as high as earlier anticipated by some philosophers.

Of even more practical importance to our understanding of music aptitude is the manner in which measures of music aptitude and intelligence, when considered together, identify students who will be most successful in musical endeavors. Two studies, one undertaken by William Young and the other by me (*A Study of the Efficacy of General Intelligence*, 1968) deal with this specific problem. Through the use of multiple regression techniques, when both the *Henmon-Nelson Tests of Mental Ability* scores and MAP scores of fifth grade students were used in my study to predict success in instrumental music instruction, the increase in precision was only negligibly better than when MAP was used alone, but it was significantly better than when the intelligence test was used alone. The same findings surfaced when MAP was used in conjunction with the *Iowa Tests of Basic Skills,* an academic achievement test battery. As a matter of fact, when all three tests were used as a group for this purpose, the multiple correlation coefficient, as might reasonably be expected, was no higher than that found for any pair of tests of which MAP was one. Ostensibly, the same results were found by William Young.

It is well known that the correlation between scores on intelligence and academic achievement tests is relatively high, almost as high as the reliability of the tests. Unfortunately, however, the correlation between MAP scores and music achievement test scores is comparatively low, approximately that of the magnitude found between MAP scores and academic achievement test scores (Gordon, *Musical Aptitude Profile,* 1995). Obviously, for whatever reason, many students are unable to take full advantage of their potential for music achievement. Parenthetically, the old tale that music aptitude and mathematical ability go hand-in-hand lacks objective credibility when MAP scores, *Iowa Tests of Basic Skills,* and *Iowa Tests of Educational Development* arithmetic and mathematics subtest scores, are used as criteria. In both cases, language arts test scores show a higher relation to music aptitude than do the quantitative tests.

Interest in learning music, especially as a predictor of musical success, has been almost totally ignored in research. However, if we accept as criteria of such an interest the degree to which one voluntarily practices an instrument, participates in extracurricular music activities, and makes use of music instruction during the summer months, we find that the correlation between each one of these factors with MAP scores is systematically higher than for those found between MAP scores and socio-economic status. Furthermore, there is a one-to-one relation between these three variables and MAP scores and the three variables and music achievement test scores. What is most striking, however, is that the correlation between MAP scores and interest in music is lower than that between MAP scores and intelligence test scores, low as the latter relation is (1995).

From the little evidence we have, we can only assume that one's interest in music does not have a great impact on one's success in musical endeavors. In keeping with the findings related to other disciplines, it appears that interest in music is of significant value only when it is accompanied by music aptitude. Because interest, which is sparked by outside factors, cannot be considered a substitute for music aptitude, it would then seem more likely that it is motivation, which is stimulated from the inside as a result of success, that is suggestive of future accomplishment in music.

Before leaving the topic of psychological characteristics, a few words concerning the personality traits of musicians are in order. Long before the supposedly corroborating research of H. J. and W. A. Pannenborg, Oswald Feis, and Ernst Kretschmer around the turn of the century, it had been assumed that musicians as a group are "emotional" and not "orderly" or "punctual." More positively, these researchers suggested that musicians have extensive artistic and linguistic abilities and that they enjoy social intercourse. The fact that some of the musicians studied during the course of the investigations, either in observational or biographical form, were alleged to be mentally unstable or given to immaturity and hysteria does not mean that all musicians demonstrate such characteristics. The emphatic claim of these investigators that mathematical ability and intelligence are closely related to music aptitude suggests that their other findings may have been somewhat in error.

More recently, Charles Lehman reported that musicianship, as displayed by high school and college students, is related to superior social adjustment. Walter B. Duda, using the *Strong Vocational Interest Blank* and other similar tests, found student teachers in music to have creative imagination and initiative. John Cooley's research does not support these contentions, nor does that of Stanley Schleuter and Robert Thayer, indicating that there is no common personality factor that is systematically associated with music aptitude or music achievement. Anthony Kemp, in the most recent comprehensive analysis of the musical temperament, does not discount the role of personality or environmental background in the making of musicians, nor does he believe that music aptitude plays a greater or lesser role in the matter. His analysis, however, indirectly supports the importance of developmental music aptitude.

The stabilized music aptitude of various ethnic groups has been of great interest to music psychologists. However, very little information has appeared in the literature during the last fifty years or so, and probably with good reason. Behavioral scientists have found that sociological studies are influenced by the nationality of subjects and by the specific part of a country in which they live. Furthermore, in studies of this type it is difficult to categorize certain groups specifically because of the extensive mixing of races, religions, and national origins. In a word, valid cross-cultural studies are virtually an impossibility, and even if they were not, it is increasingly difficult to find reasons to justify why such studies should be undertaken. Certainly the contradictions among what findings we have offer little assistance in describing music aptitude. Although the following findings are affected to an unknown degree by many such limitations, I believe that studies of this type should be included in any comprehensive historical survey of trends in the study of music aptitude.

Using the Seashore test, Z. Lenoire found African American children to be superior to whites in rhythm and tonal memory, but not inferior on the remaining measures. Joseph Peterson and Lyle Lanier report that whites scored higher on all tests, but not higher than African Americans in rhythm. Clarence T. Gray and C. Walter Bingham claim that African Americans equaled whites only on the consonance test, and in marked contradiction, two studies carried out by Guy B. Johnson reported no significant difference between the two groups. Wesley A. Peacock, however, suggests that the tests favor whites in all categories. Inconsistent results were also evidenced with the Kwalwasser-Dykema tests. Roy C. Woods and Lureata R. Martin found African Americans to be superior only in rhythm and consonance, while Viola Robinson and Mary Holmes found whites superior in all aspects.

Paul Farnsworth, using unstandardized tests of pitch, consonance, melody, and harmony, found that native-born whites were superior only in melody when compared to native-born and foreign-born Asians. Employing the Seashore tests as criteria, Thomas R. Garth and Sarah Rachel Isbell found Native Americans superior in time and rhythm. Raymond Porter reported that both Asians and whites, who shared similar environmental characteristics, scored below average on all tests. Verne Ross found Native Americans to be deficient in all respects except time, whereas Japanese were superior in both time and consonance. Finally, Walter Eells reported that Eskimos scored below average on all six Seashore subtests.

In investigations of the relation of music aptitude to religion and nationality, Keith T. Sward and Helen Sanderson used both the Seashore and Kwalwasser-Dykema tests, the former also using the Drake *Musical Memory* test. In both studies, Jewish students were discovered to be superior to all others on an overall basis. The order, as reported by Sanderson, is Jewish, German, Italian, African American, and Polish. African Americans scored higher on rhythm than any other group.

Raleigh Drake, meanwhile, in his test manual reported no significant differences in scores obtained by African American and white high school students on his *Musical Memory* test, or by African American, white, or Native Americans students on his *Rhythm* test. In the *Musical Aptitude Profile* manual, correlation coefficients representing the relation of music aptitude to race and religion are reported that are negligible. In a later investigation, the distribution of MAP scores of 658 students enrolled in two predominantly African American midwestern junior high schools was found to be almost identical to that upon which MAP norms are based (Gordon, *A Comparison of the Performance of Culturally Disadvantaged Students*, 1967).

DEVELOPMENTAL MUSIC APTITUDE

Research pertaining to the relation between developmental music aptitude and other factors is sparse when compared to corresponding research with stabilized music aptitude. The reason, of course, is that the concept of developmental music is less than twenty years old. Nonetheless, I will outline the results of relevant research that are available.

As explained, it is important to know whether scores on a music aptitude test have little or high relation to scores derived from another test that is specifically designed to serve other purposes. If it can be shown that the different types of tests have little or nothing in common, that bears on the validity of at least one of the tests and, hopefully, on both. Taking the matter further, once we believe we have a valid music aptitude test, we can more confidently use scores derived from that test to assist us in arriving at a description of music aptitude, in this case, developmental music aptitude.

There are correlations available for *Primary Measures of Music Audiation* scores and *Metropolitan Readiness Tests*-Level 2 scores for kindergarten children; for *Primary Measures of Music Audiation* scores and *Stanford Achievement Test* scores for first, second, and third grade children; and for *Primary Measures of Music Audiation* scores and *Lorge-Thorndike Intelligence Tests* verbal and nonverbal scores for third grade children (Gordon, *Primary Measures* and *Intermediate Measures*, 1979). All correlations are desirably low, approximating those between scores on the *Musical Aptitude Profile* and academic tests. The coefficients range from .15 to .30 for the Metropolitan test, from .12 to .37 for the Stanford test, and from .19 to .30 for the intelligence tests.

It would seem that whether our concern is with stabilized music aptitude or developmental music aptitude, results from music aptitude tests designed for students in either stage systematically reinforce the belief that neither general intelligence nor academic achievement of any type is a component of music aptitude.

CHAPTER 6

ESSENTIALS OF
A MUSIC APTITUDE TEST

A test author would be remiss in describing a music aptitude test simply as "a valid test of music aptitude," or as one that "measures what it purports to measure." There is no way for an author to be sure that his or her theoretical formulation of the necessary factors that define or determine music aptitude, as represented by the psychological constructs upon which a test is based, is valid. Only when positive results of various types of empirical validity investigations of the test are available can a test author offer objective support for an initial theory. In addition, a test cannot simply be declared valid. It must be shown to be valid for one or more specific purposes. That is, a test should be considered valid only when it is known that it is valid for one or more purposes.

After the subject matter of test questions is decided upon (construct validity) and the mechanical design of the test, including the manner in which subjects will give answers to questions (process validity), is determined, an author must consider aspects of the reliability (score stability) and the efficiency (time requirements) of the measures. The first step in establishing the reliability of a test is to examine the quality of each test question with regard to its difficulty level (the number of students who successfully answer each question) and its discrimination level (how well each question discriminates between high-scoring and low-scoring students on the test as a whole). Then, when the test has been revised in accordance with the results of these item-analysis techniques, the actual test reliability must be estimated through procedures such as split-halves or odds/evens, test-retest, or parallel forms methods. The primary reason that reliability merits such important consideration is that unless scores for each student in a group are consistent (highly correlated) on the same or nearly identical tests, the possibility of determining the relation of those scores to an outside criterion (validity) will be limited. Stated another way, unless music aptitude test results agree with themselves, they cannot adequately demonstrate any type of relation to another factor, such as music achievement. In this sense, reliability is thought of as a necessary, but not as a sufficient condition, for establishing objective validity for a test. As previously explained, the nature of the interrelation (intercorrelation) among tests that constitute a test battery also bears on validity, but unless test scores are reliable, the intercorrelation coefficients they give rise to have no meaning.

At the point when reliability and intercorrelation information substantiate the orientation of the test author, the relation of test scores to other factors (criterion-related or concurrent validity) is investigated. For example, it is necessary for music aptitude test scores to demonstrate a definite concurrent relation to music achievement. Because a correlation coefficient describes the extent of a relation but not the cause of a relation, a high correlation between the two criteria might indicate that the aptitude test is actually an achievement test. However, it would be of more concern to find little or no correlation between the two, because logic dictates that such a positive relation does exist. The cause of the relation must be investigated through other procedures in the process of further development of the test, specifically longitudinal predictive validity studies and diagnostic validity studies. However, additional preliminary validity evidence dealing with the concurrent relation of music aptitude scores to factors, such as intelligence test scores, that should have little association with the test, should also initially be obtained. When a low correlation is found, there is then evidence to suggest that the test is measuring what it was designed to measure.

The two primary reasons to use a music aptitude test are to evaluate a student's overall music aptitude in order to diagnose and compare a student's specific musical strengths and weaknesses (idiographic measurement) and to compare these strengths and weaknesses with those of his or her peers (normative measurement) who are enrolled in similar music classes and music performance groups. When a music aptitude test is to be used for identifying students who can profit most from and contribute most to specific music activities, the longitudinal predictive validity of the test must be investigated. That is, the preinstruction composite test score should be known to predict relative success on various music achievement criteria after sufficient instruction has taken place. Under no circumstances should the results of a music aptitude test ever prevent any student from participating in music activities. All students, whatever their levels of music aptitude, are capable of achieving some degree of success in musical endeavors.

In order to diagnose the idiographic and normative musical strengths and weaknesses of students so that their individual musical needs may be met, the subtests that constitute the music aptitude battery should not be highly related to one another, but should represent important dimensions of music aptitude that are related to actual musical skills. That is, each subtest should have high reliability and comparatively low intercorrelations with every other subtest in the battery (certainly the intercorrelation between any two subtests should not be any higher, and hopefully much lower, than the reliability of either of the two subtests), and each subtest should have a high correlation with the total test score on the battery. For a battery with high diagnostic validity, the accompanying test manual should explain the relation of a student's high and low scores, as indicated by his or her musical aptitude profile, to specific musical skills.

A well-constructed music aptitude battery may also be used to evaluate the collective potential of groups of students within the same school or school system and to design a program for educational and vocational guidance. In addition, individual teachers may develop distinctive uses for aptitude test results that have relevance to their own music programs and specific needs.

When evaluating a music aptitude test, both reliability and validity data must be examined. Validity, however, is the principal factor, because although a test may be reliable, it may lack substantial validity. Conversely, a test cannot demonstrate satisfactory validity unless it is reliable. Theoretically, the validity coefficient for a test can be no higher, and in most cases it will be considerably lower, than the square root of the reliability coefficient for the test.

Numerous types of information should be reported in a music aptitude test battery manual. Test means, standard deviations, item analyses, reliability coefficients, intercorrelation coefficients, and various types of validity should be presented. The procedures used in the standardization program and the methods of score conversions should be explained. All of these data are useful in evaluating the quality and value of a music aptitude battery.

Test means, standard deviations, intercorrelations, reliabilities, and norms should be reported for each subtest in the battery according to the groups for which the subtests were designed. In general, these statistics are best reported for individual school grades. A subtest mean should be approximately midway between the chance score (the raw score equal to the number of questions divided by the number of option responses for each question) and the total possible score. If the observed mean is much higher or lower than the theoretical mean, it is possible that the subtest is too easy or too difficult, respectively, for students in the specified grade.

Ideally, the total possible score should approximate three standard deviations above the observed mean, and a chance score should approximate three standard deviations below the observed mean. Individual subtest reliabilities should be at least .70, total tests at least .80, and composite test scores .90 and above. Intercorrelation coefficients are theoretically most desirable when they approach .00 (assuming subtest reliabilities are high), which is rarely the case, but they become suspect when they approach or exceed the reliability of the subtests themselves.

The construct validity and content validity of subtests should be considered before their objective validity is evaluated. That is to say, unless the orientation of the test administrator is in accordance with the psychological constructs and content embodied in the subtests, a teacher will have little or no confidence in the results of the subtests, even if the results demonstrate extraordinary experimental validity. In this sense, construct validity and face validity have relevance to the individual test administrator or teacher and, thus, it is primarily subjective. It should be recognized, however, that subtest reliabilities and intercorrelation coefficients lend objectivity to the determination of the construct validity of the subtests. If the subtest is not highly reliable, it may be assumed that what the test author theorizes to be music aptitude, for example, is not being appropriately measured. Moreover, if the subtest intercorrelations are exceedingly high, it is possible that what the test author considers to be several separate dimensions of music aptitude actually constitute only one music aptitude.

After the content and construct validity of a subtest is determined to be acceptable, longitudinal predictive validity and diagnostic validity should be investigated. Coefficients associated with validity can be expected to be lower than the reliability reported for a subtest, but the predictive validity for the composite score should be at least .50 if it is to be of practical use in identifying students who should be encouraged to engage in special music activities. For example, the MAP composite score reliability for a given grade of elementary school students is above .90, and the longitudinal validity of all subtests in the battery for predicting success in instrumental music over a three-year period is .75. By squaring the validity coefficient it can be determined that more than 50 percent of the reason or reasons students are successful in beginning instrumental music achievement is associated with factors relevant to their MAP scores, and that somewhat less than 50 percent of the reason or reasons they are not successful is associated with factors other than music aptitude, factors that are not taken into consideration by MAP.

Diagnostic validity coefficients are generally lower than predictive validity coefficients. In the case of the latter, the composite test score is used, and in the case of the former, individual subtest scores are used. Composite tests, primarily because they are longer, are usually more reliable and can therefore be expected to have higher validity. To be of practical diagnostic value, each subtest should correlate at least .30 with one or more relevant music achievement skills.

A raw score on a test indicates the number of questions a student answers correctly. If one student earns a raw score of 20 and another a raw score of 25, the only fact that can be discerned is that the second student scored five points higher than the first. Whether 25 is twice as good, three times as good, and so on, can most efficiently be determined when raw scores are converted to standard scores, such as percentile ranks. For example, depending on the score distribution, a raw score of 20 may be found to equal a percentile rank of 10 and a raw score of 25 may be found to equal a percentile rank of 20, or it may be that a raw score of 20 equals a percentile rank of 30 and that a raw score of 25 equals a percentile rank of 90.

A test author should report in the test manual not only the percentile rank norms for a battery of music aptitude subtests but also standard T score conversions. This is true because individual subtests in a battery will generally differ in raw score means and standard deviations. In order for each subtest in the battery to contribute equally to the composite score, each one must be given the same statistical mean and standard deviation, that is, raw scores for each subtest must be adjusted according to the overall variability of the scores for the specific subtest. For example, all seven individual subtests that constitute MAP have different raw score means and standard deviations, so in order to derive an equally weighted composite score, one in which each individual subtest contributes equally to the composite score, raw scores are converted to T scores. Thus, each subtest has a mean of 50 and a standard deviation of 10.

Finally, the procedures used in standardizing a test battery should be described in the test manual. The manner in which the test battery was administered and the various groups to whom it was administered should be reported in detail. Using such information, all subtests can be administered in similar fashion to insure a comparable and correct interpretation of the norms.

CHAPTER 7

THE MEASUREMENT OF STABILIZED MUSIC APTITUDE: STABILIZED MUSIC APTITUDE TESTS

Measurement and evaluation are different processes. A student's objective score on a music aptitude test represents measurement, whereas a teacher's subjective interpretation of that score represents evaluation. The following analogy may help. Consider a test measuring students' aptitude for speaking a foreign language composed of a few nonsense words that students are asked to listen to and learn the meaning of. Then they are encouraged to use as many of those nonsense words as they can in conversation. A student's score, rated according to the number of times each nonsense word is used and pronounced correctly by the student, becomes the objective measure of the student's potential to learn to speak a foreign language. Whether the score is high enough for the student to be considered to have the potential to learn to speak a foreign language better than other students in the group who took the test and scored lower must be decided by the teacher, and that decision represents subjective evaluation.

Subjective evaluation of an objective measure is necessary because, as is the case with any type of test, there is no one score on an aptitude test that can be classified in an absolute manner as being superior, average, or low. For this reason, subjective evaluation is also the case when the teacher decides the lower limit of a score used to determine that a student will profit little from compensatory instruction.

To assist a teacher in devising subjective evaluations, the teacher should compare each student's score with established norms. There is, of course, no assurance that a teacher's subjective evaluations of students' scores will prove to be accurate. However, a teacher should expect guidance from more than just norms. The recommendations of the test author and the results of validity studies for the test should further assist the teacher in making sound subjective evaluations based on students' objective scores.

The same holds true for music aptitude tests, which are designed for objective measurement. They yield objective scores that must be subjectively evaluated by a teacher, and it must be understood that there are no specific music aptitude scores that qualify as being superior, average, or low. Reliance on norms and validity information, as well as on guidance in interpreting test scores, all of which should be well-documented and presented in an accompanying test manual, is a necessity.

This chapter is concerned with the measurement of only stabilized music aptitude. The interpretation of stabilized music aptitude test scores is presented in chapter 9. As I have indicated in previous chapters, there have been numerous tests published for measuring stabilized music aptitude. I will discuss only the *Musical Aptitude Profile* (Gordon, 1995) and the *Advanced Measures of Music Audiation* (Gordon, 1989) however, because to the best of my knowledge, most, if not all, of the other tests are out of print or are difficult to acquire. Moreover, these are the only two current tests that have undergone extensive prepublication development in terms of design and construction as well as continuous post-publication validity investigations. The comprehensive nature of the two, particularly of the *Musical Aptitude Profile,* merits them as being unique for their intended purposes.

The Musical Aptitude Profile

The *Musical Aptitude Profile* (MAP) is an eclectic test battery, drawing from both atomistic and Gestalt omnibus theories. That is because although preference and nonpreference subtests constitute the battery and the content of all subtests consists of specially composed music performed and recorded by professional musicians,[1] the battery, nevertheless, is designed to measure seven separate dimensions of stabilized music aptitude. Moreover, the questions in all subtests, whether they are tonal, rhythm, or aesthetic/expressive subtests, include tonal and rhythm aspects, always performed with sensitive musical interpretation. The test battery has three main divisions: *Tonal Imagery, Rhythm Imagery,* and *Musical Sensitivity.* (When MAP was published, I had not yet begun my research into the nature of audiation. Thus, the word *audiation* had not yet been coined. Had the word been available, I would have used it, rather than the word *imagery*, in the titles of the main divisions of the test battery.)

The *Tonal Imagery* and *Rhythm Imagery* divisions include two subtests each, and all four are nonpreference measures. The *Musical Sensitivity* division includes three subtests, and all three are preference measures. The subtests in the *Tonal Imagery* division are *Melody* and *Harmony;* in the *Rhythm Imagery* division, *Tempo* and *Meter;* and in the *Musical Sensitivity* division, *Phrasing, Balance,* and *Style.* Directions and practice exercises are offered at the beginning of the recording of each subtest.

For each question in the *Melody* and *Harmony* subtests, the student is asked to compare a "musical answer" with a short but complete musical statement that is a few seconds in duration. The musical answer contains more notes than the musical statement. The student is asked to imagine that there are no extra notes in the musical answer and then to decide whether the musical answer without the additional notes is like the musical statement. In essence, the student is asked to decide if the musical answer is or is not a variation of the musical statement, but the word *variation* cannot be used in the directions because an understanding of that word would require music achievement. It was found that the word *notes*, even though there is no notation to be read, had to be used or else the students found the directions too complicated. If the students are in doubt about whether the musical answer is like or different from the musical statement, they are asked not to guess, but to mark the in-doubt response on the answer sheet instead.

Though I have been using the terms *musical statement* and *musical answer,* I should point out that in the directions, both are referred to as songs. Though the word *song* is a misnomer, because songs have a text, the use of the word was necessary. Students, particularly younger ones, do not understand the words *melody* or *tune.* Unfortunately, when either one of the proper words was used, students failed to understand the directions. For the same reason, the word *rhythm* had to be used in place of the word *meter* in the directions for the *Meter* subtest.

The music is performed on the violin for the *Melody* subtest and on the violin and cello for the *Harmony* subtest. The *Melody* and *Harmony* subtests are alike except that there are two parts in the *Harmony* subtest and only one part in the *Melody* subtest. In the *Harmony* subtest, the upper part is performed on the violin and the lower part is performed on the cello. The upper part of the musical statement and the upper part of the musical answer are exactly the same in every question. Extra notes are added only in the lower part. When listening to the musical answer, the student is asked to imagine that there are no extra notes in the lower part of the musical answer and then to decide whether the lower part of the musical answer is like the lower part of the musical statement.

Only the violin is used for the *Tempo* and *Meter* subtests. In the *Tempo* subtest, there is a musical statement and a musical answer. The melody is the same for both the musical statement and the musical answer. The ending of the musical answer, however, is performed either faster, slower, or at the same tempo as the musical statement, using a re-recording of the statement when the intended answer is meant to be "same" for a question. The student is asked to decide whether the musical answer is the same as or different from the musical statement. If the answer is different, the student is not asked, however, to indicate whether the ending of the musical answer is faster or slower than the ending of the musical statement. When the students were asked to make that choice in the process of the development of the subtest, the reliability of the measure decreased dramatically.

In the *Meter* subtest there is a musical statement and a musical answer. The musical answer may be the same as or different from the musical statement. If the musical answer is different, it is because of a difference in meter. The tonal dimension remains the same in all cases. For both *Rhythm Imagery* subtests, if the students are in doubt about whether the musical answer is the same as or different from the musical statement, they are asked not to guess. They are told to mark the in-doubt response on the answer sheet.

The violin and cello are the stimuli for the *Phrasing* subtest, and in that subtest, the same original melody is performed twice, but with different musical expression. Tempo rubato, dynamics, tone quality, or intonation, or two or more together, are altered in the second performance of the melody. The student is asked to decide which of the two renditions of the melody sounds better. It is important to be aware that the word "best" is not used in the directions for any of the preference subtests, because both renditions in every pair were designed with intentional faults. Unless this was the case, the questions were found to be too easy and reliability decreased. Only the violin is used in the *Balance* and *Style* subtests. In the *Balance* subtest, two original melodies are performed. The beginnings of each melody are the same, but the endings are different as a result of tonal and/or rhythm changes. The student is asked to decide which of the two endings better complements the beginning. In the *Style* subtest, the same original melody is performed twice, but at different tempos. All other musical aspects of the melody are the same, and as a matter of fact, the same bowings and fingerings were used in both renditions. The student is asked to decide which of the two tempos for the melody sounds better.

Again, when in doubt, the student is asked to mark the in-doubt response. Because it is a valid test of stabilized music aptitude, no formal music training is required of students in grades four through twelve in order to score high on the *Musical Aptitude Profile*. Moreover, if students have had prior formal music training, it will not affect their test results either positively or negatively. The same test is used for all students, and may be administered to groups of students or individually. Because it is a test of stabilized music aptitude, the *Musical Aptitude Profile* needs to be administered only once to students throughout their school career.

It takes one 50 minute period to administer each of the main divisions of the *Musical Aptitude Profile.* The actual listening time for every subtest is approximately 15 minutes. Each of the four nonpreference subtests—*Melody, Harmony, Tempo,* and *Meter* —includes 40 questions, and each of the three preference subtests—*Phrasing, Balance,* and *Style* —includes 30 questions, making a total of 250 questions for the complete battery. It is recommended in the MAP manual that the battery be admin-istered in three 50-minute periods on three different days. The days need not be consecutive, and the testing days may be even weeks or months apart during the academic year without affecting the results. The two *Tonal Imagery* subtests are on one recording and are administered during the first 50-minute period; the two *Rhythm Imagery* subtests are on anoth-er recording and are administered during the second 50-minute period; and the three *Musical Sensitivity* subtests are on another recording and are administered during the final 50-minute period.

The 40 questions in each of the four nonpreference subtests are in pairs. That is, they are numbered 1A and 1B, 2A and 2B, and so on through 20A and 20B. The musical statement is the same for 1A and 1B, for 2A and 2B, and so on. In preliminary research it was found that to listen to and respond to 40 different musical statements, each followed by a musical answer that might be like, same as, or different from the musi-cal statement, was too demanding for students of all ages. This would require that the students attend to 80 test phrases within a span of 12 minutes for each subtest, considering that the directions and practice exercises take approximately three minutes for each subtest, or to 160 test phrases during a half hour when two subtests are administered as suggest-ed in the test manual. It was found that the reliability of all four subtests decreased significantly under these conditions. Moreover, to expose students to many different musical phrases in rapid succession would be to force them to attempt to memorize, rather than to audiate, the phrases. As a result, the subtests would be more related to music achievement than to music aptitude. It is interesting to note in table 35 of the MAP manual that the B questions are neither more nor less difficult than the A questions, and that the B questions are neither more nor less discriminating than the A questions, all having positive discrimination values. (If more high-scoring students than low-scoring students answer a question correctly, it will have a positive discrimination value and thus increase the reliability and probably the validity of a test. If more low-scoring students than high-scoring students answer a question correctly, it will have a negative discrimination value and so will decrease the reliability and probably the validity of a test.) Among other implications, the difficulty and discrimination findings offer indirect support for the validity of MAP as a music aptitude test rather than a music achievement test, because if the B questions were found to be consistently easier and some negatively discriminating, the role of memorization, or simply recognition, would be the most likely cause.

It was not found to be necessary to pair the questions in the *Musical Sensitivity* subtests, because, unlike the nonpreference subtests, concentration on specifics is not necessary. All that is required in the preference subtests are general aesthetic impressions.

Another unique feature of the *Musical Aptitude Profile* is the inclusion of the in-doubt response. As explained in the recorded directions, students are asked not to guess if they are unsure of the correct answer for a question. When a student marks the in-doubt response, the student is not penalized, but simply receives no credit for the answer. On the other hand, if the student guessed the answer and it is incorrect, no credit would be deducted either. The value of using the in-doubt response is that a student will cease thinking about an answer and be ready to listen to the next question, which may be easier. Each subtest is designed so that very easy and easy questions are heard periodically.

It was found in early prepublication research of MAP that by including the in-doubt response, the decrease in test reliability was not significant and that in fact test validity increased significantly. This finding is surprising, because it is far more usual that as reliability decreases, validity decreases, and as reliability increases, so does validity. The theoretical limit of the validity of a test can be no higher than the square root of the reliability of the test. With regard to MAP, the reason that reliability decreases is that students are inconsistent in their use of the in-doubt response, and the reason validity increases is because students guess less frequently, making the resulting scores more accurate because they are not undeservedly high. On average, slightly less than 10 percent of the answers on the complete battery of seven subtests are in-doubt responses. The inclusion of the in-doubt response undoubtedly contributes to the unusually high validity of the *Musical Aptitude Profile*.

Several researchers have investigated different theoretical aspects of the in-doubt response. Stanley Schleuter and Robert Thayer were concerned that students with low self-esteem might tend to use the in-doubt response excessively and receive lower music aptitude scores than they deserve. Both found this not to be the case. Students with various types of normal personalities all use the in-doubt response. Schleuter, in a later study, observed the same incidence of the use of the in-doubt response with college and university students, on the one hand, and students in grades 4 through 12, on the other. Oddly, he found that nonmusic majors in universities used the in-doubt response fewer times than did university music majors. Florence Culver found the criterion-related validity of MAP in its present form to be higher than when the battery was experimentally altered and "in doubt" was removed as an option response. Neil Levendusky hypothesized that if the in-doubt response is functioning as intended, it should be used more frequently with difficult than with moderately difficult or easy questions. Using the difficulty levels reported for the questions in the MAP manual, he compared the number of times the in-doubt response was used in association with difficult and easy questions. He proved his hypothesis and concluded that the in-doubt response as used in the *Musical Aptitude Profile* has theoretical validity, implying that the battery has higher validity because the in-doubt response is operative.

Of concern to some persons is the practical validity of the *Musical Sensitivity* subtests. Although they understand and approve of the use of specially composed music, particularly for the questions in the preference subtests, they contend that the decision about whether to rate the first or second part of each question as sounding better was made arbitrarily. That belief is not correct, because as explained in detail at the end of chapter 3, the procedure for determining appropriate answers to the preference questions was complex. The process required the writing of many versions of the three subtests and took almost eight years. I would be remiss not to tell you that I, to this day, still disagree with six of the designated correct responses. This means, of course, that my aesthetic/expressive aptitude is not as high as those who attain higher or perfect scores. Even if a few of the answers for the preference test questions are inappropriate, however, that does not mean that the *Musical Sensitivity* division of the *Musical Aptitude Profile* is of no value. It simply means that the preference subtests are not perfect.

There are those who contend that the preference subtests represent music achievement rather than music aptitude, because professional musicians shared in the development of the subtests along with students. However, the majority of students who participated in the development of the test battery did not have any formal training in music, other than what might have been typically offered in general music classes, and thus their decisions about answers to the preference questions could not have been based on information that might have been put forth in formal music instruction. Yet their answers for the preference questions in the final version of MAP agreed with those made by the professional musicians, which could indicate that the professional musicians based their decisions on factors associated more with music aptitude than with music achievement. It should not be overlooked that because all test questions are composed of original music, and not versions of familiar music written by established composers, the possibility that the preference subtests are music achievement or recognition tests is further lessened.

Various concerns have been expressed by reviewers in this country and abroad about the validity of the preference subtests (for example, see the *Seventh Mental Measurements Yearbook*, edited by Oscar Buros). For instance, it has been said that students are asked to compare classical, contemporary, and jazz/popular styles of music in the *Phrasing* subtest and feel forced to choose the "accepted" standard as the better one, ignoring musicality altogether. However, students are not asked to do that. Though different styles of music are heard throughout the *Phrasing* subtest, the style of music remains consistent within the two parts of each test question. Only tempo rubato, dynamics, tone quality, and intonation are made to fluctuate in each question. The student must decide which rendition of two performances that are in the same style is better in terms of musical syntax. Style is held constant for both parts within a question for the *Phrasing* subtest, just as all variables other than the ending are held constant for both parts within a question in the *Balance* subtest, and all variables other than tempo are held constant for both parts within a question in the *Style* subtest. Actually, if you care to take the time to listen, you will find that the slower rendition of the pair in each question in the *Style* subtest is virtually in "slow motion." Such a task was not easy for the violinists to accomplish.

Given the inordinate amount of attention directed toward multicultural music in present-day music education circles, it is no wonder that many teachers misunderstand the difference between multicultural music and multicultural musicianship and, as a partial result, discredit the *Music Sensitivity* subtests for being discriminatory against minorities. Given the explanations offered above and the results of objective research presented in chapter 5, that would hardly seem to be the case. Again, it is a matter of fact, not opinion, that regardless of where students attend school or of the nature of their cultural backgrounds, *Musical Aptitude Profile* scores, including results derived from the three preference subtests, for any group of students will be normally distributed. All culturally homogeneous groups of fifty or more students will have similar numbers of students scoring high, average, and low.

Although the answers to the preference subtest questions are not arbitrary, the titles of the subtests are. The words *phrasing, balance,* and *style* mean different things to different persons. I was required to give the subtests titles, however, and the three titles that I decided upon were found to cause the least confusion among students taking the subtests. Meanwhile, some interesting findings were disclosed during the period of experimentation with different sets of directions for the subtests. It was discovered that as long as students were given practice exercises in following the directions, their scores remained relatively the same, even when the titles of the preference subtests were changed. That was true even when numbers (test 1, test 2, etc.) or letters (test A, test B, etc.) were used. In further research it became clear that as long as students heard the practice exercises, only minimal directions were required to allow them to understand how to proceed. In the final analysis, the longer directions were included in the published version of the battery, because in a prepublication questionnaire, a substantial number of test administrators said they would be uncomfortable with only brief directions.

There are other interesting aspects of the design of the *Musical Aptitude Profile* that might be discussed. During the period in which the battery was being developed, different instruments and combinations of instruments were used to perform the music in the questions. Only for the nonpreference subtests, did woodwind and brass instruments prove to be as good as the string instruments that were used in the final version of the battery. That is, the correlations between sets of scores when different instruments were used as stimuli were as high as the subtest reliabilities. Thus, consideration was given to interchanging instrumentation within and among the nonpreference tests in an attempt to bring variety to the listening process. That idea was discarded, however, because students began to make false inferences from the alternation of instruments. The students were concerned that different instruments were used for a reason they did not understand, and so many construed that it might be related to answering questions correctly. To explain in the directions that this was not the case only complicated matters. Primarily for this reason, then, only string instruments were used. In the *Harmony* subtest, a keyboard instrument proved to be unsatisfactory because the lower part of each musical statement and musical answer could not be emphasized without making the questions sound unmusical. For the preference subtests, woodwind, brass, and keyboard instruments presented additional problems when they were used as stimuli, particularly in the *Phrasing* and *Style* subtests, and to some extent in the *Balance* subtest. The musicians could not be flexible enough to make the necessary subtle changes of tone quality and dynamics, nor could they make the intended musical faults in the questions sound slight enough so that the faults would not be immediately obvious to all students. Perhaps the nature of the instruments themselves, especially in the use of vibrato for the woodwinds and brasses and reverberation in the use of keyboard instruments, precluded the possibility of attaining such standards. Whether string instruments were used solo or in ensemble made no difference, except in the *Phrasing* subtest. However, a string quartet rather than a duet could have been used for the *Phrasing* subtest, and a violin and cello rather than solo violin could have been used for the *Balance* and *Style* subtests.

As I have explained, in order to be sure that the musical answer sounded exactly the same as the musical statement for those questions so designated in the *Rhythm Imagery* subtests, the musical statement was re-recorded to serve also as the musical answer. After that re-recording was made, the musical answer, itself, was re-recorded twice. One re-recording became the musical statement and the other became the musical answer. As a result, there is no tone-quality difference between the recording of the musical statements and the musical answers. It was found that without those precautions, some students could discern the timbre difference between the musical statement and the musical answer. They would then use that information as a clue for answering the question, without having to listen to whether the musical statement and the musical answer were the same or different in tempo or meter, as explained in the directions.

Carl E. Seashore designed his tests, as most other test authors have done, so that the first question in each test is the easiest and the last is the most difficult. The questions become progressively more difficult from the beginning to the end of the test. That procedure insures higher reliability, but not necessarily higher validity, than the test would otherwise have. The subtests in the *Musical Aptitude Profile* are designed differently. Very easy, easy, moderately difficult, difficult, and very difficult questions are randomly scattered throughout each subtest in the battery. Hence, a student with low or average music aptitude does not lose interest or become frustrated in taking the subtest because it has become too difficult. The student soon discovers that there are questions throughout the subtest that can be answered with ease. That procedure, in combination with the inclusion of the in-doubt response, increases the validity of the subtest.

The rhythm subtests were the most difficult ones in the battery to develop. In the first version of MAP, there was only one rhythm test. The student was asked to decide whether the musical answer was the same as or different from the musical statement. If the musical answer was different, however, it was for one of three reasons: either the musical answer was performed at a faster or slower speed (a change of tempo), the musical answer was performed with one note more or one note less (a change of meter), or one note in the musical answer was shorter or longer (a change in melodic rhythm). When the musical answer was different, the student was directed to indicate why it was different. The student had to choose among "tempo," "meter," and "melodic rhythm." Approximately half the number of students who took the test were able to decide correctly whether the musical answer was the same or different from the musical statement, but almost none knew why it was different. As a result, the reliability of the test approached zero. Thus, the design of the test was ultimately changed to its present form, to include two subtests.

After the design of the test was changed, the initial versions of the two subtests were still found to be too difficult for the majority of students, regardless of their age. For example, in the *Tempo* subtest, if the musical answer was different from the musical statement, the student was asked to indicate whether the ending of the musical answer was faster or slower than the ending of the musical statement. Again, the reliability of the test approached zero. There are two probable reasons for this. The first and more important of the two is that young children in the developmental music aptitude stage are typically deprived of informal guidance in rhythm and so when, as a group, their rhythm aptitude stabilizes, it is impoverished and generally low. Second, it seems that to understand even the words "faster" and "slower" requires at least some music achievement, and therefore the use of these words is inappropriate for directions. It was not until students were asked to indicate "same" or "different" without explaining the nature of the difference, and not until the faster and slower endings were exaggerated in terms of speed, that the *Tempo* subtest began to exhibit acceptable reliability.

Also, when the word *meter* was used rather than the word *rhythm* in the directions for the *Meter* subtest, the reliability of the subtest decreased drastically. It was when the word *meter* was no longer used and the heavy beats, which I call macrobeats, were accented in performance by the violinist that the reliability of the *Meter* subtest increased to its present acceptable level. In this connection, it is interesting to note that the same need for dynamic accents in the *Meter* subtest of the *Musical Aptitude Profile* also became apparent in the development of the *Rhythm* subtests of the *Primary Measures of Music Audiation* and the *Intermediate Measures of Music Audiation*. For the two developmental music aptitude tests, it is necessary to have clicks, representing macrobeats, underlying the melodic rhythm of all questions.

Difficulties in developing the *Tempo* and *Meter* subtests of the

Musical Aptitude Profile should have been anticipated, because the design of each subtest is unique. The *Meter* subtest, in which two phrases of meter are compared, has been shown to be a more valid measure of rhythm aptitude than one in which two phrases of melodic rhythm are compared (Gordon, *An Investigation of the Intercorrelation Among Musical Aptitude Profile and Seashore Measures*, 1969; and Rolland Raim). To compare the melodic rhythm of two phrases is to emphasize memorization rather than audiation, making such a test one of music achievement. Actually, in order to make accurate comparisons of melodic rhythm, a feeling of meter as the underlying structure must be audiated. Responding to meter is natural, basic, and simple, whereas making judgments about melodic rhythm, especially without the audiation of meter, is mechanical and complex. The *Tempo* subtest measures the most fundamental of rhythm aptitudes. Unless a consistent tempo can be audiated, the possibility of demonstrating a high level of rhythm aptitude is questionable. Just as meter is basic to melodic rhythm, so tempo is basic to meter. Without a sense of audiation for tempo and meter, acceptable achievement in any form of melodic rhythm is doubtful. It is probably because of a lack of tempo and meter audiation that so many students are taught to count numbers and that so many musicians continue to count numbers throughout their professional careers. As will be explained in chapter 9, the *Tempo* and *Meter* subtests together offer a type of comprehensive diagnosis unlike that found in any other stabilized music aptitude test battery.

Among the many investigations of the *Musical Aptitude Profile* cited in the bibliography, the three most impressive longitudinal predictive validity studies are summarized below in chronological order. The initial one was the first of its type (Gordon, *A Three-Year Longitudinal Predictive Validity Study*, 1967). In all, 241 students took part in the study. Every student in at least one fourth or fifth-grade classroom in one or more selected cities in Iowa and one city in Wisconsin was given a minimum of one group music lesson each week during the academic year. The students were required to participate in that one group instrumental lesson, as a curricular activity, for a period of three years. In addition, the students were encouraged to participate in other music activities, depending upon their motivation and achievement. Because all students in a classroom were required to study a musical instrument, they constituted a heterogeneous group in terms of stabilized music aptitude. The students had no previous experience with music except that which they might have been exposed to in general music.

The *Musical Aptitude Profile* was administered to the students before any instrumental music instruction was begun. Because of the nature of the study, neither the music teachers nor any other person associated with the study was informed of the students' scores until the study was completed. At the end of each year of the three years of the study, all students' instrumental music achievement was measured and then correlated with their pretraining MAP scores. This was done automatically with the use of a computer. Thus, unlike a concurrent or criterion-related validity study in which a music aptitude test and a music achievement test are administered within a short period of time, making it impossible to determine causation, if a high correlation is found between pretraining music aptitude scores and post-training instrumental music achievement scores in a longitudinal study, the cause of the relation is obvious. Because the students had had no formal music instruction before they took MAP, and because a substantial amount of time had elapsed before their instrumental music achievement was measured, their high music aptitude had to be the cause of their high music achievement, and their average or low music aptitude had to be the cause of their average or low music achievement. As an ancillary part of the study, the effects of training on *Musical Aptitude Profile* scores were investigated.

Every participating student was provided with a new musical instrument at no cost. The instruments included flutes, clarinets, saxophones, trumpets, French horns, cornets, trombones, and baritones. Each student was permitted to choose an instrument to study. The teachers chose the methods books and music to be used in instruction in their own schools.

The following five criteria were used for measuring the music achievement of the students: 1) judges' ratings of melodic, rhythmic, and expressive aspects of recorded performances of etudes prepared in advance by the students with guidance from their teachers; 2) judges' ratings of melodic, rhythmic, and expressive aspects of recorded performances of etudes prepared in advance by the students, again without guidance from their teachers; 3) judges' ratings of melodic, rhythmic, and expressive aspects of recorded performances of etudes that the students sight read; 4) the students' scores on a given level of the *Iowa Tests of Music Literacy* (Gordon, 1991); and 5) teachers' ratings of the students' music achievement. The judges rated the students' music achievement using a five-point rating scale for each etude, and their reliability exceeded .90 every year.

The predictive validity coefficients for each of the seven ᶜ MAP with regard to all criteria, except criterion 5, increaseᵈ ˙ through the third year of the study. The coefficients fᶜ ite score for the final year of the study were .58, .7ι criteria 1 through 5, respectively. When all criteria predictive validity was .75. That indicates that approxι of the reason or reasons students are successful in beginning instrumental music is accounted for in the composite score of the *Musical Aptitude Profile*. Of the remaining 45 percent, less than 5 percent can be attributed to error of measurement, and approximately 5 percent may be attributed to general intelligence. Thus, approximately 35 percent of the nature of the variance remained unknown at that time. Since then, as is discussed in chapter 10, it has been discovered by using the *Instrument Timbre Preference Test* (Gordon, 1984) that approximately 25 percent of the then-unknown variance can be accounted for if a student learns to play an instrument for which he or she has a preference in terms of the tone quality and range.

With regard to the effects of training on MAP scores, an increase of only .06 of one standard score point (the standard score range being from 20 to 80) was found for students studying a musical instrument when their scores were compared to those of students who did not receive such training.

The second study (Gordon, *Taking into Account Musical Aptitude Differences*, 1970) took place over a period of two years. It was designed primarily to investigate the diagnostic validity of the *Musical Aptitude Profile* battery, that is, to determine whether students' instrumental music achievement is greater when their teachers make use of their MAP scores before and during instruction than when their teachers do not use that information as an aid in instruction.

The *Musical Aptitude Profile* was administered to approximately 400 students who entered the fourth and fifth grades in all Kenosha, Wisconsin, county schools. A few of the students had or were taking piano lessons, but none of them had had any previous instruction on a woodwind or brass instrument. Of those students, 190 voluntarily elected to participate in beginning instrumental music instruction for a period of two years. Each student was allowed to study an instrument of his or her choice.

The participating students were grouped into four music aptitude levels (high, above average, below average, and low) according to their composite scores on MAP. After students had been classified at each music aptitude level according to the instrument that each selected, their school grade, and their sex, they were assigned to either an experimental or a control group. Each group comprised a randomly stratified sample of students based on the factors described, and the groups were of comparable size. The teachers of students in the experimental groups were given the students' MAP scores, but the teachers in the control groups were not. aid in the adaptation of instruction that took into account the musical strengths and weaknesses of individual students, every teacher was given supplementary instructional materials and was introduced to the section in the MAP manual that offered suggestions on the interpretation and use of test results. The research was further controlled by having each of the seven teachers instruct both an experimental and a control group. The students were required to participate in at least one half-hour group instrumental music lesson of heterogeneous instrumentation each week, and all were encouraged to participate in other music activities in and out of school.

In addition to the composite score on *Level One* of the *Iowa Tests of Music Literacy,* five instrumental etudes served as validity criteria. Two of the etudes were prepared with teacher help, two without teacher help, and one was sight read. Each of the recorded etudes was evaluated by two judges at the end of each year using a five-point rating scale.

After the second year of study, the differences in mean scores on each of the six criteria combined for each of four music aptitude levels favored the students in all experimental groups. The differences were of practical as well as statistical significance. When the groups were considered separately, the predictive validity coefficients were .60 for all experimental groups combined and .58 for all control grouped combined, suggesting that music aptitude is a greater factor than instructional techniques in successful achievement in instrumental music. That, of course, does not discount the importance of the diagnostic value of the *Musical Aptitude Profile* in terms of guiding students to make the most of their potential.

It is interesting to note that even after two years of instructing the students, the teachers were not fully aware of the level of music aptitude of each of the students in the control groups. Correlations between the teachers' estimates of the students' music aptitudes and their *Musical Aptitude Profile* scores were only .29 for *Tonal Imagery,* .29 for *Rhythm Imagery,* .34 for *Musical Sensitivity,* and .43 for the composite score. Teachers' need for a valid test of stabilized music aptitude could not be made more compelling. Warren Hatfield came to a similar conclusion when he investigated the diagnostic value of MAP for use with instrumental music majors enrolled in a university.

The third longitudinal study of the validity of the *Musical Aptitude Profile* spanned a five-year period (Gordon, *Fifth-Year and Final Results,* 1975). It was precipitated by a short investigation of the potential for music achievement among students in disadvantaged schools (Gordon, *A Comparison of the Performance, 1967),* where it was found that the potential for music achievement is similar among groups of students who are classified as attending economically disadvantaged schools and those attending other schools.

Unfortunately, of the 658 disadvantaged students in the study, o~

of the 55 who attained *Musical Aptitude Profile* composite scores above the 90th percentile participated in school music performance groups or performed on a musical instrument. Because such a small number of those students participated in music activities, it was not practical to investigate the comparative extent to which disadvantaged and more advantaged students achieve in music. Therefore, the purpose of the final longitudinal study to be described was to determine whether, if given similar educational opportunities, students who attend disadvantaged schools achieve in music at levels comparable to those of students in other schools with corresponding stabilized music aptitudes.

The *Musical Aptitude Profile* was administered to all fifth and sixth grade students in four disadvantaged inner city schools, composed mainly of minorities and people of color, and in three other schools in Des Moines, Iowa. Each student who volunteered to take instrumental music lessons and to participate in school music activities was lent a relatively new musical instrument. The available instruments were divided among the 82 volunteers in the disadvantaged schools and among the 96 volunteers in the more advantaged schools. Two teachers were assigned to the disadvantaged schools and two teachers were assigned to the other schools. Neither group of students was favored in terms of instructional materials or instructional time. Because of the length of the study and because many families moved to other school districts in the city and others moved out of the city, only 28 disadvantaged students and 35 heterogeneous students remained in the study throughout the five years.

After each year of instruction, a sequential level of the *Iowa Tests of Music Literacy* was administered to all students, and the students performed three etudes, all of which served as validity criteria. Two judges evaluated the recorded performances of the etudes using a five-point rating scale. The significance of the differences between the achievement means of the disadvantaged students and the other students was examined each year.

At the completion of the first year, the mean for every validity criterion significantly favored the more advantaged group and students with high music aptitude, regardless of their environmental backgrounds. By the end of the fifth year, however, when all criteria were combined in terms of a multivariate analysis, the overall mean differences significantly favored the disadvantaged students and, again, all students with high music aptitude.

It was concluded from the continuing results of the study that if given appropriate compensatory instruction over a period of years, initially deficient students who attend disadvantaged schools can ultimately surpass more advantaged students in instrumental music achievement.

Moreover, disadvantaged students who possess below average stabilized music aptitudes can ultimately achieve standards in instrumental music achievement similar to those demonstrated by more advantaged students who possess above average music aptitudes. Of particular importance, however, is that overall, students with above average and high MAP scores, regardless of their environmental backgrounds, can attain higher levels of instrumental music achievement than students with below average MAP scores.

THE ADVANCED MEASURES OF MUSIC AUDIATION

The *Advanced Measures of Music Audiation* is a recorded test of stabilized music aptitude that is designed for use with high school students and for college and university music and nonmusic majors. Since its publication, however, it has been found to offer satisfactory reliability when used with students as young as those in seventh grade or who are twelve years old (David Fullen). The two most important purposes of the test are to assist professors and administrators in 1) establishing objective and realistic expectations for the music achievement of college and university music and nonmusic majors and 2) efficiently and diagnostically adapting music teaching in classroom, ensemble, and private instruction to the individual musical differences among college and university students.

Included on the recording are the directions for taking the test, three practice exercises, and the 30 questions that constitute the test. The original music composed for each test question was programmed on an Apple Macintosh computer and performed by a professional musician on a Yamaha DX-7 synthesizer. Whether administered to a group or to an individual student, the test requires no more than 20 minutes of overall administration time. The recording is only 16 minutes long.

Each question consists of a short musical statement followed by a short musical answer. The student is asked to decide whether the musical statement and the musical answer are the same or different for each question. If the musical answer is different from the musical statement, the student is then asked to decide whether the difference is a result of a tonal change or a rhythm change. There may be one or more tonal changes or one or more rhythm changes in a musical answer. Never, however, are there both a tonal change and a rhythm change in a musical answer.

What is meant by a tonal change and a rhythm change is made clear in the practice exercises. If the musical answer is the same as the musical statement, the student fills the blank in the "same" column on the answer sheet after the number for the question. If the musical answer is different from the musical statement because of a tonal change, the student fills the blank in the "tonal" column, and if the musical answer is different from the musical statement because of a rhythm change, the student fills the blank in the "rhythm" column. If a student is unsure of an answer, he or she is directed not to guess; the blank should be left unfilled for that question. The in-doubt response is not an option.

In each question the musical statement and the musical answer have the same number of notes. Thus, a student cannot arrive at a correct answer by simply counting and comparing the number of notes in the musical statement and the musical answer. Moreover, the difference between the musical statement and the musical answer may occur at the beginning, in the middle, and/or at the end of the musical answer. When a change is at the beginning, the question becomes an easy one; when it is at the end, it becomes a moderately difficult one; and when it is in the middle, it becomes a difficult one. The more changes in a musical answer, the easier, of course, the question.

A musical answer may be different from a musical statement as a result of a tonal change of one or more pitches, tonality, and/or keyality, or as a result of a rhythm change of one or more durations, meters, and/or tempos. Various tonalities, keyalities, meters, and tempos, as well as tonal and rhythm modulations, are represented in the questions. The music in some of the questions is indicative of contemporary sound, that is, what might be called atonal or arrhythmic or what I refer to as multitonal and multimetric music. The questions are not clustered in terms of difficulty levels or in terms of tonality, keyality, meter, or tempo.

Initially, the music that constitutes the questions was performed by musicians using actual musical instruments. Except for the designated difference, it was soon discovered that it was impossible for a musician to perform all the other parts of each musical statement and musical answer exactly the same way. Because unintended as well as intended differences in expression, intonation, and rhythm were present in the musical answer when the music was performed by a musician on an actual musical instrument, the validity of the test was in jeopardy. Thus, the questions had to be programmed on a computer and performed on an electronic instrument. The result was that all parts of each musical statement and musical answer are perfectly consistent except for the designated difference.

Typically, subtests are used in a test battery that is designed to yield two or more scores related to different dimensions of music aptitude. That is not the case for the *Advanced Measures of Music Audiation*, which is actually one intact test. Nonetheless, because of the unique process of scoring the test, a *Tonal* score, a *Rhythm* score, and a total score are derived from the same 30 questions. Though it would add to the validity of the test if preference measures were included, that, according to college and university administrators, would have made the test too long and so unsuitable for use in most institutions of higher learning.

The *Advanced Measures of Music Audiation* is misunderstood by some persons to be a music achievement test. It is a music aptitude test. There are various reasons for this. First, the skills measured by the test are not formally taught to students. Second, because it is original, a student could not have achieved familiarity with the music used in the test questions. Third, although because of formal or informal music instruction some students may have theoretical knowledge of the words *tonal* and *rhythm*, most students will quickly acquire the necessary understanding when listening to the practice exercises. It is conceivable that the rapidity with which and the extent to which a student learns how the words *tonal* and *rhythm* are used for taking the test, regardless of how much music instruction the student may have had previous to the administration of the test, are a measure of the student's music aptitude, but that should be appropriately reflected in the test results. Of course, if a teacher should teach to the test, AMMA, like any other test, regardless of whether it is an aptitude test or achievement test, would become invalid.

Considerable experimentation was undertaken to determine the most desirable length of silent time needed to separate the musical answer from the musical statement. Given too much time, a student might be able to imitate or even memorize the musical statement before comparing it to the musical answer. Should that happen, the test would probably become a measure of music achievement. Four seconds were found to be optimal for allowing a student enough time to audiate, but not to imitate or memorize, the music. That is, four seconds of silent time is not enough for a student to repeat the music in any question at the actual tempo at which it was heard. There is, however, just enough time for a student to audiate the musical statement before the musical answer is heard. Audiation is accomplished by the student as he or she syntactically makes generalizations about the essential features of what was heard in the musical statement and then retains that information in audiation while listening to the musical answer. That the student must be listening simultaneously for either a tonal change or a rhythm change further encourages the more mature student in the stabilized music aptitude stage to audiate rather than to imitate or to memorize.

A developmental music aptitude test, for example PMMA and IMMA, consists of a *Tonal* subtest and a *Rhythm* subtest. The *Tonal* subtest is without rhythm and the *Rhythm* subtest is without variable pitch. Thus, the student hears tonal aspects and rhythm aspects separately from each other, and so is required to respond only to tonal questions in the *Tonal* subtest or to rhythm aspects in the *Rhythm* subtest. A stabilized music aptitude test for school-age students, for example MAP, also includes a separate tonal subtest and a separate rhythm subtest. The student, however, hears tonal aspects and rhythm aspects in the tonal subtests but responds only to tonal aspects, and likewise hears tonal aspects and rhythm aspects in the *Rhythm* subtests but responds only to rhythm aspects. In the *Advanced Measures of Music Audiation,* also a test of stabilized music aptitude but one intended for college and university students, there are no separate tonal and rhythm subtests, and, again, tonal aspects and rhythm aspects are heard simultaneously. The student, however, responds to tonal aspects and rhythm aspects in the same question. I am unable to explain why these differences in test design are essential; I can only say that as a result of extensive research in test development and comparative studies of test reliability and validity, that the differences are necessary. To complicate the issue, as I will be explaining in chapter 8, the design of a developmental music aptitude test for very young children, three and four years old, must have characteristics in common with a stabilized music aptitude test designed specifically for young adults and adults in order for it to demonstrate satisfactory reliability and validity. To unravel the reasons for this situation requires extensive research, and there should be rich rewards for those who investigate the matter as well as for all serious music educators.

Because they are both tests of stabilized music aptitude, a teacher has a choice between using the *Musical Aptitude Profile* or the *Advanced Measures of Music Audiation* with students in grades seven through twelve. The main difference between the two is that MAP offers an extensive diagnosis, seven subtest scores, of students' musical strengths and weaknesses, whereas AMMA offers only two test scores, and those two scores are highly related. With regard to the composite score, which is the most valuable part of AMMA because of its length, the MAP complete score is more reliable, but it is not consistently more valid. For the specific purpose of identifying students with high music aptitude who should be engaged in school music activities but are not, and when administration time is limited, I recommend that AMMA be given to groups at large. After students with high music aptitude have been identified, MAP may be administered only to them. Should time permit, however, it would be prudent to administer MAP to all students in general music classes.

The procedure for scoring the *Advanced Measures of Music Audiation* is unique. To begin, a constant of 20 points is added to the student's *Tonal* test score and to the student's *Rhythm* test score. Then, scoring each question again, if the musical answer is the same as the musical statement, or if there is a rhythm change and the student made an error by indicating that a tonal change took place, one point is subtracted from the student's *Tonal* test score. The same logic is applied when sameness or a tonal change is mistaken for a rhythm change. Then one point is subtracted from the student's *Rhythm* test score.

The adjusted scores on the *Advanced Measures of Music Audiation* should not be construed to be corrected-for-guessing scores. The scores are adjusted on the basis of how well a student positively and negatively audiates tonally and rhythmically. To simply and without qualification correct a score for guessing by adding or subtracting a point for a given answer is quite different from and less valid than the procedure described above.

The unadjusted and adjusted tonal test scores correlate .89, the two sets of rhythm scores correlate .87, and the two sets of total scores correlate .93. The amount of unique variance associated with each adjusted score suggests that the adjusting of scores is justified. Further, the reliabilities of the adjusted scores are .89 for the *Tonal* test, .90 for the *Rhythm* test, and .92 for the total test. The corresponding reliabilities for the unadjusted scores are .76, .76, and .80. Those coefficients are indicative of the negative correlations of -.51 and -.49 between the number of points subtracted and the adjusted scores on the *Tonal* test and the *Rhythm* test, respectively.

Another difference between the *Musical Aptitude Profile* and the *Advanced Measures of Music Audiation* is that, as stated heretofore, AMMA does not include a provision for the in-doubt response. The reason, of course, is that AMMA is the only test in which scores are adjusted, and therefore the in-doubt response would detract from its established scoring procedure. Nonetheless, in the directions for the test students are encouraged, as they are in the other tests, not to guess if they are unsure of the correct answer to a question. They leave the answer blank on the answer sheet, and unanswered questions do not affect a test score either positively or negatively. The question remains, however, whether the validity of a test is enhanced more when the in-doubt response is included as an option response or when scores are adjusted in the manner described. To design a study and to construct authentic parallel test forms to answer that research question would certainly be a challenge.

Studies have been undertaken to investigate the validity of the established scoring system for the *Advanced Measures of Music Audiation*. In one study (Gordon, *Advanced Measures of Music Audiation*, 1989), AMMA score distributions of European students were compared to those of American students who participated in the test standardization program. Virtually no differences were found. In another study (Gordon, *Taking Another Look*, 1997), a recorded instrumental etude performed by music majors and professional musicians studying in exemplary music conservatories in America and Europe served as the validity criterion. Seven alternative procedures for scoring AMMA were compared to one another and to the established procedure to determine which of the eight demonstrated highest validity. Some of the other scoring processes included unadjusted scores, scores without constants, and other types of adjusted scores. The most interesting alternative, the opposite of the established procedure, was to subtract a point from a student's rhythm score instead of the tonal score when the student believed a tonal change was heard when there was actually a rhythm change or no change, and to subtract a point from a student's tonal score instead of the rhythm score when the student believed a rhythm change was heard when there was actually a tonal change or, again, no change. It was found that although there were advantages to some of the other approaches, overall, the established procedure was most promising.

As I have mentioned, there is a problem with AMMA that remains consequential. It is that there is a high intercorrelation between scores on the *Tonal* test and the *Rhythm* test. That problem comes about mainly because, to keep the test brief, the questions that have "same" as the correct answer are included in calculating both the *Tonal* score and the *Rhythm* score. Thus, in the study just described, one of the alternate scoring procedures was to eliminate the ten questions with "same" as the correct answer in the derivation of scores. Although the intercorrelation coefficient between the two tests was drastically reduced, the overall reliability and validity of the *Tonal* test, the *Rhythm* test, and the total score was measurably reduced, thus eliminating that alternative as a scoring procedure.

Although it was found in one study (Gordon, *Is it Only in Academics,* 1992-93) that 385 highly select music students and professional musicians attending the Bela Bartok special high school for music in Budapest, Hungary, attained significantly higher AMMA scores than did older conservatory students enrolled in various institutions across the United States, it was apparent that the results of a longitudinal predictive validity study of the test would be more compelling. In that more extensive one-year study (Gordon, *Predictive Validity Study of AMMA*, 1990), AMMA was administered to 114 undergraduate and graduate music majors in an urban university at the beginning of the academic year. At the end of that school year, the students recorded their performances of the same etude used in the Hungarian/American study, and the quality of their performances was rated by one professional musician and two professors of music education. The correlations between the combined judges' ratings and the students' AMMA scores obtained one year earlier were .77 for the *Tonal* test, .75 for the *Rhythm* test, and .82 for both tests combined. Those coefficients approximate the validity coefficient obtained for the *Musical Aptitude Profile* in the three-year longitudinal predictive validity study described heretofore.

---

1 The violinists are Stuart Canin and Charles Trager and the cellist is Paul Olefsky. Mr. Canin was the first American to win the Paganini International Violin Competition in Genoa, Italy, in 1959. Mr. Trager was the first American to be awarded the Henry Wieniawski International Violin Competition in Poznan, Poland, in 1962. Mr. Olefsky has received, among many other honors, the Michels Memorial Award.

CHAPTER 8

THE MEASUREMENT OF DEVELOPMENTAL MUSIC APTITUDE: DEVELOPMENTAL MUSIC APTITUDE TESTS

The concept that music aptitude is developmental to age nine appears reasonable to most persons, professionals in a variety of disciplines and laypersons alike. The idea that there can be a developmental music aptitude test that is not a music achievement test, however, is difficult, particularly for some professional music educators, to understand. They think that because a child's score can improve on a developmental music aptitude test, that test must be a music achievement test. It must be understood, however, that children have not been formally or informally taught what is asked of them on a music aptitude test.

In a developmental music aptitude test, children are asked to listen to a series of two tonal patterns or a series of two rhythm patterns and to decide whether the two patterns they have heard sound the same or different. It is not likely that young children would have been taught this kind of skill at home or in typical classroom instruction. Most often, children in school and preschool are taught to sing or to chant by imitating what their teacher or peers have performed. In classroom instruction, young children are seldom asked to listen to or to sing a tonal pattern without rhythm and only occasionally to chant a rhythm pattern using a single pitch, and as we now know from music learning theory, for patterns to become familiar, children must hear and perform them solo. Despite this, children who reach a certain level of developmental music aptitude do respond to tonal patterns without rhythm and to rhythm patterns without variable pitches on a valid test of developmental music aptitude, regardless of their previous instruction. They accomplish this through audiation.

It is important to understand that although children may have learned, in classroom instruction, to be skillful at memorizing, in a developmental music aptitude test, the period of silence between the first and second patterns in a pair to which young children respond is too short to allow enough time for them to imitate or memorize, in real time, the first pattern before they hear the second. It is true that some children taking the test may have been guided, previously, in audiating essential pitches and durations in patterns. In the classroom instruction they might have received, however, provision would have been made for them to hear the relevant tonality, keyality, meter, and tempo of patterns before they were asked to perform them. In a developmental music aptitude test, children are given at most only a suggestion of keyality and tempo before they hear and respond to each pair of patterns. This means that whatever their previous training, children's capacity to discern tonality, keyality, pitch center, meter, tempo, or macrobeats and microbeats to serve as a syntactical base becomes an essential and valid measure of each child's level of developmental music aptitude.

Despite clear evidence that previous instruction does not act as a false indicator on a valid test of developmental music aptitude, what children absorb and learn in early childhood informal music guidance in preschool or at home and what they are taught through formal music instruction at home or in school forms the foundation for the scores they attain on a developmental, as well as a stabilized, music aptitude test. Only when the content of a developmental music aptitude test duplicates what is typically taught in the classroom will the test become one of music achievement.

Young children's music aptitude fluctuates according to the quality of their music environment. That is why a music aptitude test designed for young children is called developmental. Children's music aptitudes change whether or not they have received, or are receiving, formal or informal music instruction, regardless of the type and quality of that instruction. By simply listening to music and performing as and when they choose to do so, children's music aptitude can be affected. Without any exposure at all to music, or if the exposure is inappropriate, developmental aptitude not only stagnates, it actually decreases. When, however, children receive an abundance of appropriate informal guidance and formal instruction in music, the chances are that their developmental music aptitude will increase. How high a child's music aptitude can become depends on the potential with which the child was born.

Conceivably it may even rise back to its birth level. Of course, it requires significantly less effort by adults to allow a child's developmental music aptitude to decrease than it does to help the child move back toward his or her aptitude level at the time of birth.

The importance of appropriate informal guidance and formal instruction in music for young children from birth to age nine cannot be overemphasized. Because a child's music aptitude becomes stabilized after age nine and cannot be increased, from that time on, an adult can help a child achieve in music only to the extent that his or her level of stabilized music aptitude will allow. For that reason alone, a developmental music aptitude test should be administered to young children periodically. Not only will test results serve diagnostic purposes, they will also identify children with high developmental music aptitude who require constant attention if that level is to be maintained. In addition, music aptitude test results have been shown to be very useful when there is disagreement between a child's score and the score a parent or teacher believes the child should have received. The process of discovering the source of the discrepancy has enormous value to the child's educational progress.

I have already explained that approximately half the number of students with high stabilized music aptitude are not identified as such throughout their school careers. Those who are known identify themselves because they are motivated to achieve. Typically, they are then later recognized by their teachers as a result of their music performance skills. Unfortunately, young children rarely identify themselves as having high music aptitude, and only in rare instances do they have the opportunity to distinguish themselves through music performance skills. For this reason, the importance of frequent administrations of a developmental music aptitude test cannot be overstated.

This chapter is concerned with the measurement of developmental music aptitude, and the interpretation of developmental music aptitude is presented in chapter 9. I believe that there are only three published tests that are specifically designed to measure developmental music aptitude. They are the *Primary Measures of Music Audiation* (Gordon, 1979), the *Intermediate Measures of Music Audiation* (Gordon, 1982), and *Audie* (Gordon, 1989). PMMA is designed for children in kindergarten through grade three, IMMA is designed for children in grades one through four, and *Audie* can be used with children as young as three and four years of age. I will describe each test in this chapter and will make clear the differences in how they may be used to measure developmental music aptitude. The relationships among developmental and stabilized music aptitude tests will be discussed in chapter 9.

THE PRIMARY MEASURES OF MUSIC AUDIATION

The *Primary Measures of Music Audiation* is a recorded test of short musical phrases. It may be administered to children in kindergarten through grade three on an individual basis or in groups as large as those that constitute typical classrooms. The test has two parts: *Tonal* and *Rhythm.* Each part is recorded separately, and each recording includes practice examples and 40 test questions. A child does not need to know how to read, to read music notation, or to recognize numbers in order to use the answer sheet for either subtest, nor is prior achievement in music required to answer the questions.

Children answer the questions by making circles around pictures of faces on an answer sheet. A circle is drawn around a pair of faces that look the same if the two tonal patterns or rhythm patterns heard on the recording sound the same. If the two patterns sound different on the recording, a circle is drawn around a pair of faces that look different. Because many young children do not know what is meant by the words *pattern* or *phrase,* the word *song* is used in the directions read to the children who are taking the test. To further assist the children, the word *first* is announced on the recording before the first pattern of each pair is performed, and the word *second* is announced before the second pattern of each pair is performed.

In order to make clear to children how to mark their answer sheets, the name of an object is announced on the recording before each set of patterns is heard, and children can quickly locate that object on their answer sheet. Children then mark their answers by making a circle around the same or different pair of faces under the picture of the object that was named on the recording. The order of the objects announced and of the pictures is, of course, the same. Because pictures are substituted for numbers, children do not need to know how to count to demonstrate their developmental music aptitude.

The recording for each subtest includes approximately 12 minutes of listening time, and each subtest requires approximately 20 minutes to administer. The *Tonal* subtest is given on one day and the *Rhythm* subtest on another, the two days preferably being within one week but no more than two weeks apart. It was found in prepublication research that young children cannot keep pace with recorded directions. Unlike students nine years of age and older, a few less mature children may need help in understanding the test directions as they are being read. Other children may feel that they need to ask questions about the directions. This is why, in place of recorded directions, either a classroom teacher or music specialist reads the directions to the children and administers the test.

Each question in both subtests that constitute the *Primary Measures of Music Audiation* was programmed by a professional musician on an Apple Macintosh computer and performed on a Yamaha DX-7 synthesizer. Young children are more attentive when they hear an electronic instrument than when they hear an actual musical instrument played or one typically used by children, such as a bell-type instrument. In the preliminary research with PMMA, the reliability of both subtests increased significantly when a synthesizer was used in place of a standard musical instrument. More important, the use of rhythm instruments affected the validity of the *Rhythm* subtest, because controlled duration is not possible using a rhythm instrument. When such an instrument is used, none of the questions in the *Rhythm* subtest can be performed accurately, because after the attack, the distinction between an intended duration and a rest cannot be made. The only difficulty discovered with the use of a synthesizer for the *Rhythm* subtest was that accents cannot be performed. As will be explained, that problem was solved through the use of a rhythm programmer click track.

The development of the *Primary Measures of Music Audiation* was begun in 1971. Over the eight-year period until its publication, the test underwent several revisions that are described in the test manual. Initially, a taxonomy of tonal patterns and rhythm patterns was created from the content of the *Iowa Tests of Music Literacy*. Then the difficulty levels and growth rates of the patterns were investigated. On the basis of the results of the first study (Gordon, *Toward the Development of a Taxonomy*, 1974), the taxonomy was revised and lengthened, and methods of experimental procedures and data analyses were improved. The difficulty levels and growth rates of the patterns were investigated again in a second study (Gordon, *Tonal and Rhythm Patterns*, 1976). The taxonomy was revised and lengthened once again, and then a third and final study was completed (Gordon, *A Factor Analytic Description*, 1978).

In the final study, 1114 tonal patterns and 486 rhythm patterns were analyzed. As in the first two studies, the tonal patterns and rhythm patterns were classified according to tonality and meter. Throughout a school year, one group of students listened to all of the recorded tonal patterns and another group listened to all of the recorded rhythm patterns. The statistically derived numerical values associated with each of the patterns were transformed into three difficulty levels: easy, moderately difficult, and difficult, and into three growth rates: positive, static, and negative. A positive growth rate indicates that the pattern becomes easier to audiate as students increase in age, a static growth rate indicates that the pattern becomes neither easier nor more difficult to audiate as students increase in age, and a negative growth rate indicates that the pattern becomes more difficult to audiate as students increase in age. The content of the *Primary Measures of Music Audiation* includes only those tonal patterns and rhythm patterns that were found to be easy to audiate and had static growth rate. With few exceptions, all of the easy major and harmonic minor tonal patterns, and with no exceptions, all of the easy rhythm patterns in every meter, are included in PMMA. Of course, although only easy patterns were used in the test questions, the test questions assume different difficulty levels depending on how the patterns are paired in a test question. It has been discovered since the publication of PMMA, that if the order of the test questions is changed in either subtest, the difficulty level of the test questions remain relatively stable. Overall, the easy questions remain easy, the moderately difficult ones remain moderately difficult, and the difficult ones remain difficult. With only very few exceptions, children find it easier to identify two patterns in a pair that sound the same and more difficult to identify those that are different.

The child's capacity to give syntactical meaning to the test questions is the basis of the rationale behind the *Primary Measures of Music Audiation.* To do well on the test, the child must organize isolated pitches into tonal patterns, which are then audiated in relation to a pitch center, in a keyality and/or tonality. Similarly, the child must organize isolated durations into rhythm patterns, which are audiated in relation to macrobeats, in a consistent tempo and/or meter. The higher the level at which a child audiates, the higher the child's developmental music aptitude. For tonal patterns, the lowest level is pitch center and the highest is tonality, and for rhythm patterns, the lowest level is macrobeats in a consistent tempo and the highest is meter. The musical syntax of a test question can be distinguished if a child is capable of audiating a pitch center or macrobeats in a consistent tempo.

The discrimination between two pitches without reference to a pitch center, keyality, or tonality, and the discrimination between two durations without reference to macrobeats in a consistent tempo and meter, does not necessarily require musical thought. If at least a pitch center or macrobeats in a consistent tempo are not audiated, acoustics play the prominent role in the test. The audiation of tonality and meter are typically associated with formal music instruction and stabilized music aptitude, whereas the audiation of a pitch center and macrobeats in a consistent tempo are typically associated with informal guidance and developmental music aptitude. The more and the sooner a child in the developmental music aptitude stage attempts to audiate in terms of tonality and meter, the higher the child's developmental music aptitude. The use of words such as *up* and *down* and *higher* and *lower* in pitch discrimination tests, and the understanding of words such as *longer* and *shorter* and *even* and *uneven* in time discrimination tests, requires formal music achievement. However, the ability to discriminate between two pitches less than a half step apart, to discriminate between two durations less than a fraction of a second different in length, to identify the numeral associated with a changed pitch, and to discriminate between isolated sounds in a timbre test or dynamics test is not functionally related to either informal guidance or formal music instruction or to either developmental music aptitude or stabilized music aptitude.

The *Primary Measures of Music Audiation* yields a *Tonal* score, a *Rhythm* score, and a total score. Each question in the *Tonal* subtest includes two tonal patterns, and each question in the *Rhythm* subtest includes two rhythm patterns. The pitches in the tonal patterns are performed in beats of equal length, and the durations in the rhythm patterns are performed on the same pitch. All of the tonal patterns, which are from two to five pitches long, are performed at the same tempo. At least one tonal pattern in every pair includes the resting tone or tonic, depending on whether the listener is audiating a tonality, keyality, or both, and in some questions one or both patterns may end on the resting tone or tonic. (A tonic is represented by a letter name, such as C or G, that relates to a keyality, whereas a resting tone is represented by a syllable, such as "do" or "la," that relates to a tonality.) Through the audiation of the resting tone or tonic, the child is guided in inferring syntax for each tonal pattern.

In the rhythm questions, although each pattern includes the same number of durations (which prevents the child from counting to arrive at the correct answer), the macrobeats may or may not be systematic in number or length, because an eighth note remains constant among different meters as well as in the same meter. When each macrobeat is performed on the synthesizer as part of a rhythm pattern, it is reinforced at a relatively low dynamic level with a click performed on the rhythm programmer, the click having, of course, a different timbre than the rhythm pattern itself. Because macrobeats are emphasized, the child is guided in inferring syntax for each rhythm pattern in relation to meter or macrobeats. That is particularly important for questions in which the patterns are different but include the same number of macrobeats. As with the *Rhythm Imagery-Tempo* subtest of the *Musical Aptitude Profile,* in which macrobeats had to be accented even though it is a stabilized music aptitude test, the reliability of an experimental version of the *Rhythm* subtest of the *Primary Measures of Music Audiation,* in which macrobeats were not accented, also decreased to a point where the subtest became practically useless.

As explained, only tonal patterns in major and harmonic minor tonalities that were identified in the research as easy to audiate were included in the *Tonal* subtest, and, although they are not clustered according to tonality, more major than harmonic minor patterns are included. Easy patterns in other tonalities were not used because there were not a sufficient number that included the characteristic tone or tones of a given tonality, such as the raised sixth and lowered seventh in Dorian tonality and the lowered second and lowered seventh in Phrygian tonality as compared to harmonic minor tonality, or the raised fourth in Lydian tonality and the lowered seventh in Mixolydian tonality as compared to major tonality.

Both tonal patterns in a pair have the same number of pitches and are intended to be audiated in the same tonality, major or harmonic minor, and keyality, C or A. The two tonics are established immediately in the practice examples. To encourage audiation, an arpeggiated form of a tonic pattern is strategically placed in questions throughout the tonal subtest. In some questions where the patterns are not the same, the difference may be the result of only one pitch change or as many as all pitches in a pattern being changed. A single change may occur at the beginning, middle, or end of a pattern. The difference may also be a result of melodic contour. Such variations contribute to the different difficulty levels of the questions and, thus, to the increased reliability of the subtest. In general, those pairs of patterns in which the last pitch is the same but the first pitch is different are less difficult than those in which the first pitch is the same and the last pitch is different. A question with tonal patterns moving in contrary motion is easier than one with the two moving in oblique or similar motion. Tonal patterns moving in similar motion are most difficult.

Because fewer rhythm patterns than tonal patterns were studied in the research, all rhythm patterns, regardless of meter, that were identified as being easy to audiate and having static growth were included in the *Rhythm* subtest. That all meters are represented in the subtest is actually of great benefit, because most young children in the developmental music aptitude stage audiate rhythm in terms of meter as it relates to the pairing and lengths of macrobeats. Rhythm is affected by a change in the length of durations. A change may occur at the beginning, middle, or end of the second rhythm pattern. The more differences in durations, the easier the question, regardless of where the changes take place. However, in the majority of questions that include patterns that are different, the differences are the result of differences in meters. Questions in which the patterns are in the same meter but have different rhythm are more difficult than questions in which the patterns are in different meters. The most difficult questions are those in which the rhythm is similar but macrobeats are placed differently, made evident because the clicks occur at different times.

There is no provision for children to indicate that they are in doubt about a correct answer to questions in either the *Tonal* or *Rhythm* subtest. Although the in-doubt response functions well when used with the *Musical Aptitude Profile,* it does not prove to be satisfactory when used with a developmental music aptitude test. It was found in early research that approximately half the young children in a group will tend to use the in-doubt response even though some of them know the correct answer, because of their lack of self confidence. Many of those who do not know the correct answer will quickly mark their answer, often with a great deal of assurance. Thus, children are encouraged to answer every question, even when they are unsure of the correct answer, by making their best guess. Questions of different difficulty levels are randomly scattered throughout both subtests.

The split-halves reliabilities for the *Tonal* subtest range from .85 to .89, from .72 to .86 for the *Rhythm* subtest, and from .90 to .92 for the total test. These coefficients are of about the same magnitude as those for the preference subtests of the *Musical Aptitude Profile.* A detailed description of all types of reliabilities, means, standard deviations, inter-correlations, and other relevant statistical information may be found in the test manual. A unique aspect of the test is that not only are reliabilities reported for each subtest and the total test separately, but there are separate reliabilities for children five, six, seven, and eight years of age. As would be expected, the split-halves reliabilities are higher than the test-retest reliabilities, and, except for the oldest children, *Tonal* subtest reliabilities are higher than *Rhythm* subtest reliabilities. As observed in tests of stabilized music aptitude and music achievement, the means for rhythm subtests are consistently lower than the means for tonal subtests. I have no objective explanation for this, but for whatever the reason or reasons, measures of developmental music aptitude present no contradiction to this curious phenomenon.

In addition to the two longitudinal predictive validity studies of the *Primary Measures of Music Audiation,* there have been many concurrent or criterion-related validity, content validity, and process validity studies of the test (for example, studies by William Bell, Richard DiBlassio, Alicia Clair Gibbons, Christine Hobbs, John Holahan, Janet L. S. Moore, Doris Norton, Thomas Clark Saunders and John Holahan, Jeffery Rhone, and Christine Hughes Simmons) in addition to my own. Some of the concurrent studies were designed to determine if PMMA is sensitive to informal guidance or formal instruction in music and related arts that young children might have received or are receiving. Others were designed to investigate the effects of socio-economic influences and learning disabilities on PMMA scores. With regard to process validity and construct validity, the adequacy of the test directions and the suitability of the timbre used to perform the tonal patterns was of main concern.

The two longitudinal predictive validity studies are similar in design, the second intended to serve as a cross validation of the first. The first, which I conducted, is reported in the test manual, and the second was undertaken by Louis Woodruff.

My study took place in a parochial school in Plymouth Meeting, Pennsylvania, where all students were required to study the violin for one year, with the assumption that they would elect to continue lessons after the first year. There were 26 children in the group who were seven or eight years of age. Shortly after some students had been given violins and others had already had some lessons, the *Primary Measures of Music Audiation* was administered to them. At the end of the school year, violin performances of the children were recorded and evaluated by two judges. Separate five-point rating scales were used to measure intonation, rhythm accuracy, and musical expression. The three scores for each child were combined and the two judges' ratings were combined, and that total was correlated with scores on PMMA. The result was a predictive validity coefficient of .73, and it is interesting to note that the coefficient is higher than that derived for the first year of the three-year longitudinal study of the *Musical Aptitude Profile*. That finding tends to corroborate the idea that developmental music aptitude is a more potent factor than stabilized music aptitude in predicting music achievement.

At the end of the year, the teacher rated what he or she considered to be the overall music aptitude of each child. Those ratings correlated .46 with the PMMA total score. As impressive as that concurrent validity coefficient may seem, it is considerably lower than the corresponding predictive validity coefficient. As was found in the MAP two-year longitudinal predictive study relating to stabilized music aptitude, it appears that even after a teacher has closely observed children's musical development for a year or more, the teacher knows less about the developmental music aptitude of the children than can be determined objectively by a valid music aptitude test before instruction has begun.

Two classes of five-year-old children who were attending the Hunter College elementary school in Manhattan, New York, participated in the Woodruff study. There were 13 children in one class and 10 in the other. None of the children had received violin instruction before the beginning of the study. They did, however, participate in pitch, rhythm, and motor games as preparation for studying the violin. Once formal instruction began, the same teacher, using the Suzuki method, taught the two classes in group lessons of 18 to 30 minutes over a twelve-week period. During the course of instruction, the children were taught, among other things, to play the first two phrases of *Twinkle, Twinkle, Little Star* with rhythm variations. At the end of the instruction period, each child performed the two phrases with variations. The performances were recorded and the children's tonal and rhythm skills were evaluated by two judges. The correlations between the combined judges' ratings of both types of achievement and the total PMMA score was .59 for the larger group and .15 for the smaller group. Woodruff could not explain the sizable difference in the coefficients. Nonetheless, considering that the instructional period was so short and the children were so few in number, the predictive validity for the larger group is exceptionally high.

As was explained in regard to stabilized music aptitude tests, another type of validity, called inverse or indirect, is important, particularly for a developmental music aptitude test. That is, it is essential to know that the content of a music aptitude test does not duplicate the content of other tests that are designed for other purposes, such as tests that measure academic achievement and general intelligence. If it is found that a music aptitude test and another type of test are measuring the same factor or have a factor in common, that is, if the scores on the two tests correlate highly, the content of one or both of the tests is called into question, because without content validity, experimental validity is difficult to justify. Inverse or indirect validity is assumed for a test if it demonstrates a low correlation coefficient with another type of test. As reported in chapter 5, scores on PMMA have no more than 15 percent, and usually much less, in common with academic achievement and intelligence test scores. Thus, the data confirm the belief that the words *talented* and *gifted* are not synonymous, although they are very often used as if they were. A so-called talented child is one who is very musical or artistic, whereas a so-called gifted child is one who has a high level of intelligence or a great deal of academic knowledge. Talented children are not necessarily gifted, and gifted children are not necessarily talented.

THE INTERMEDIATE MEASURES OF MUSIC AUDIATION

Approximately two years after the *Primary Measures of Music Audiation* was published, it became apparent that a more advanced version of the test was needed. Because music teachers were made aware of the levels of and changes in the developmental music aptitudes of their students by using PMMA, they were able to provide instruction that was more appropriate to the individual musical differences found among their students. In turn, because instruction had become more efficient, their students began to achieve much higher scores on PMMA than those typically earned by students of the same age who were receiving less appropriate or inappropriate instruction. When an inordinate number of students score high on a test, not only does the reliability of the test decrease, but the test no longer discriminates well among high and above-average students. A more advanced test must be used for more sophisticated students, keeping in mind that the content of the more advanced test must in no way contribute unwittingly to making it a measure of music achievement.

The need for an advanced version of the *Primary Measures of Music Audiation* was satisfied by the creation of the *Intermediate Measures of Music Audiation*. The two tests are designed and organized in the same manner. The directions for taking the tests are alike, and both include a *Tonal* and *Rhythm* subtest. The only difference in design between PMMA and IMMA is in the difficulty of the test questions, thus insuring that IMMA maintains and continues the tradition of PMMA of measuring developmental music aptitude and not music achievement. Only those tonal patterns and rhythm patterns that were found in the three studies cited heretofore to be difficult to audiate and had static growth constitute the content of the *Intermediate Measures of Music Audiation*. That an obvious need evolved for an advanced developmental music aptitude test supports the idea that music aptitude is developmental and that it can be raised back toward its birth level with appropriate informal guidance and formal instruction.

The *Intermediate Measures of Music Audiation* is intended to be used with a group in which half or more of the children score above the 80th percentile on the *Tonal* subtest, the *Rhythm* subtest, or both, of the *Primary Measures of Music Audiation*. IMMA discriminates most precisely among children with above-average and high developmental music aptitudes, whereas PMMA discriminates most precisely among children with average and low developmental music aptitudes. Further, PMMA should be used with children five through eight years of age, and IMMA should be used with children six through nine years of age. Recently, IMMA norms have been developed for students in the fifth and sixth grades as a result of findings that the reliabilities of even the subtests for these students are satisfactory.

Changes in developmental music aptitude, in terms of either raw scores or percentile ranks, cannot be evaluated by comparing students' scores on the *Primary Measures of Music Audiation* with their scores on the *Intermediate Measures of Music Audiation*. Differences that occur in students' developmental music aptitude must be interpreted by comparing students' scores on two or more administrations of PMMA or on two or more administrations of IMMA. The variability in the score distributions for the corresponding subtests and the total scores of the two batteries is highly dissimilar.

To gather normative data for the *Intermediate Measures of Music Audiation,* the results of a random sample of 675 children six years of age, 656 children seven years of age, 653 children eight years of age, and 752 children nine years of age were used. A complete description of the standardization sample may be found in the test manual.

An analysis of data gathered from the IMMA standardization program indicated that the test-retest reliabilities are higher than the split-halves reliabilities. The opposite is the case for PMMA. That is, the split-halves reliabilities for PMMA and the test-retest reliabilities for IMMA are comparable. A possible explanation is that whereas the content of IMMA relates to developmental music aptitude, about half the number of children who are given IMMA are closely approaching the stabilized music aptitude stage. However, although the *Musical Aptitude Profile,* a test of stabilized music aptitude, demonstrates split-halves reliabilities that are higher than test-retest reliabilities, it should be remembered that the content validity and construct validity of MAP and IMMA are quite different. Such combinations of test design and music aptitude stage typically produce important but unexplainable interactions. Perhaps research will some day tell us why.

Because the design and purposes of the *Primary Measures of Music Audiation* and the *Intermediate Measures of Music Audiation* are so much alike and an ample number of studies have been undertaken that pertain to the concurrent or criterion-related validity of PMMA, it has not appeared that the investigation of those types of validities for IMMA are vital, nor that they are as important as the longitudinal predictive validity studies that will be described henceforth. Thus, only two concurrent validity studies have been conducted, and they are summarized below. Detailed accounts of the data may be found in the test manual.

The first study was conducted in a private school for boys. Without prior knowledge of the children's IMMA scores, the general music specialist was asked to use a five-point scale to rate each of the children in her classes in terms of overall music aptitude. There were 24 children in the first grade, 23 in the second, 29 in the third, and 31 in the fourth. The teacher was well acquainted with the children because they attended her music classes two to three times each week. The concurrent validity of IMMA was estimated by the correlation of the teacher's rating with the children's IMMA scores. The separate validity coefficients for each group ranged from .40 to .47 for the *Tonal* subtest, from .22 to .25 for the *Rhythm* subtest, and from .35 to .45 for the total test score.

In the second study, before IMMA was administered, the band director in a public elementary school was asked to rate, on the basis of their overall music aptitude, the 21 fourth-grade students who elected to study a musical instrument. The teacher had taught the beginning instrumental students for slightly less than one year. As in the first study, the teacher probably rated the students' music achievement, not really knowing what their music aptitude might be. Either way, the intent of securing concurrent validity was not affected. Again, the teacher's ratings and the students' IMMA scores were correlated. The IMMA validity coefficients were .81 for the total score, .69 for the *Rhythm* subtest, and .42 for the *Tonal* subtest. The differences in the coefficients for the two subtests probably reflects the comparative importance the teacher placed on tonal and rhythm achievement when rating the students.

There are two IMMA longitudinal predictive investigations, one a one-year study and the other a two-year study. The one-year study will be described first (Gordon, *A Longitudinal Predictive Validity Study*, 1984). All 33 boys nine years of age who attended a private academy were required to study the violin for one semester and the recorder for the other semester. During the first semester, approximately half the class studied the violin and the other half studied the recorder. At the beginning of the second semester, the boys changed teachers and studied the other instrument. The *Intermediate Measures of Music Audiation* was administered to all of the boys before instruction was begun. At the end of each semester, every boy sang two songs and played two songs on the violin or recorder. The performances were recorded, and two judges evaluated the melodic accuracy, rhythmic accuracy, and musical expression of each performance using three five-point rating scales. To investigate the effects of instruction on IMMA scores, IMMA was administered again at the end of the year.

At the conclusion of the first semester, predictive validity coefficients ranged from .63 to .76 for the instrumental and vocal performances of students in the recorder group, and from .54 to .74 for the instrumental and vocal performances of students in the violin group. At the conclusion of the second semester, coefficients ranged from .62 to .79 for the instrumental and vocal performances of students in the recorder group, and from .63 to .92 for instrumental and vocal performances of students in the violin group. Overall, these predictive validity coefficients approximate the longitudinal coefficients found in association with the *Primary*

Measures of Music Audiation and the *Musical Aptitude Profile.* As to the effects of instruction on IMMA scores, the mean gains from year to year were less than one point, and the correlations between the two sets of scores were not less than .90 for either of the two sets of subtests and the total scores.

As was previously explained, IMMA comprises developmental music aptitude content and design and so is sensitive to the informal guidance and formal instruction young children receive. Nonetheless, considering the slight differences between the preinstructional and post-instructional mean scores when the test is re-administered yearly to students nine and ten years of age, it appears that IMMA can also function as a test of stabilized music aptitude. Though extensive research is needed to confirm the idea, it would seem that developmental and stabilized music aptitudes are more a matter of what is embodied in the musical mind than what is encapsulated in the tests themselves.

The two-year longitudinal predictive validity study took place in three public elementary schools in upstate New York (Gordon, *Predictive Validity Studies*, 1989). The long-range validity of the *Instrument Timbre Preference Test* (described in chapter 10) and the *Intermediate Measures of Music Audiation* were studied in combination with each other. The *Intermediate Measures of Music Audiation* and the *Instrument Timbre Preference Test* (ITPT) were administered to all 181 fourth grade students who were planning to enter beginning instrumental music classes in the fifth grade, and IMMA was administered again after one year of instruction. Regardless of their IMMA scores, the students were encouraged to learn to play musical instruments that were suggested by their scores on the timbre preference test. Of the 181 students, 30, designated as the experimental group, agreed to study the instrument suggested by their ITPT results and instruments were provided for them free of charge. The remaining 151 students constituted the control group.

The students received one 30-minute group instrumental lesson each week taught by two teachers, and each instructional class included students from both the experimental and control groups. The teachers knew which students were members of the experimental and control groups, but they did not know the students' scores on IMMA. As in the first longitudinal study, the students performed etudes that were recorded and rated by two judges. The achievement of the students in the two groups was compared at the close of each of the four semesters over the two-year period, and it was found that the students in the experimental group consistently obtained significantly higher mean performance ratings. As important as that finding is, what is germane here is the predictive validity of IMMA for all students combined, which ranged from .41 after the first semester of the first year to .60 after the second semester of the second year. A comparison of the means for the IMMA *Tonal* and *Rhythm* subtests indicated that the average scores changed less than one point, suggesting that the effects of instruction on IMMA are almost meaningless for students who are in the stabilized music aptitude stage.

AUDIE

Audie is a developmental music aptitude test specifically designed for children three and four years old. There are recorded directions and practice exercises for each of the two subtests, *Tonal* and *Rhythm,* and each subtest includes ten questions. Audie is a character that talks and sings short songs, including one special short song. The child says "yes" when Audie's special song is heard on the recording and "no" when a different song is heard. In the *Tonal* subtest, if Audie does not sing his special song, it is because a pitch is changed in the melodic pattern although the rhythm component has remained the same. In the *Rhythm* subtest, if Audie does not sing his special song, it is because a duration is changed in the melodic pattern although the tonal component has remained the same. A parent or teacher marks the answer sheet according to the child's responses.

More than five years were devoted to designing and developing *Audie.* Several experimental versions were administered by a teacher or researcher to children as a group, and others were administered by a parent or a teacher to children individually. The experimental versions differed in the type and length of the test directions, in the type and the music content of the questions, in the way the questions were asked, and in the way children were guided in responding to the questions.

It was found in the development of the test that a young child's span of concentration on consecutive questions was limited, and ten questions for each subtest were found to be as many as a typical child can attend to without becoming totally distracted. Thus, because of the brevity of the subtests, it was determined that percentile rank norms would assist very little in interpreting results, which is why only criterion scores are used.

The *Tonal* subtest was administered to 317 three and four-year old children and the *Rhythm* subtest to 312 children of the same ages. All of the children were in preschool, where they received informal guidance and formal instruction in music by a variety of teachers. Mean differences between the three and four-year-old children were not found to be significant. The means for both subtests were 6.8, and Kuder-Richardson # 20 reliabilities were .68 and .69 for the *Tonal* and *Rhythm* subtests, respectively. Other than Patricia M. Ryan's concurrent validity study and Cynthia Crump-Taggert's predictive validity study, both of which demonstrate encouraging results, no extensive experimental validity has been established for either subtest. Through practical use of the test in conjunction with teaching procedures and teachers' subjective observations, it has been ascertained that children who obtain scores of 9 or 10 on either subtest may be considered to have high developmental music aptitude, that scores of 6 to 8 suggest average developmental music aptitude, and that scores from 0 to 5 suggest low developmental music aptitude. The primary value of the test, however, is to monitor the changing levels of each child's developmental music aptitudes.

In summary, there are several possible choices one has when considering which test to use with students of a given chronological age. With students in junior high school and high school, either the *Musical Aptitude Profile* or the *Advanced Measures of Music Audiation* may be used, depending upon whether the extensive diagnostic information MAP provides is of importance at the time. With students in grades four through six, either the *Musical Aptitude Profile* or the *Intermediate Measures of Music Audiation* is satisfactory, although MAP offers greater reliability, and therefore greater precision, than IMMA. Also, MAP is designed to provide greater diagnostic information than the two subtests of IMMA provide. Finally, either the *Primary Measures of Music Audiation* or the *Intermediate Measures of Music Audiation* is suitable for students in grades one through three. Which test is most appropriate must be decided on the basis of the score distributions that PMMA yields. If an analysis of PMMA scores indicates that a large number of students score above average on one or both subtests, PMMA should no longer be used, and one or both IMMA subtests should be administered to students thereafter.

CHAPTER 9

THE INTERPRETATION OF STABILIZED AND DEVELOPMENTAL MUSIC APTITUDE TEST RESULTS

A well-developed music aptitude battery is accompanied by a thorough test manual. The manual should include at least the following: 1) The purposes and description of the test, 2) the development of the test, 3) the rationale, content, and design of the test, 4) how to administer the test, 5) how to score the test, 6) how to interpret and use the test results, and 7) the technical properties of the test. Without knowledge of any one of these topics, it would be difficult to evaluate the music aptitudes of students to whom the tests were administered.

The manuals for the *Musical Aptitude Profile,* the *Advanced Measures of Music Audiation,* the *Intermediate Measures of Music Audiation,* the *Primary Measures of Music Audiation,* and *Audie* cover each of these topics, and most of the topics have been discussed in earlier chapters of this book. What remains to be presented in this chapter is a detailed explanation of the purposes of the tests, the scoring of the tests, and the interpretation and use of test scores for the improvement of instruction. Because there is so much in common between the two tests of stabilized music aptitude and the three tests of developmental music aptitude (although the purposes, as I have previously explained, are not precisely the same), I will limit my discussion to only the *Musical Aptitude Profile* and the *Primary Measures of Music Audiation.*

Corresponding information for the other tests can be quickly generalized or may be secured from the relevant manuals.

STABILIZED MUSIC APTITUDE AND THE MUSICAL APTITUDE PROFILE

The *Musical Aptitude Profile* has one major purpose: to act as an objective aid in the evaluation of students' music aptitudes so that the teacher can better provide for all students' individual musical needs. The value of a test is determined by the extent to which it results in improved instruction and more effective use of human potential. When employed with wisdom and judgment, test scores on MAP can be used with confidence for the following purposes:

1. TO ENCOURAGE STUDENTS WITH HIGH STABILIZED MUSIC APTITUDE
   TO PARTICIPATE IN MUSIC ACTIVITIES

The test should be used positively to identify, objectively and efficiently, students with high music aptitude in elementary, middle, junior high, and senior high school who can profit from membership in instrumental and choral music performance organizations. It is important that these students with exceptionally high music aptitude who do not volunteer to study music be encouraged to do so. The aim is not to discourage students with low or average music aptitude from taking music lessons or otherwise participating in music activities. All students, regardless of their levels of music aptitude, who have the desire to study music should not only be allowed, but should be encouraged, to become involved in music.

2. TO ADAPT INSTRUCTION TO MEET THE INDIVIDUAL NEEDS OF
   STUDENTS

To achieve that purpose, scores on the same subtest for different students are compared and scores on different subtests for the same student are compared. By compensating for the lower stabilized music aptitudes of some students while enhancing the higher stabilized music aptitudes of others, all students should then be able to demonstrate music achievement commensurate with their music potential.

3. TO FORMULATE IMMEDIATE AND FUTURE EDUCATIONAL PLANS

Some students excel in many subjects, some only in one. Scores on the *Musical Aptitude Profile* may help the student who has many strengths to decide where educational emphasis might best be placed now and in the future. Through a comparison of a student's stabilized music aptitude scores and performance ability in music with his or her achievement in science, mathematics, or history, for example, the student might be properly advised to enrich his or her background and enroll in music composition, theory, and history classes and/or to participate in small ensembles and specialized performance groups. The student may be guided to choose music as an avocation or to enter a school of music as a result of the student's standing on MAP as well as his or her past and current achievement in music.

4. TO EVALUATE THE STABILIZED MUSIC APTITUDES OF GROUPS OF STUDENTS

School supervisors and music directors can evaluate objectively the overall music potential of different performance ensembles within a school system and in comparison with a national sample of select music students. As a result of such knowledge, adequate planning and the appropriate and impartial allocation of resources can be undertaken that will contribute to more realistic goals for a specific music ensemble.

5. TO PROVIDE PARENTS WITH OBJECTIVE INFORMATION

Whether parents overestimate or underestimate the music aptitude of their child, an unbiased and objective analysis of the child's stabilized music aptitude helps in many cases to produce a more informed and reasonable attitude on the part of parents. Just as objective information is needed by some parents as a basis for encouraging their children with high music aptitude to participate in music activities, so objective information may also be necessary to make other parents aware that high expectations for their children may be unreasonable. In both cases, MAP results serve extremely important and useful functions.

One of the most important results of standardizing a test is the establishment of norms. The following procedures were used in developing the norms for the *Musical Aptitude Profile*. To simplify the categorization of school districts, the nine regions of the U. S. Office of Education were organized into three groups: 1) Northeast and Mideast, 2) Southeast, and 3) Great Lakes, Southwest, Rocky Mountains, Far West, and noncontiguous states. The schools in each of the three groups were identified as rural, small-town, urban, or suburban. Then the socio-economic level of each school was determined. The goal of establishing norms for MAP was achieved by administering the entire test battery to more than 12,000 students in 20 school systems in 18 states. Because MAP was administered to all students in grades four through twelve in every participating school, the sample upon which the norms are based represents a typical and natural proportion of musically select and randomly selected students. Thus, norms were derived for musically heterogeneous students (musically select and unselected combined) in each grade, 4 through 12. In addition to those nine sets of norms, three sets of norms were derived for only musically select students: one for elementary school students, grades 4 through 6; another for middle and junior high school students, grades 7 through 9; and the other for senior high school students, grades 10 through 12. A complete description of the standardization program is presented in the MAP manual.

A raw score is a simple count of the test questions answered correctly by a student. A raw score lacks precise and definitive meaning, because such meaning depends on the length and difficulty of the test as well as on the scores of other students who have taken the test. It cannot be said with certainty that a raw score of 10 is twice as good as a raw score of 5, nor can it be said that a raw score of 10 on one test is necessarily equal to a raw score of 10 on another test. In fact, a raw score of 5 on one test may be superior to a raw score of 10 on another test. For this reason, the combined raw scores for all students in grades 4 through 12 who participated in the standardization program were converted to normalized standard score equivalents for each of the seven subtests of the *Musical Aptitude Profile.* The standard score scale has a mean of 50 and a standard deviation of 10.

First, the raw scores for each of the subtests (*Melody, Harmony, Tempo, Meter, Phrasing, Balance,* and *Style)* were converted to standard scores. Then the standard scores for each of the total tests (*Tonal Imagery,* including *Melody* and *Harmony; Rhythm Imagery,* including *Tempo* and *Harmony;* and *Musical Sensitivity,* including *Phrasing, Balance,* and *Style)* were derived by averaging the standard scores of subtests in each total test. Similarly, the standard scores for the composite score were derived by averaging the standard scores of the three total scores. Weighted frequency distributions of the standard scores for the subtests and the average standard scores for the total tests and the composite test were derived for students in each grade and for the three groups of musically select students. After the distributions were plotted and smoothed graphically, standard score/percentile rank equivalents were derived.

Standard scores are important for two reasons. First, standard scores have standard meaning. Given the same standard score mean and standard deviation for two or more tests, that standard score has the same meaning for all of the tests. For example, if the standard score scale for each of the tests is based on a mean of 50 and a standard deviation of 10, on any test a standard score of 50 is an average score. A standard score of 60 is one standard deviation above the mean, and a standard score of 40 is one standard deviation below the mean. A standard score of 70 is two standard deviations above the mean, and a standard score of 30 is two standard deviations below the mean. A standard score of 80 is three standard deviations above the mean, and a standard score of 20 is three standard deviations below the mean. A standard score of 70 equals the 98th percentile, a standard score of 60 equals the 84th percentile, a standard score of 50 equals the 50th percentile, a standard score of 40 equals the 16th percentile, and a standard score of 30 equals the 2nd percentile. Second, and more important, when all of the subtests in a battery are converted to the same standard score scale, all of them become equally important. As a result, when some subtest scores are combined into a total test score, or when all subtests scores are combined into a composite test score, each subtest score contributes equally to the total test score and to the composite test score. Moreover, only when each subtest is based on the same standard score scale may the standard error of a difference between a student's two or more subtest scores be computed and interpreted correctly.

For ease in evaluating a student's stabilized music aptitude as determined by MAP, standard scores are transformed into percentile ranks. Through the direct use of percentile ranks, all students' scores, whether or not they happen to be the equivalents of average scores or standard deviations, can be interpreted quickly. There are percentile ranks for each of the seven subtests, the three total tests, and the composite test. Thus, there are eleven sets of percentile rank norms for musically select and unselected students combined in grades 4 through 12. There are also eleven sets of percentile rank norms for only musically select students in each grade group, 4 through 6, 7 through 9, and 10 through 12.

Two scoring masks are required to score the *Musical Aptitude Profile,* one for each side of the answer sheet. The process requires that raw scores, standard scores, and percentile ranks all be computed and reported. The student's name and his or her scores and percentile ranks are entered on the class record sheet, which is provided by the publisher, before they are entered on the music aptitude profile chart found in the music cumulative record folder, which is also provided by the publisher. Directions for the entire procedure are given in the MAP manual. Particularly important is the plotting of the students' scores on the music aptitude profile chart, as illustrated on the following page.

As can be seen on the music aptitude profile chart, the student's name and eleven standard scores and percentile ranks are written in the appropriate spaces above the chart. As shown in the illustration, and as explained in the folder itself, a student's scores can be easily plotted on the chart by marking percentile ranks with dots in the appropriate columns. The dots are then connected with straight lines. Broken and unbroken lines or different-colored lines may be used for different norms groups.

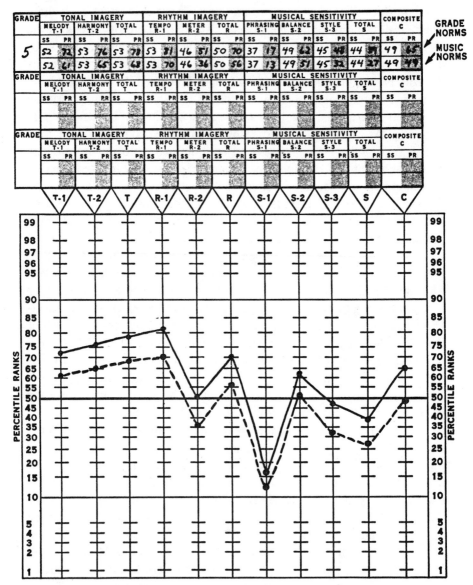

After each student's test results are entered on the class record sheet and on the music aptitude profile chart, students' music aptitudes may be evaluated. Test results, which are measures, may be evaluated normatively, by using the class record sheet, or idiographically, by using the music aptitude profile chart. When test results are evaluated normatively, each student is compared to every other student in the group. That is, the percentile ranks for each student's test scores are compared to the percentile ranks for the same test scores of all other students in the class, all of which are based on the norms group. When test results are evaluated idiographically, the percentile ranks for each student's test scores are compared to one another. In an idiographic evaluation, a student is not compared with other students. That is, although the percentile ranks were derived normatively, the differences among only an individual student's results are compared.

For the purpose of identifying students with exceptionally high overall music aptitude, a normative comparison should be made. Each student's percentile rank for the composite test score should be evaluated in terms of grade norms for musically select and non-music students combined. Either the class record sheet or the music aptitude profile chart may be used for that purpose. Validity studies are not designed to indicate a single criterion score that separates students with exceptionally high music aptitude from all other students. Such studies are useful only in determining whether higher scoring students ultimately achieve more in music than do lower scoring students. Nonetheless, from practical experience using the *Musical Aptitude Profile,* it has been discovered that students who score at the 80th percentile and above on the composite test score possess exceptionally high overall music aptitude. That is, such students are capable of attaining and maintaining much higher music achievement levels than students who score below the 80th percentile on the composite test score. To be even more precise, only those students who score at the 80th percentile and above on the three total tests should be identified as having exceptionally high overall music aptitude, and it is important to note that future musical success is more dependent on a high score on the *Rhythm Imagery* total test than on either the *Tonal Imagery* or *Musical Sensitivity* total test. Although a composite test score at or above the 80th percentile indicates that a student has exceptionally high overall music aptitude, it does not suggest the type of musical endeavor in which a student will be most successful. It would seem that, given suitable psychological and physical characteristics, a student with exceptionally high overall music aptitude might have the potential to be a successful vocalist, instrumentalist, soloist, ensemble member, conductor, composer, arranger, or whatever he or she chooses.

Of course it is possible, though not likely, that in any given group a teacher might be instructing (particularly a very small one), there may not be any students whose composite test score is at or above the 80th percentile. In that case, MAP scores need to be examined in pragmatic terms. The highest scoring students, whatever their scores might be, should be recognized as those who have the greatest potential in the group for profiting from special musical instruction.

For diagnosing the musical strengths and weaknesses of individual students, both idiographic and normative comparisons should be made. The use of the plotted music aptitude profile chart is best for those purposes. Every student's percentile ranks for each of the seven subtest scores in terms of grade norms for musically select and non-music students combined should be examined, and the normative comparison should be made first. It is not uncommon to find a student scoring at or above the 80th percentile on only one or two subtests, and if a student scores at or above the 80th percentile on one subtest, he or she may be considered to have exceptionally high aptitude for that specific dimension of music. After it has been determined on which, if any, of the seven dimensions of music a student excels, an idiographic comparison of the student's subtest scores should be made to complete the diagnostic analysis by comparing percentile ranks on each of the seven MAP subtests to one another. Then the student's musical strengths should be ranked. Given all of that information, the teacher not only may begin to adapt instruction to the individual musical strengths and weaknesses of the students as a group, but may also begin to adapt instruction to the individual musical needs of each student. In adapting instruction to students' individual musical needs, it is important for a teacher to remember and to take into consideration that although, for example, a student's rank on one subtest may be higher than his or her rank on another, the student's rank on the higher of the two subtests may not be any higher than that of 30 percent of all students in the norms group. Further, when adapting instruction to a student's individual musical needs, it is prudent to begin to compensate for the student's musical weaknesses before enhancing the student's musical strengths, although both should be given equal attention over time. The teacher should not expect a student's stabilized music aptitude percentile ranks to increase as a result of receiving appropriate instruction. A student's music achievement can never surpass his or her potential to achieve as determined by his or her stabilized music aptitude. Specific suggestions for adapting instruction to students' individual musical differences and needs may be found in the test manual (Gordon, *Musical Aptitude Profile*, 1995, 56-63).[1]

For assisting students in formulating immediate and future educational plans, a normative comparison should be made. Each student's percentile ranks for the three total test scores and the composite test score should be evaluated in terms of musically select norms for the appropriate school grade level: elementary, middle or junior high, or senior high.

Either the class record sheet or the music aptitude profile chart may be used for that purpose. In addition, all other objective and subjective information, including that of a non-musical as well as of a musical nature, that has been collected in the student's cumulative record folder should be examined. A student who scores at or above the 80th percentile on the composite test and on each of the three total tests in terms of musically select norms should be encouraged to engage in or to continue to engage in special study in music.

Older students about to graduate and choose a vocation will need to know whether their expectations are realistic. While maintaining professional integrity, a teacher might motivate high-scoring students to follow music as a vocation and encourage low-scoring students who have a desire to continue their study of music to do so as an avocation. The decision to advise a student to consider music as a vocation rather than as an avocation requires serious thought and must not be made in haste. Regardless of a student's enthusiasm, economic conditions and opportunities associated with professional music must not be overlooked by adults or ignored by an overly enthusiastic student.

Some students excel only in music and others excel in one or more disciplines. Thus, all students need guidance and counseling throughout their educational careers. Younger students who will not be graduating in the immediate future, for example, will need advice about if and when they should study music theory, music history, or music composition in conjunction with their applied music lessons and participation in music ensembles. Moreover, depending on total test score comparisons, some students may need to take compensatory instruction in rhythm, perhaps by participating in small ensembles or classes in movement and dance, while others may need to avail themselves of enrichment classes in composition or in the interpretation of music, either in group or private instruction.

To provide parents with objective information about their children's music aptitudes, a normative comparison should be made. Although the child's overall music aptitude can be expected to be of primary concern to parents, parents should also be shown a plotted profile of their child's percentile ranks for the three total test scores and the composite test score in terms of grade norms for all students combined. It is best if the evaluation of those test results is discussed in a parent-teacher conference. Regardless of the nature of a student's scores, the teacher should initially place emphasis on the highest of those scores as it relates to the others, and an idiographic analysis should be of primary concern. The main purpose here is to inform parents of their child's music aptitude scores as a way to assist them in developing realistic expectations for their child and to suggest how they can support their child in further instruction of all types. Interpreting their child's musical strengths and weakness is at least of equal, and in many cases, of greater value to parents than explaining how their child measures up in a class.

Many parents may not be aware that their child has exceptionally high overall music aptitude. If the child scores at the 80th percentile or above on the MAP composite test, it should be explained to parents that their child is in at least the upper 20 percent of all students of the same age in terms of potential to achieve in music. There are parents who will not respond to the subjective judgment of a teacher in such a matter, but who will respond to the objective scores earned by their child on a music aptitude test. Many times teachers can engender the confidence of parents by substantiating their opinions with facts, and that, of course, will contribute to their continuing working relationship. Teachers should remember that if parents are not made aware of their child's unusual potential for music achievement, they may not give their child the necessary support and encouragement. Such care is vital if children are to make the most of that potential.

Unfortunately, there are some parents who develop unsound ideas about their children's music potential. In such a situation, children suffer because they are forced to practice an unreasonable amount of time each day, they feel intimidated by their lack of progress, or they are actually punished for not making noticeable progress. Children become motivated and benefit musically and technically from practice only to the extent that they have the potential to do so. Many adults grow up disliking music because of their unpleasant childhood associations with forced practice or performance.

Teachers and administrators may desire to compare the overall music aptitudes of musically select and non-music students in the same school building, in the same school system, in different school systems, or in comparison with national norms. Through such comparisons, scheduling and administrative procedures may be developed or re-examined with confidence, contributing to the music achievement of all students. Such comparisons are not acceptable for evaluating the skills of teachers, however.

For comparing the music aptitude of groups of students, normative comparisons should be made using either school grade norms or musically select norms that are documented on the class record sheet. Musically select students may be defined, as they were in the analysis of the standardization data, as those who are members of school music performance organizations (such as band, orchestra, choir, and small or jazz ensembles) or who are taking private instrumental or singing lessons.

Using the norms provided with the *Musical Aptitude Profile,* there is only one valid way in which group comparisons can be made. A frequency distribution of MAP results must be compiled for each group of students to be compared. Then score ranges in terms of variability should be examined. Percentile ranks for the highest and lowest scoring students in each group provide the basic information necessary for making those comparisons. Under no circumstances should means of percentile ranks, standard scores, or raw scores reported in the norms for *individual* students be used in making *group* comparisons.

DEVELOPMENTAL MUSIC APTITUDE AND THE PRIMARY MEASURES OF MUSIC AUDIATION

The *Primary Measures of Music Audiation* has one general purpose: to serve as an objective aid to teachers in their evaluations of students' developmental music aptitudes. With such objectively-based evaluations, better curriculum planning and instruction will take place, and the result will be the best use of human potential. When used with wisdom and judgment, test scores on PMMA can be used periodically for the following purposes:

1. TO EVALUATE THE COMPARATIVE TONAL AND RHYTHM APTITUDES OF EACH YOUNG CHILD

By making an idiographic analysis, that is, by comparing each child's *Tonal* and *Rhythm* subtest scores to each other, appropriate informal guidance and formal instruction can be provided to meet every child's individual musical needs at all developmental periods. For example, if a child's *Tonal* subtest score is higher than his or her *Rhythm* subtest score, the child's weakness in rhythm aptitude can be compensated for and the child's strength in tonal aptitude can be enhanced.

2. TO EVALUATE THE TONAL AND RHYTHM APTITUDES OF EACH YOUNG CHILD IN COMPARISON WITH THE TONAL AND RHYTHM APTITUDES OF OTHER CHILDREN OF SIMILAR AGE

Through normative comparison, that is, by comparing each child's *Tonal* and *Rhythm* subtest scores with those of other children, further appropriate informal guidance and formal instruction can be provided to meet the child's individual musical needs at all developmental levels. For example, although a child's tonal aptitude may be higher than his or her rhythm aptitude, the child's tonal aptitude may not be higher than that of 20 percent of all students in the norms group. The degree and type of idiographic and normative interaction of each child's scores suggest the most suitable ways of providing informal guidance and formal instruction in music. For example, when it is known that one score is significantly higher than the other, but both are comparatively low for one child, and if one score is significantly higher than the other and the lower one is only slightly above average for another child, the guidance and instruction both children receive may be structured specifically to meet each child's individual musical strengths and weaknesses.

3. TO IDENTIFY YOUNG CHILDREN WHO CAN PROFIT FROM THE OPPORTUNITY TO PARTICIPATE IN ADDITIONAL GROUP STUDY AND SPECIAL PRIVATE INSTRUCTION IN AND OUT OF SCHOOL

Such study might include lessons on a musical instrument and participation in a movement or dance class, in a singing or instrumental ensemble, or in creativity and improvisation activities. The *Primary Measures of Music Audiation* is not designed to exclude an interested young child, however low the child's PMMA scores may be, from participating in any type of music activity, but to guide and encourage children to engage in specific appropriate activities.

The purposes of tests of stabilized music aptitude and those of developmental music aptitude are not the same. The identification of students with exceptionally high music aptitude usually takes precedence with the *Musical Aptitude Profile,* whereas the diagnostic analysis of children's test scores is fundamental for the *Primary Measures of Music Audiation.* That is not to say that the diagnosis of students' stabilized music aptitudes is unimportant.

The norms provided for PMMA are based on a carefully selected but relatively small stratified group of children. All of the children who participated in the standardization program attended one of nine elementary schools in West Irondequoit, New York. The use of such a small sample afforded me the opportunity to administer and re-administer the tests myself to all of the children over a period of five weeks and to conduct ancillary research. It should be pointed out, however, that experience with PMMA by many teachers throughout this country and the world involving thousands of children has verified the accuracy of the norms derived from the small and geographically limited standardization sample. This offers further support for the validity of the *Primary Measures of Music Audiation* as a test of music aptitude rather than as one of music achievement

The tests were administered to 873 children in kindergarten through grade 3, more than 95 percent of the children in those grades being in

West Irondequoit. The enrollments by grade were 127 in kindergarten, 202 in the first grade, 280 in the second grade, and 264 in the third grade. The children to whom the tests were administered were heterogeneous in their socio-economic status (approximately 7 percent were inner-city Rochester children), academic achievement, and IQ, and to other unmeasured factors, and thus were fairly representative of elementary school children in general. The complete description of the standardization program is reported in the test manual.

The norms sample was chosen to serve two fundamental purposes: first, to offer evidence of the statistical properties of the tests, and second, to provide objective support to teachers in the evaluation of children's developmental music aptitudes when local norms are not available. Because results on a test of developmental music aptitude are a product of both innate and informal and formal environmental influences, which cause test scores to fluctuate, extensive national norms for the *Primary Measures of Music Audiation* would be difficult, or perhaps impossible, to acquire. Monthly norms would be more advantageous, and beginning-of-the-year, middle-of-the-year, and end-of-the-year norms would be minimal requirements. This is most realistically satisfied through the development of local norms, a natural outgrowth of continuous administrations of a developmental music aptitude test. Further, local norms are adequate, if not superior, for normatively and idiographically comparing each child's relative standing on the two subtests in the battery. In establishing norms for a test, the number of persons tested is not nearly as important as the manner in which the students are selected.

The *Tonal* and *Rhythm* subtests were scored separately for children in kindergarten and each of the three grades. In addition to determining a raw score for each child, the raw scores on the two subtests were added together to derive a composite score. That resulted in three sets of scores: one for the *Tonal* subtest, one for the *Rhythm* subtest, and one for the composite test for children in each of the four groups. Each raw score distribution was plotted and smoothed graphically, and the percentile ranks for the raw scores were recorded for children in kindergarten and each of the three grades.

In deriving the composite test score, raw scores were not weighted through the use of standard scores. This is because the standard deviations for the *Tonal* and *Rhythm* subtests differ by no more than one and a half points for kindergarten children to as little as a quarter of a point for children in the second grade. Because those differences are so small, because the variance of a composite score is not affected by the means of the contributing subtest scores, and because the fact that there are only two subtests constituting PMMA makes obvious the contribution of each subtest to the mean of the composite score, it was decided that the additional step of converting raw scores to standard scores was unnecessary. Moreover, in the measurement and evaluation of developmental music aptitude test scores, patterns of growth on each of the subtests, rather than on the composite test score, are of greatest significance.

Because there are no standard scores for the *Primary Measures of Music Audiation,* the scoring of the test is relatively simple. After the answer sheets are scored, the students' names, scores, and percentile ranks are entered on the class record sheet, which is provided by the publisher, before they are entered on the music aptitude profile charts, also provided by the publisher. Then the children's music aptitudes may be evaluated.

As is the case for evaluating stabilized music aptitude, for periodically evaluating the comparative developmental tonal and rhythm aptitudes of each child, idiographic and normative comparisons should be made. Typically, one of a child's subtest scores will be higher than the other. The teacher must, of course, have more information than that, because to adapt informal guidance and formal instruction to the individual musical needs of the child, the teacher must also understand the interaction between the two subtest scores. For example, the guidance and instruction given to a child who has a *Tonal* percentile rank of 18 and a *Rhythm* percentile rank of 82 should be different from that given to a child who has a *Tonal* percentile rank of 58 and a *Rhythm* percentile rank of 82. Both children have lower developmental tonal aptitude than developmental rhythm aptitude, but the rhythm aptitude for one child is quite low, whereas it is slightly above average for the other. The use of the plotted music aptitude profile chart, illustrated on page 150, is best for diagnosing and adapting guidance and instruction to the musical strengths and weaknesses of each young child. Notice that there is ample provision on the chart to plot the progress of a child's developmental music aptitude four times. Where a child is making progress and where his or her deficiency is becoming even greater can quickly be observed on the plotted profile.

Consideration of children's chronological age is not as important in adapting guidance and instruction to children's individual musical differences as is their musical age, as measured by the *Primary Measures of Music Audiation.* To determine how high or low a child has scored on each subtest, the child's score results should be interpreted in terms of local norms or, if they are not available, in terms of the norms provided in the PMMA manual. If a child receives a percentile rank of 80 or higher on a subtest, the child may be regarded as having exceptionally high developmental music aptitude in that dimension measured by the subtest;

if a child receives a percentile rank between 21 and 79 on a subtest, the child may be regarded as having average developmental music aptitude in that dimension (51 to 79 being above average and 21 to 49 being below average); and if a child receives a percentile rank of 20 or lower on a subtest, the child may be regarded as having low developmental music aptitude in that dimension. If, after informal guidance or formal instruction is provided for a year, re-administration of PMMA shows that a child's percentile rank has remained essentially the same on a subtest, the guidance or instruction the child received may be considered appropriate and the child is probably demonstrating normal growth (in order for a child's percentile rank to remain the same when he or she enters a higher school grade, the raw score must increase). If a child's percentile rank increases upon re-administration of PMMA, the guidance or instruction the child has received may be considered compensatory. If a child's percentile rank decreases upon re-administration of PMMA, the informal guidance or formal instruction the child has received was neither suitable nor complementary to his or her innate developmental music aptitude and, thus, may be considered inappropriate. In that case, the guidance or instruction that the child is receiving should be re-assessed and most probably changed. Extra-musical factors might also be considered.

An immediate attempt should be made to raise the lower of the child's two subtest scores. Moreover, regardless of how high a child's percentile rank on the other subtest might be, emphasis should be placed next on attempting to raise the higher of the two scores. That rule applies whether the child is in the same school grade or has been promoted to a higher school grade when PMMA is re-administered. Just how long different types of guidance and instruction should be experimented with for a given child cannot be objectively determined. The decision must be a subjective one made by the teacher, who should use all of the information, both musical and extra-musical, at his or her command. Consultation with the child's parents is always recommended as a way to help evaluate the guidance and instruction that is taking place in the home and otherwise outside of school. Unlike stabilized music aptitude scores, developmental music aptitude scores can be expected to fluctuate, and every attempt should be made to raise them. Specific suggestions for adapting informal guidance and formal instruction to children's individual musical needs as they are revealed by *Primary Measures of Music Audiation* results may be found in the test manual (Gordon, *Primary Measures of Music Audiation*, 1979, 70-84).[2]

For identifying children with exceptionally high overall developmental music aptitude, a normative comparison should be made. Each child's percentile rank for the composite test score should be evaluated in terms of local or standardized norms, using either the class record sheet or the music aptitude profile cards for that purpose. If a child receives a percentile rank of 80 or higher, the child may be considered to have comparatively high overall developmental music aptitude. Only those children who receive a percentile rank of 80 or higher on both the *Tonal* and *Rhythm* subtests, however, should be regarded as having exceptionally high overall developmental music aptitude. (In this regard it should be explained again that if more than 80 percent of students in a class who take the *Primary Measures of Music Audiation* score above the 50th percentile on one or both subtests, one or both subtests of the *Intermediate Measures of Music Audiation* should then be administered, because the PMMA subtest or subtests would no longer be valid for measuring their high levels of developmental music aptitude.)

PROFILE CARD FOR THE PRIMARY MEASURES OF MUSIC AUDIATION

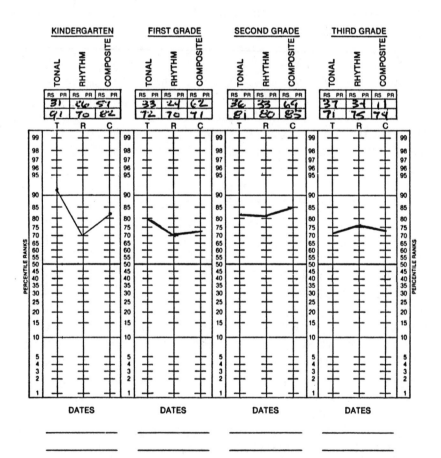

A young child with high overall developmental music aptitude should be encouraged, though not forced, to take part in special music activities in and out of school. *Primary Measures of Music Audiation* test results in no way indicate which type of special activity might be best or which instrument might best suit a child, but all such children should be encouraged to participate in movement and dance classes, because they are as valuable as private instrumental lessons, if not a necessary readiness, for private or group instrumental instruction. A young child who does not score at the 80th percentile or above on the composite test score should not be discouraged from or forced to take part in special music activities, either informal or formal. The composite test percentile rank is only one of several factors that should be considered before a young child is encouraged to participate in special music activities. For example, before the study of a musical instrument is considered, a child's emotional development and motor skills should be evaluated. Nonetheless, the PMMA composite test percentile rank should be given serious initial attention, because it is objective, it measures audiational understanding (the basis of music aptitude), and its results are totally without prejudice.

RELATIONS BETWEEN AND AMONG DEVELOPMENTAL AND STABILIZED MUSIC APTITUDE TESTS

As explained previously, there are different tests to choose among when one is measuring the music aptitudes of children and students of different chronological ages. Either the *Primary Measures of Music Audiation* or the *Intermediate Measures of Music Audiation* may be used for children in grades 1 through 3, either the *Intermediate Measures of Music Audiation* or the *Musical Aptitude Profile* may be used with students in grades 4 through 6, and either the *Musical Aptitude Profile* or the *Advanced Measures of Music Audiation* may be used with students in grades 7 through 12. The primary reasons for using one or the other tests have been outlined in earlier chapters. To offer additional assistance in deciding which test might be more appropriate for use, however, the statistical relations reported in six studies between and among the four test batteries are described below.

In the first study, the relation between PMMA and IMMA was investigated (Gordon, *Primary Measures of Music Audiation*, 1979). The data are based on the test results of 126 children in grades one through four in a public elementary school in Great Valley, Pennsylvania. PMMA was administered to the children approximately one month prior to the administration of IMMA, and the correlation coefficients that were found among the corresponding subtest and composite test scores for the two batteries are outlined below.

	Tonal	Rhythm	Composite
Grade 1	.58	.53	.62
Grade 2	.68	.56	.72
Grade 3	.62	.64	.66
Grade 4	.51	.60	.74

The substantial correlations shown here indicate that the two test batteries have much in common. In fact, the coefficients are almost as high as the split-halves reliabilities for IMMA. That the correlations are not any higher is probably due to curvilinear score distributions, most probably because most of the children, particularly the older ones, scored relatively high on PMMA. For this reason, these data emphasize the need to use IMMA to discriminate precisely among children who have high and exceptionally high developmental music aptitudes.

The second study took place in West Irondequoit, New York (Gordon, *Primary Measures of Music Audiation*, 1979). The relation of scores on PMMA and MAP of 227 fourth-grade students was investigated. The tests were administered in random order over a period of three weeks, and the results are reported in the following table.

Musical Aptitude Profile	Primary Measures of Music Audiation		
	Tonal	Rhythm	Composite
Tonal Imagery-Melody	.39	.33	.43
Tonal Imagery-Harmony	.29	.24	.31
Tonal Imagery-Total	.34	.51	.55
Rhythm Imagery-Tempo	.25	.42	.44
Rhythm Imagery-Meter	.42	.34	.47
Rhythm Imagery-Total	.35	.53	.56
Composite	.40	.52	.61

Because PMMA is not designed for young children, fourth-grade students found the test to be easy. As a result, the reliabilities of the PMMA subtests were lower for the nine-year-old students. Nonetheless, because of the differences between developmental and stabilized music aptitude tests, the data offer objective evidence that PMMA has more in common with IMMA than it has with MAP, and that PMMA and IMMA have about as much in common as do IMMA and MAP.

In a third study, students' scores on IMMA and MAP were correlated (Gordon, *Primary Measures of Music Audiation*, 1979). The test results of 92 students in grade 4 in Troy, New York, were used for that purpose. Only the *Tonal Imagery* and *Rhythm Imagery* total tests of MAP were administered to the students. The coefficients reported below suggest that IMMA has as much in common with MAP as it has with PMMA. Thus, we can conclude that although it is designed for children in the developmental music aptitude stage, IMMA can function as a valid test of stabilized music aptitude as well as a valid test of developmental music aptitude for upper elementary school children.

Musical Aptitude Profile	Intermediate Measures of Music Audiation	
	Tonal	Rhythm
Tonal Imagery-Melody	.54	
Tonal Imagery-Harmony	.50	
Tonal Imagery-Total	.58	
Rhythm Imagery-Tempo		.52
Rhythm Imagery-Meter		.60
Rhythm Imagery-Total		.63

An unusual investigation involving PMMA, IMMA, and MAP constitutes the fourth study, which was designed to determine if the psychological constructs of developmental and stabilized music aptitudes can be substantiated objectively (Gordon, *A Factor Analysis*, 1986). The three test batteries were administered in random order over a period of one semester to all 110 students in fourth grade in five classes in three elementary schools in Annville, Pennsylvania. The test results were not only correlated, but were factor analyzed. The unrotated and rotated principle factor matrices, which cross-validate each other, are reported below. As would be expected, factor I in the unrotated analysis is a general factor. Factors II and III are bipolar. Nonetheless, factor I in the unrotated analysis and factor II in the rotated analysis represent stabilized music aptitude, because MAP subtests load on those factors. The two minor differences between the factors is that factor I in the unrotated analysis includes the three MAP preference subtests and factor II in the rotated analysis includes the *Rhythm* subtest of IMMA. Factor II in the unrotated analysis and factor I in the rotated analysis represent developmental music aptitude, because, with the exception of the IMMA *Rhythm* subtest, all PMMA and IMMA subtests load on those factors. Factor III in both analyses may be identified as representing a unique factor, because all three MAP preference subtests load on those factors.

Unrotated Analysis

| | Factors | | |
	I	II	III
MUSICAL APTITUDE PROFILE			
Tonal Imagery-Melody	.71	-.26	.20
Tonal Imagery-Harmony	.58	-.31	.27
Rhythm Imagery-Tempo	.77	-.30	.11
Rhythm Imagery-Meter	.73	-.28	.11
Musical Sensitivity-Phrasing	.62	-.11	-.52
Musical Sensitivity-Balance	.73	-.01	-.32
Musical Sensitivity-Style	.66	.03	-.42
INTERMEDIATE MEASURES OF MUSIC AUDIATION			
Tonal	.41	.85	.15
Rhythm	.40	-.38	.54
PRIMARY MEASURES OF MUSIC AUDIATION			
Tonal	.36	.87	.12
Rhythm	.40	.85	.14

Rotated Analysis

| | Factors | | |
	I	II	III
MUSICAL APTITUDE PROFILE			
Tonal Imagery-Melody	.06	.70	.34
Tonal Imagery-Harmony	-.02	.68	.20
Rhythm Imagery-Tempo	.03	.71	.44
Rhythm Imagery-Meter	.03	.67	.42
Musical Sensitivity-Phrasing	.00	.14	.80
Musical Sensitivity-Balance	.17	.29	.72
Musical Sensitivity-Style	.16	.18	.75
INTERMEDIATE MEASURES OF MUSIC AUDIATION			
Tonal	.95	.02	.10
Rhythm	-.08	.75	-.13
PRIMARY MEASURES OF MUSIC AUDIATION			
Tonal	.94	-.05	.09
Rhythm	.94	.01	.10

Considering the established predictive validities of the three test batteries, the factor analytic results support the existence of developmental music aptitude, as measured by PMMA and IMMA, and of stabilized music aptitude, as measured by MAP. It may be concluded further that developmental and stabilized music aptitudes bear a moderate relation to each other, music preference and nonpreference measures differ from each other, and music preference measures are in the domain of stabilized music aptitude.

The fifth study was an investigation of the relation of AMMA and MAP (Gordon, *Advanced Measures of Music Audiation*, 1989). The complete MAP battery was administered to 20 undergraduate music majors at the University of Louisville, approximately one year before AMMA was administered to them in the standardization program. The correlations between the MAP total and composite scores and all three AMMA scores are reported below.

Musical Aptitude Profile	Advanced Measures of Music Audiation		
	Tonal	Rhythm	Composite
Tonal Imagery-Total	.73	.70	.74
Rhythm Imagery-Total	.67	.71	.72
Musical Sensitivity-Total	.46	.43	.57
Composite	.71	.76	.78

The correlations were found to be much higher than anticipated, particularly because the sample was small and homogeneous and the two test batteries were not administered concurrently. An encouraging fact is that the MAP *Musical Sensitivity* total test score, which includes all three preference subtests, correlates least with all scores on AMMA, which does not include any preference measures. Thus, high as the coefficients are, there is, as there should be, a substantial amount of uncommon variance between the two batteries.

In the sixth and final study, only the four nonpreference MAP subtests were administered, this time to 33 undergraduate music majors at Texas Christian University approximately one year before AMMA was administered to students who were participants in the standardization program (Gordon, *Advanced Measures of Music Audiation*, 1989). The correlations are outlined on the following page.

Although they are of like magnitude, the results of the Texas study are even more compelling than those of the Kentucky study, because they are more clear-cut. The two MAP tonal subtests are more highly correlated with the AMMA tonal subtest than they are with the AMMA rhythm subtest. Similarly, the two MAP rhythm subtests are more highly correlated with the AMMA rhythm subtest than they are with the AMMA tonal subtest.

Musical Aptitude Profile	Advanced Measures of Music Audiation		
	Tonal	Rhythm	Composite
Tonal Imagery-Melody	.76	.64	.81
Tonal Imagery-Harmony	.73	.59	.77
Rhythm Imagery-Tempo	.46	.70	.68
Rhythm Imagery-Meter	.60	.70	.85

---

1 More general suggestions may be found in *Learning Sequences in Music: Skill, Content, and Patterns* by Edwin E. Gordon (Chicago: GIA, 1997).

---

2 More general suggestions may be found in *Learning Sequences in Music: Skill, Content, and Patterns* by Edwin E. Gordon (Chicago: GIA, 1997).

CHAPTER 10

TESTS OF MUSIC ACHIEVEMENT, TIMBRE PREFERENCE, AND IMPROVISATION READINESS

The emphasis throughout this book has been on music aptitude. Important as music aptitude is, however, there are other factors that are also significant indicators of success in musical endeavors, and an understanding of the research in the psychology of music would be incomplete without thorough knowledge of these factors. For example, one may have the aptitude to achieve high standards in music but may lack corresponding music achievement. Thus, one would be hampered to some degree from enjoying and participating in music to the fullest extent possible. Obviously, just as we need to diagnose students' musical potential in terms of their musical strengths and weaknesses, we need to understand whether students' actual music achievement reflects their capabilities. It is for that reason that music achievement tests serve a need in music education.

There are various types of music achievement tests. The majority are written by classroom teachers to assess how well their students have learned the specific material they have been taught. Music achievement tests may measure, for example, knowledge of music theory, knowledge of music history, music-reading skills, and music-performance skills.

Professional test writers, as well as teachers, construct all types of music achievement tests. There are differences between a teacher-made test and a published standardized test, however, because a teacher-made test is designed for a specific group of students and so the content it includes is limited to what the students have been taught. On the other hand, a published standardized test is typically designed to measure students' general knowledge of music, and therefore the content it includes covers a variety of music skills as well as a comprehensive summary of musical knowledge. Thus, the two types of tests are used for different purposes. A teacher-made music achievement test is best suited to the grading process, whereas a published standardized music achievement test is used primarily for determining students' relative accomplishments in music compared to a large sample of students of their own age and in the same grade.

The results from a published standardized test are useful to a teacher who desires to know how one student or an entire class compares to peers across the country. While it may be true that a teacher believes a given class is being taught well or that a specific student is exceptional, a teacher may discover that this is not the case when a published standardized test is used. It should not be construed, however, that the standardized test is able to identify with certainty the cause of less-than-satisfactory music achievement; all it can do is alert the teacher and school administrators to possible problems that they may have not known existed.

Another significant difference between a teacher-made test and a published standardized test is that the former is rarely constructed in the form of a battery of tests, whereas the latter, when it is developed with care and an understanding of the educational process, does include a series of relevant subtests. Aside from the fact that a published standardized test battery is more prone to objectivity, because of its uniform administrative and scoring procedures, than is a teacher-made test, which, by its very nature is subjective, the objective test battery serves well to diagnose students' strengths and weaknesses in music achievement. Given that information, direct comparisons can be made between and among each student's potential and achievement in two or more specific domains of music, and that means that students' individual musical needs can be identified.

Research and publication relating to music achievement tests have not been as prolific as that relating to music aptitude tests. Moreover, the design of published music achievement tests is generally less sophisticated than standardized published achievement tests in other academic disciplines, and the reason for this may be the lack of agreement among teachers about what should be included in a music curriculum and how best to achieve recommended goals. Perhaps the most problematic aspect of the majority of music achievement tests has been that they are designed as multi-use tests, on the assumption that a given test can be used for school students of all chronological ages and various musical ages. Even more problematic is the idea that the same test can be administered over and over again to the same students, year after year, as a way to investigate educational growth, and in some cases, to award grades. It was not until a researched-based music learning theory was developed that provided the foundation for the creation of the *Iowa Tests of Music Literacy* (Gordon, 1991) that the possibility of establishing a multi-level music achievement test battery was fulfilled.

THE IOWA TESTS OF MUSIC LITERACY

The *Iowa Tests of Music Literacy* (ITML) is a multi-level battery designed to measure simple to complex dimensions of music achievement. Through the use of such a battery, the measurement and evaluation of students' tonal and rhythm audiation and notational audiation may be made from semester to semester or from year to year, using test levels that are most appropriate to students' current music achievement. A wide-range, single-level test repeatedly administered to students for the purpose of measuring and evaluating their music achievement is an inefficient test. Such a test must include a reasonable number of questions that are too difficult for younger students as well as a reasonable number that are too easy for older students. Multi-level tests, on the other hand, are not nearly as inefficient as wide-range, single-level tests, because students are asked to consider only those questions that may be properly expected to challenge them. As a consequence, a given level of a multi-level battery of subtests includes a variety of questions that relate to specific dimensions of music achievement that are associated with particular sequential aspects of a well-organized music program, with the result, of course, that the test is more reliable and, thus, more valid than would be a wide-range, single-level test.

ITML includes six subtests classified into two divisions: *Tonal Concepts* and *Rhythm Concepts*. The three subtests in the *Tonal Concepts* division are *Audiation/Listening, Audiation/Reading,* and *Audiation/ Writing*. The three subtests in the *Rhythm Concepts* division are also *Audiation/Listening, Audiation/Reading* and *Audiation/Writing*.

The specific purposes of the *Iowa Tests of Music Literacy* are 1) to diagnose a student's comparative strengths and weaknesses in six dimensions of tonal and rhythm audiation and notational audiation, 2) to compare students' achievement in audiation and notational audiation with their potential to achieve as indicated by their music aptitude scores, 3) to evaluate students' continuous and sequential achievement in tonal and rhythm audiation and notational audiation, and 4) to determine students' relative overall standing in tonal and rhythm audiation and notational audiation.

There are six recorded levels of the *Iowa Tests of Music Literacy,* including practice exercises and directions for taking the test. Each of the six levels includes six subtests that are similarly titled from level to level, because they measure parallel concepts at each level, but the content of each subtest grows in complexity at each level.

The content of the test questions consists of tonal patterns for the tonal subtests and rhythm patterns for the rhythm subtests, all of which are performed on a synthesizer. For the tonal *Audiation/Listening* subtests, students indicate, by filling in ovals on the answer sheet, the tonality they hear performed on the recording. In the lower levels of the battery, only major and harmonic minor tonalities are presented, whereas in the higher levels, students are presented with patterns in Dorian, Phrygian, Lydian, Mixolydian, and Locrian tonalities, and with patterns that are multitonal and pentatonic. For the tonal *Audiation/Reading* subtests, students indicate, by filling in ovals on the answer sheet, whether the notated patterns they see on the answer sheet are the same as those they hear performed on the recording. The same sequence of tonalities and multitonality and pentatonicism is used, and accidentals, treble and bass clefs, and chord symbols are introduced as they become more complex from level to level. For the tonal *Audiation/Writing* subtests, students complete the notation of the tonal patterns they hear performed by filling in blank spaces on the answer sheet. Only major and harmonic minor tonalities and multitonality are used in the writing subtests, and accidentals, treble and bass clefs, and part-music are introduced in the writing subtests as the levels of complexity increase.

For the rhythm *Audiation/Listening* subtests, students indicate, by filling in ovals on the answer sheet, the meter they hear performed on the recording. In the lower levels of the battery, only usual duple and triple meters are presented, and in the higher levels, multimetric patterns are presented in combined and unusual meters. For the rhythm *Audiation/Reading* subtests, students indicate whether the notated patterns they see on the answer sheet are the same as those they hear performed on the recording. The same sequence of meters and multimetricity is used, and various measure signatures are introduced as the subtests become more complex. For the tonal *Audiation/Writing* subtests, students complete the notation of the rhythm patterns they hear performed by filling in blank spaces on the answer sheet. Usual, unusual, and combined meters and multimetricity are introduced, and different measure signatures are introduced as the levels of complexity increase.

The *Iowa Tests of Music Literacy* was first published in 1970, and the national standardization of the battery was undertaken that year, following the procedures used for the standardization of the *Musical Aptitude Profile*. The program included 18,680 students, and norms were established for grades 4 through 12. The battery was revised in 1991, but because no great changes were known to have taken place in the teaching of school music during those years, it was decided that the enormous effort it would have required to conduct a supplementary standardization program to establish new norms would not be necessary. This conclusion was borne out by the results of a study conducted in 1993 that included the participation of 6,598 students throughout the United States (Gordon, *A Comparison of Scores on the 1971 and 1993 Editions,* 1994). In a practical sense, all statistical data were found to be ostensibly the same for the 1971 and 1993 groups. The means were not systematically dissimilar, and the differences for all corresponding subtests were found to be less than one standard score point. Overall reliability for the subtests in all six levels for all grades was in the .70s; for the total tests, in the .80s; and for the composite test, in the .90s. When compared to the reliabilities of the subtests, the intercorrelations among them were found to be low to moderate.

Of course, it is the validity of a test that is most important. As with most standardized published tests, responsibility for investigating the objective validity of a test remains with the author and other researchers. The appropriateness of the design and content of ITML, however, must be determined subjectively by those considering the use of the test battery. In addition to my study already described in chapter 5 (*Fifth-Year and Final Results,* 1975), there are seven studies pertaining to the objective validity of the *Iowa Tests of Music Literacy* (Roger Foss; James Mohatt; Robert Romaine; Stanley Schleuter; Warren Swindell; Robert Thayer; and Thelma Volger). I will briefly describe one of them.

James Mohatt administered all six levels of the *Iowa Tests of Music Literacy* to 122 students who comprised the entire eighth grade in Burlington, Iowa. Then, over a period of months, students' practical understanding of music, which directly corresponds to what is measured in ITML, was intensively measured and evaluated through listening activities and musical performance. While they were listening to actual musical compositions in various styles, students were asked to identify the tonality and meter of the music. Next, they participated in tonal and rhythm sight-singing, and finally, they took tonal and rhythm dictation. Students' scores on the listening and performance activities were correlated with their corresponding scores on ITML, and it was found that except for all levels of the rhythm *Audiation/Listening* subtests, the validity coefficients ranged from .31 to .71, the majority being .40 and higher.

THE INSTRUMENT TIMBRE PREFERENCE TEST

It will be remembered that in the three-year longitudinal predictive validity study of the *Musical Aptitude Profile* described in chapter 7, the correlation between fourth and fifth-grade students' MAP composite scores before instrumental music instruction was begun and the evaluation of five combined music achievement criteria after the students had received three years of instrumental music instruction was .75. If the coefficient of .75 is squared, it can be determined that students' music aptitudes account for approximately 55 percent of the reason for their success in beginning instrumental music. Stated another way, pre-instructional MAP scores predict success in beginning instrumental music with approximately 55 percent accuracy, that is, 55 percent better than chance. The percentage does not refer to specific students, but, rather, to the reason or reasons for the success of all students considered together.

It appears that students' success in beginning instrumental music is predicted about as well using either a developmental music aptitude or a stabilized music aptitude test. In a one-semester longitudinal predictive validity study of the *Primary Measures of Music Audiation* (Gordon, *Primary Measures of Music Audiation*, 1979) described in chapter 8, pre-instructional PMMA composite scores predicted success in violin performance of students seven and eight years of age with a coefficient of .73. In a one-year longitudinal predictive validity study of the *Intermediate Measures of Music Audiation* (Gordon, *A Longitudinal Predictive Validity Study*, 1984) also described in chapter 8, pre-instructional IMMA composite scores predicted success in violin and recorder performance of students eight and nine years of age with the majority of coefficients ranging from .62 to .79.

When it was initially discovered that approximately 55 percent of the reason behind students' success in beginning instrumental music is attributable to their music aptitude scores, no attempt was made to identify experimentally the nature of the remaining 45 percent of the variance. However, when the music aptitude tests and the criterion measures are corrected for attenuation, and even when other possible contributing factors, such as students' physical and psychological well-being or their home and cultural environments, are considered, approximately 35 percent of the nature of the variance still remained unknown. Recently, however, with the development of the *Instrument Timbre Preference Test* (Gordon, 1984), a significant portion of that variance has been accounted for, because it was discovered in the development of the ITPT that students become highly motivated and more successful when they learn to perform with good tone quality on instruments that have a timbre and range they like.

The primary purpose of the *Instrument Timbre Preference Test* (ITPT) is to assist teachers and parents in helping a student choose an appropriate woodwind, brass, or string instrument to learn in beginning instrumental music instruction. Whether students do or do not have a timbre preference, more than 40 percent of students who have a composite score above the 80th percentile on the *Musical Aptitude Profile* and the *Intermediate Measures of Music Audiation* do not volunteer for instrumental study. One of the reasons could be that they have not identified the instrument they would like to learn to play.

ITPT includes seven synthetic timbres of the same brief melody performed with the same musical expression, on a synthesizer. The different timbres are produced by changing and combining footages (octaves) and by modifying tone color through filtering. Each of the seven synthesized timbres is intended to represent the sound of one or more instruments. Because the melody has a range of an eleventh, it is possible to produce a broad spectrum in each timbre.

The seven timbres are organized into 42 recorded test questions on the *Instrument Timbre Preference Test.* Each of the seven timbres is paired twice with every other timbre, so that each timbre is heard once as first in the pair and once as second in the pair. The student is asked to listen to each test question and to indicate on an answer sheet which of the two timbres he or she prefers. Because the melody is always the same and the musical expression is held constant, timbre is the only changing factor in each test question. The melody does not become boring, because it is unusual and brief.

There are several reasons for the use of synthesized sounds rather than the sounds of actual instruments. 1) It is not possible for different, or even the same, musicians to perform a melody on different instruments with the same expression. As a result, it was found that when actual instruments were used, students were attentive to and based their preferences on the quality of the musical expression with which the melody was performed, rather than on the timbre and range of the instrument on which it was performed. 2) It was not possible to include all of the different stylistic timbres (such as commercial, studio, symphonic, jazz, and country) for each instrument on the recording. If only one style of tone quality were selected, it might be the one that some students did not like, even though they had a preference for the sound of the instrument when it was played in another style. 3) Although a student might claim to prefer a specific timbre when an actual instrument is used, the student's preference may be more a matter of familiarity than of preference. Moreover, a student may choose a timbre that he or she hears performed on an actual instrument because that instrument is associated with male or female performers, because the student may know that playing a specific instrument entitles one to membership in a select organization that offers many extra-musical opportunities, because the student's parents favor that instrument, because one of the student's relatives plays that instrument, because a friend plays or wants to play that instrument, because a famous artist plays that instrument, or because the student associates that instrument with a favorite piece of music.

Because of the non-traditional design of ITPT, it is not possible to investigate its reliability in terms of internal consistency, for either split-halves or odds-evens. As I explained previously, each of the times one of the seven timbres is heard on the test it is paired with one of the other six timbres. For the purpose of estimating reliability, the twelve questions that include the same timbre could have been divided into test halves of six questions each. However, then the test halves would not be homogeneous, because each timbre would have been heard first in combination with each of the other timbres in one test half and second in combination with each of the other timbres in the other test half. Thus, the coefficient of stability (test-retest) is the more appropriate type of reliability for investigating the stability of ITPT.

Eleven groups of 305 students in grades 3 through 8 in three public and private schools in the Philadelphia, Pennsylvania, area participated in the establishment of the statistical data for the *Instrument Timbre Preference Test*. The reliabilities for the seven individual timbres ranged from .46 to .89, with the majority found to be well above .70, but the intercorrelations among the individual test questions were even more impressive. That is, when questions with reversed timbres were correlated, all coefficients were negative, ranging from -.12 to -.38, suggesting students' consistency of preference for the same timbre regardless of whether it was heard as the first or as the second of the pair in a question.

Thus far I have designed three longitudinal predictive validity studies of the *Instrument Timbre Preference Test*, and I will summarize each of them. The one extensive investigation that bears on the construct validity of the test is best read in entirety (Gordon, *A Study of the Characteristics*, 1991).

The first of the two-year longitudinal predictive validity studies was conducted in Henrietta, New York (Gordon, *Final Results of a Two-Year Longitudinal Predictive Validity Study*, 1986). Here, the *Instrument Timbre Preference Test* and the *Musical Aptitude Profile* were administered to all students. In the first year of the study, 57 students (the experimental group) in beginning instrumental music classes elected to learn to play a woodwind or brass instrument for which they had demonstrated a timbre preference on ITPT. The 111 students in the control group chose to play a woodwind or brass instrument that was not suggested by their ITPT scores. The students received one 30-minute group lesson each week. Students in the individual experimental and control groups were taught together in every class. At the end of the first and second years of the study, the students performed three etudes on their instruments, and their performances were recorded and evaluated by two independent judges.

After the first year of instruction, students in the experimental group scored significantly higher than did students in the control group on the achievement criteria. In the experimental group, 24 (48 percent) of the students discontinued instruction, whereas 64 (58 percent) of the students in the control group decided not to continue instruction. After the first year, the combined predictive validity of the *Instrument Timbre Preference Test* and the *Musical Aptitude Profile* for students in the experimental and control groups together was .81. After the second year of instruction, the students in the experimental group again scored significantly higher than did students in the control group on the achievement criteria. Twenty-two students (39 percent) in the experimental group and 28 students (25 percent) in the control group completed two years of instruction and the overall the predictive validity of ITPT and MAP in conjunction with each other was found to be even higher, .85, for the second year. The data indicate that approximately 72 percent of the reason for students' success in beginning instrumental music is a result of a combination of their music aptitude and favorable circumstances that encourage and allow them to play an instrument for which they have a timbre and range preference. That is, when used in conjunction with the *Musical Aptitude Profile,* the *Instrument Timbre Preference Test* increases the accuracy of prediction of success in beginning instrumental music by approximately 16 percent over the accuracy when the aptitude test alone is used. Because there are no numerical scores associated with ITPT, it is, of course, not possible to derive norms for the test or to determine how well the test would predict success apart from MAP. Nonetheless, from a subjective analysis of the data it was determined that students who demonstrate a preference for a given timbre 10 or more of the 12 times it is heard on the recording should be encouraged to play the instrument or instruments associated with that timbre, and if they choose a given timbre 2 or fewer of the 12 times it is heard on the recording, they should be discouraged from playing the instrument or instruments associated with that timbre.

The second of the two-year longitudinal predictive validity studies was conducted in Guilderland, New York (*Predictive Validity Studies,* Gordon, 1989). The *Instrument Timbre Preference Test* and the *Intermediate Measures of Music Audition* were administered to all 292 students in fourth grade. When the students entered fifth grade, 181 of the students elected to learn to play a musical instrument in group lessons. All were told that if they studied a woodwind or brass instrument suggested by their ITPT results, they would be lent an instrument free of charge for two years. Of the 181 students, 30 accepted the offer (the experimental group) and the remaining 151 did not (the control group). The students received one 30-minute group instrumental lesson each week taught by two teachers.

At the end of the first semester of the first year, 49 students in the control group (32 percent) discontinued instruction, and 2 students in the experimental group (6 percent) declined to continue participation. At the end of the second semester, 39 of the 102 students in the control group (38 percent) discontinued instruction, and 9 of the 28 students in the experimental group (32 percent) no longer wanted to participate. At the end of the first semester of the second year, 31 of the initial 151 students (21 percent) remained in the control group and 17 of the initial 30 students (57 percent) remained in the experimental group, and at the end of two years of instruction, there were 26 students (17 percent) in the control group and, again, 17 students (57 percent) in the experimental group who remained.

As in the previous study, the students performed and recorded etudes at the conclusion of each semester that were then evaluated by two judges. The mean differences in achievement criteria were found to be consistently significant, all favoring the experimental group, and the combined predictive validity coefficient for the *Instrument Timbre Preference Test* and the *Intermediate Measures of Music Audiation* at the end of the two years was .80, which accounted for 60 percent of the variance compared to 72 percent in the first study. Though a difference of 12 percent in accuracy was found between the two studies, which may be due to whether a test of developmental or stabilized music aptitude is used in conjunction with ITPT, it seems clear that knowledge of timbre preference is an important component in predicting student success in instrumental music. It seems equally clear, however, that the use of timbre preference in guiding student study will not compensate for a student's low level of music aptitude.

An ancillary aspect of the study had to do with administering ITPT before instruction and again after two years of instruction. The correlations between the two sets of scores for each of the timbre preferences ranged from .52 to .63. These data suggest that not only can instrument timbre preference be measured reliably, but that it tends to remain consistent over a period of time, that is, the coefficients describing the stability of ITPT results gathered two years apart approximate those reported for the reliability of the preferences themselves.

The one-year longitudinal predictive validity study (Gordon, *Selecting an Appropriate String Instrument for Study*, 1994) was specifically directed to investigating timbre preference for string instruments. The *Instrument Timbre Preference Test* was administered to 355 fourth-grade students who were enrolled in five elementary schools in Haverford, Pennsylvania. Of the 355 students, 28 students (the experimental group) volunteered to study a string instrument for which they showed a timbre preference on ITPT, and 44 students (the control group) decided to learn to play a string instrument for which they did not show a preference. It is interesting, though not atypical, that nearly one-third of the students in the control group did not demonstrate any timbre preference on ITPT. The students received one group lesson each week, and after one year of instruction, 6 students (21 percent) in the experimental group discontinued instruction, whereas 14 students (32 percent) in the control group discontinued instruction.

At the end of one year of instruction, all 52 students who remained in the program performed and recorded two familiar songs taught in class without the use of notation, and the performances were rated by two judges. All of the mean differences for the achievement criteria favored the experimental group, particularly in musical expression.

It was not possible to administer the *Intermediate Measures of Music Audiation* to all students in the experimental and control groups, but many students who were not studying a string instrument managed to find the time to take the music aptitude test. As a result of that and additional supplementary analyses of the data, several ancillary investigations were undertaken. The following is a summary of the results of those investigations: 1) More students prefer timbres associated with upper-range woodwinds and strings than with lower-range brasses and strings. 2) Students who prefer timbres associated with upper-range woodwinds and strings tend to dislike timbres associated with lower-range brasses and strings. 3) Students who demonstrate superior achievement in beginning string instruction prefer timbres associated with cello, trombone, baritone, and French horn, and they tend to dislike timbres associated with double-reed instruments. 4) Having or not having a timbre preference bears no relation to music aptitude. 5) There are as many students with high music aptitude who do not participate in beginning instrumental music instruction as there are students with high music aptitude who do. 6) Students with low music aptitude are not apt to discontinue beginning instrumental music instruction any more than are students with high music aptitude. 7) Student preference for the musical range of an instrument the student is learning to play seems to be no less important than a preference for the timbre of that instrument for high achievement in beginning instrumental music.

There are, of course, studies that have been conducted by researchers other than me that bear on the validity of the *Instrument Timbre Preference Test*. One is a study of the predictive validity of ITPT (Mark Belczyk), two others are studies of the construct validity of ITPT (Sally Weaver and David Williams), and a third one relates to the experimental validity of ITPT (Charles Schmidt and Barbara Lewis).

Belczyk discovered that when the *Instrument Timbre Preference Test* is used in conjunction with the *Intermediate Measures of Music Audiation*, ITPT increases the predictive validity of the developmental music aptitude test. Weaver, however, did not always find agreement between the responses of musicians and the information reported in the ITPT manual with regard to the sounds of actual musical instruments and the actual instruments the synthesized timbres are intended to represent. That, as explained heretofore, was one of the primary reasons synthesized timbres rather than actual instruments were used as stimuli for ITPT. Nonetheless, whether the validity of ITPT might increase with alternate timbre sounds is a topic worthy of study.

Schmidt and Lewis administered ITPT to adults, not to students of the age the test is intended for, and found that there was a lack of agreement between a subject's preference for an ITPT timbre and the actual musical instrument the subject played. As is explained in the test manual, that is the reason ITPT was developed: a significant number of professional musicians play instruments for which they do not show a timbre preference or who have a timbre preference for an instrument they wish they had studied and could play. This has no bearing on the longitudinal predictive validity of the *Instrument Timbre Preference Test*, however. What are really needed are replications of mindful predictive validity studies with groups of students of various cultural backgrounds and environments, but studies undertaken without real purpose that do not require the expense of effort and time contribute very little to the understanding of relevant aspects of the validity of a test, let alone to the understanding of music aptitude or music education.

Worthy questions might include the following: 1) Does a score of 12 for a timbre preference indicate a significantly greater preference for that timbre than a score of 11 or 10? 2) Does a score of 0 for a timbre preference indicate a significantly weaker preference for that timbre than a score of 1 or 2? 3) Which musical instrument is most appropriate for a student to learn when the student has multiple timbre preferences? 4) Does a student's dislike of one timbre have any affect on or relation to his or her preference for another timbre? 5) When there is more than one musical instrument associated with one timbre preference, which would be most appropriate for the student to learn? 6) Which instruments, other than woodwinds, brasses, and strings, might be associated with the seven timbres?

THE HARMONIC IMPROVISATION
READINESS RECORD

The *Harmonic Improvisation Readiness Record* (Gordon, 1996) consists of harmonic patterns in various tonalities, all in the same simple rhythm, that were programmed on an Apple Macintosh computer and performed by a professional musician on a Yamaha DX-7 synthesizer. Students are asked to listen to pairs of harmonic patterns, each of which includes three chords, and to mark on an answer sheet whether the two harmonic patterns sound the same or not the same. If students are not sure of the correct answer, they are told to mark the question-mark column, indicating that they are in doubt. There are two important purposes for using the *Harmonic Improvisation Readiness Record* (HIRR): 1) to objectively determine whether individual students have the necessary harmonic readiness to learn to improvise and 2) to assist teachers in adapting instruction to students' individual musical differences when teaching improvisation.

The *Harmonic Improvisation Readiness Record* is not considered to be either a music aptitude test or a music achievement test. The reasons are several. To begin, HIRR has some characteristics of both music aptitude and music achievement tests, as well as other characteristics that are unrelated to either type of test. It will be remembered that although raw scores and percentile ranks on music achievement tests typically change as students get older, students in the stabilized music aptitude stage tend to maintain their relative standing from year to year in terms of percentile ranks on a test of stabilized music aptitude (even though their raw scores increase with chronological age). That is not the case for students who take a developmental music aptitude test, because, as with music achievement tests, both their raw scores and percentile ranks fluctuate. In contrast, it has been discovered that HIRR mean remains ostensibly the same for students in both the developmental and stabilized stages of music aptitude and for professional and non-professional musicians alike. The HIRR raw score mean for persons young and old, ages eight through adulthood, centers around 28 (there are 43 questions in the test).

Even more startling is that in an unpublished on-going investigation (*An Investigation of Children's Readiness to Improvise Harmonically: The Primary Harmonic Improvisation Readiness Record*) of a modified version of HIRR designed for use with very young children, Beth Bolton of Temple University has found the means and reliabilities to be 27.4 and .84, respectively, for kindergarten children, and 28.2 and .88, respectively, for children in first grade. The musical content of the test questions was not changed. Bolton simply adapted the original HIRR answer sheet to look like the one that is used in the administration of the *Primary Measures of Music Audiation,* and she discarded the recorded directions in favor of reading them aloud. Because the in-doubt response was eliminated as a possible answer, the length of time for children to decide on their answers was increased.

The fact that HIRR can be used effectively without the modification of content with students as young as those in third grade as well as with professional musicians is a phenomenon that is difficult to explain. The mean scores for HIRR are almost identical for elementary, junior high/middle, and high school students; for adults; and for music teachers and professional musicians. Perhaps, for whatever the reason or reasons, HIRR constitutes a combination of developmental and stabilized music aptitude and music achievement tests. A curious fact that was uncovered in the development of HIRR is that students and adults find harmonic patterns that include the subdominant chord in all tonalities easy to audiate (a matter belonging in the realm of music aptitude) but difficult to perform (a matter associated with music achievement), particularly in harmonic minor tonality.

The answer to the question of whether the *Harmonic Improvisation Readiness Record* is associated more with music aptitude or music achievement became more elusive when the music aptitude scores that were available for students in the eight schools included in the HIRR standardization program were correlated with their HIRR scores. The correlations of scores on HIRR with scores on the *Primary Measures of Music Audiation* and with scores on the *Intermediate Measures of Music Audiation,* both tests of developmental music aptitude, resulted in coefficients ranging from .02 to .19 in three schools and from .40 to .53 in two schools. With the *Advanced Measures of Music Audiation,* a test of stabilized music aptitude, the coefficients ranged from .04 to .66 in three schools.

The norms provided with the *Harmonic Improvisation Readiness Record* are based on a typical proportion of 8,285 music and non-music students in grades three through twelve who were attending school in the northeastern and southeastern United States. For students in grades three through six, the mean was 27.2 and the reliability .83; for students in grades seven and eight, the mean was, again, 27.2 and the reliability .86; and for students in grades nine through twelve, the mean was 28.1 and the reliability .87.

As with all tests, it is the practical validity of the *Harmonic Improvisation Readiness Record* that is of central importance. Given its relatively recent publication, there has been only one validity study of HIRR, and it is of a concurrent nature. It took place in a parochial school in Havertown, Pennsylvania, with two classes each in the fourth and fifth grades. The 49 fourth-grade students were administered the *Harmonic Improvisation Readiness Record* and the *Intermediate Measures of Music Audiation,* and the 46 fifth-grade students were administered the *Harmonic Improvisation Readiness Record* and the *Musical Aptitude Profile.* Within one month, all students were asked to listen to recordings of six four-measure songs without words or accompaniment that they had not heard before. The songs, performed twice, were in major, harmonic minor, Dorian, and Mixolydian tonalities, and in duple and triple meters. After hearing each song for the second time, each student was then asked to sing a response that sounded like the song but was not an imitation. The directions to the student were as follows. "You will hear a series of short songs twice. When each is over, I will not ask you to sing it. I will only ask you to sing something like it. Please listen to the first song." The responses of all students were recorded. The intent of the investigation was to see how well the students maintained the implied harmonic progression of each song while singing a melodic variation of that song. Using the following rating scale, I evaluated the performances of the songs as follows:

5   Performs a melody with all sequentially correct implied harmonic changes and with appropriate rhythm

4   Performs a melody with some sequentially correct implied harmonic changes and with appropriate rhythm

3   Performs a melody with some sequentially correct implied harmonic changes but with inappropriate rhythm

2   Performs a melody incorporating some implied harmonic changes but not necessarily in a consistent style

1   Performs an unrelated melody with a sense of tonality

0   Does not perform or simply chants

The HIRR mean for the 95 fourth and fifth-grade students combined was 28.8, and the correlation coefficient representing the relation of their HIRR scores and the combined ratings of their performances of all six songs was .68. The mean, as expected, is similar to that for older and younger students, and the validity coefficient indicates that there is approximately 46 percent in common between students' ability to improvise and their scores on the *Harmonic Improvisation Readiness Record.* Thus, HIRR can provide objective information to a teacher that pertains to the teaching of improvisation to individual students, enabling the teacher to then take into consideration students' individual musical needs when adapting the instructional process.

Additional study of the data indicated that the correlation between HIRR and MAP scores ranged from .37 to .60, and the correlation between HIRR and IMMA scores ranged from .37 to .66. That is, the correlation between HIRR scores and ratings of achievement in harmonic improvisation is not noticeably different from the correlation between HIRR scores and developmental and stabilized music aptitude scores. Thus, the answer to whether HIRR is more related to music aptitude or music achievement remains undetermined.

In a further attempt to solve the dilemma, a factor analyses of the students' HIRR scores, their music aptitude scores, and their improvisation performance ratings was undertaken for each grade separately. The results of the rotated principal factor matrixes are outlined on the following page.

In the fourth-grade analysis, HIRR and improvisation ability load on factor I, whereas the two developmental music aptitude tests stand alone on factor II. In the fifth-grade analysis, the three stabilized music aptitude tests stand alone on factor I, and HIRR and improvisation ability load on factor II. From these data, it would seem conclusive that the *Harmonic Improvisation Readiness Record* is a function of music achievement and not of either developmental or stabilized music aptitude. Replications of the study and ancillary studies, however, as well as results of studies of the longitudinal predictive validity of HIRR, are needed to warrant such a judgment.

With regard to an ancillary study, I have just designed a new test, the *Rhythm Improvisation Readiness Record,* in an attempt to gather further information about the overall nature of improvisation readiness. It might be that being aware of chord changes is necessary, but not sufficient, for establishing readiness to learn to improvise harmonically. To know when chord changes actually occur in syntactic time may be equally, or perhaps, even more important to the process of audiation. Should that prove to be the case, and if it demonstrates acceptable psychometric qualities, the new test will be published in the near future to serve as a necessary companion to HIRR.

Grade 4

	Factors	
	I	II
HARMONIC IMPROVISATION READINESS RECORD	.90	.27
INTERMEDIATE MEASURES OF MUSIC AUDIATION		
Tonal	.27	.78
Rhythm	.10	.87
IMPROVISATION PERFORMANCES	.94	.13

Grade 5

	Factors	
	I	II
HARMONIC IMPROVISATION READINESS RECORD	.33	.82
MUSICAL APTITUDE PROFILE		
Tonal Imagery-Total	.67	.43
Rhythm Imagery-Total	.94	.02
Musical Sensitivity-Total	.73	.33
IMPROVISATION PERFORMANCES	.10	.92

In conclusion, I would like to say that my initial intent in writing this book was to summarize the research pertaining to the nature and description of music aptitude so that it may be understood by all who are concerned with the topic. I was well on my way toward that end before the *Harmonic Improvisation Readiness Record* and the research it required came into being. At this point, it may be that we know most of what we will ever know about music aptitude or that we are on the threshold of finally understanding the nature and description of music aptitude in its entirety. Perhaps HIRR represents a generic form of music aptitude for which researchers have been searching for more than a century. Whatever the case may be, it is the process of seeking an answer rather than arriving at an answer that is the most exciting and makes the most sense.

GLOSSARY

Atomistic Theory The theory that music aptitude is comprised of multiple capacities.

Audiation Hearing and comprehending in one's mind the sound of music that is not or may never have been physically present. It is neither imitation nor memorization. There are six stages of audiation and eight types of audiation.

Aural/Oral The first (most elementary) level of discrimination learning and the foundation for all other levels of discrimination learning and for inference learning. At this level of learning students use a neutral syllable to learn by rote to perform tonal patterns and rhythm patterns.

Aural Perception Hearing music for which the sound is physically present.

Battery of Tests A set of subtests designed as a unit and to be administered as a group.

Chance score A score obtained by guessing answers.

Composite score A total score for all subtests in a test battery.

Composite Synthesis-reading The highest (most advanced) level of discrimination learning. At this level of learning students learn by rote to read comprehensively, using tonal syllables and rhythm syllables, series of tonal patterns and series of rhythm patterns that were taught at lower levels of learning.

Composite Synthesis-writing The highest (most advanced) level of discrimination learning. At this level of learning students learn by rote to notate comprehensively, using tonal syllables and rhythm syllables, series of tonal patterns and series of rhythm patterns that were taught at lower levels of learning.

Concurrent Validity The correlation between test scores and criterion values obtained at about the same time.

Construct Validity The degree to which a user of a test believes the test to be designed as an accurate measure of a trait.

Content Validity The degree to which a user of the test believes questions reflect an understanding of the information that a test was designed to measure.

Content Learning Sequence Tonal content learning sequence includes all tonal classifications and functions. Rhythm content learning sequence includes all rhythm classifications and functions. The classifications and functions are taught sequentially in combination with skill learning sequence.

Correlation The relation between factors. The cause of the relation must be determined experimentally.

Correlation Coefficient An index that indicates the degree of relation between factors. A perfect positive relation equals +1.00, no relation equals 0.00, and perfect negative relation equals -1.00.

Creativity The spontaneous audiation and use of tonal patterns and rhythm patterns without restrictions.

Creativity/ Improvisation One level of inference learning. Creativity/improvisation may take place with verbal association (using tonal syllables to perform tonal patterns and rhythm syllables to perform rhythm patterns) or without verbal association (using a neutral syllable to perform tonal patterns and to perform rhythm patterns). At this level of learning students create and improvise using familiar patterns, those learned by rote in discrimination learning, and unfamiliar patterns.

Criterion- Referenced Test A test that a student either passes or fails according to a predetermined standard.

Criterion-Related Validity The correlation between test scores and criterion values obtained at about the same time.

Developmental Music Aptitude Music potential that is affected by the quality of environmental factors. A child is in the developmental music aptitude stage from birth to approximately nine years old.

Diachronic Audiation	Concern with music that has been heard and will be heard.
Diagnostic Validity	The correlation between individual subtest scores and related specific capabilities.
Discrimination Learning	The lower of two generic types of skill learning. In discrimination learning students are taught skills, content, and patterns by rote. Discrimination learning includes the following levels and sublevels of learning: aural/oral, verbal association, partial synthesis, symbolic association-reading, symbolic association-writing, composite synthesis-reading, and composite synthesis-writing. Discrimination learning is the readiness for inference learning.
Duration	A part of a rhythm pattern. For example, each eighth note in a rhythm pattern of two eighth-notes is a duration.
Empirical Validity	Validity data based on objective evidence from experimental or observational studies.
Enrhythmic	Two rhythm patterns that sound the same but are notated differently. Also, two measure signatures that are used to notate the same sounding meter. Enrhythmic is to rhythm notation and audiation what enharmonic is to tonal notation and audiation.
Essential Durations	The important durations in a rhythm pattern that are retained in audiation to give meaning to the complete rhythm pattern.
Essential Pitches	The important pitches in a tonal pattern that are retained in audiation to give meaning to the complete tonal pattern.
Evaluation	Subjective interpretation, which may or may not be based on an objective measure, such as a test.
Extrinsic Meaning	Meaning in music that is based on its programmatic aspects and the moods it may suggest. The meaning is not intrinsic to the music.

Factor Analysis	A set of procedures for analyzing complex relations among a group of factors. Common, group, and/or unique factors may be discovered or verified.
Formal Music Instruction	A curriculum in which music skill and content are structured and sequenced, as in learning sequence activities. Students' music responses are planned and directed by the teacher.
Generalization-aural/oral	The first (most elementary) level of inference learning. At this and all other levels of inference learning students learn to audiate familiar and unfamiliar tonal patterns and rhythm patterns in unfamiliar order. The aural/oral level of discrimination learning is the direct readinesses for the generalization-aural/oral level of inference learning.
Generalization-symbolic	One level of inference learning. At this level of learning students learn to read and to notate familiar and unfamiliar tonal patterns and rhythm patterns in unfamiliar order. The symbolic association and composite synthesis levels of discrimination learning are the direct readinesses for the generalization-symbolic level of inference learning.
Generalization-verbal	One level of inference learning. At this level of learning students learn to verbally associate and synthesize familiar and unfamiliar tonal patterns and rhythm patterns in unfamiliar order. The verbal association and partial synthesis levels of discrimination learning are the direct readinesses for the generalization-verbal level of inference learning.
Gestalt Theory	The theory that music aptitude is comprised of only one general capacity.
Identification	Unfamiliar patterns are identified, whereas familiar patterns are recognized. The ability to recognize patterns in discrimination learning forms the foundation for the ability to identify patterns in inference learning.
Idiographic Evaluation	Comparing a student's music achievement to his or her music aptitude or past music achievement.

Idiographic Grading	Grading a student by comparing his or her music achievement to his or her music aptitude or his or her current music achievement to his or her past music achievement.
Imitation	Repeating music that was heard without giving it musical meaning. Imitation may be immediate or delayed.
Improvisation	The spontaneous audiation and use of tonal patterns and rhythm patterns with restrictions.
Inessential Durations	The unimportant durations in a rhythm pattern that are not necessarily retained in audiation and do not give meaning to the complete pattern.
Inessential Pitches	The unimportant pitches in a tonal pattern that are not necessarily retained in audiation and do not give meaning to the complete pattern.
Inference Learning	The higher of two generic types of skill learning. In inference learning students are guided by the teacher to learn skills, content, and patterns by teaching themselves. Students are not taught by rote in inference learning. Inference learning includes the following levels and sublevels of learning: generalization-aural/oral, generalization-verbal, generalization-symbolic, creativity/improvisation-aural/oral, creativity/improvisation-symbolic, theoretical understanding-aural/oral, theoretical understanding-verbal, and theoretical understanding-symbolic.
Informal Guidance	A sequenced curriculum of acculturation, imitation, and assimilation designed to encourage children who are in music babble to respond naturally and spontaneously to music. In informal guidance, children are not forced to respond to music. Children are simply exposed to music.
Intact Macrobeat	A macrobeat in unusual meter that is not long enough to be divided into microbeats. It can be divided only into divisions of a microbeat. An intact macrobeat is the durational equivalent of a microbeat.

Intercorrelation   The relations among subtests in a test battery, typically described by intercorrelation coefficients.

Intrinsic Meaning   Meaning in music that is based on the intrinsic elements (for example, the tonality and meter) of music.

Item Analysis   The study of the statistical properties of a test question, such as item difficulty and discrimination values.

Item Difficulty   The percent of students who answer a test question *correctly.*

Item Discrimination   A comparison of the percentage of more capable and less capable students who answer a test question correctly.

Key Signature   That which is actually a "do" signature. A key signature is seen in notation, whereas a keyality is audiated. A key signature does not indicate any one keyality. For example, the key signature of three flats may indicate Eb keyality in major tonality, C keyality in harmonic minor or Aeolian tonality, F keyality in Dorian tonality, G keyality in Phrygian tonality, Ab keyality in Lydian tonality, Bb keyality in Mixolydian tonality, and D keyality in Locrian tonality. Nevertheless, although "do" is not the resting tone in all of those tonalities, Eb is "do" in all of them.

Keyality   The pitch name of the tonic. A keyality is audiated, whereas a key signature is seen in notation. C is the keyality in C major, in C harmonic minor and Aeolian, in C Dorian, in C Phrygian, and so on. A tonic is associated with a keyality, whereas a resting tone is associated with a tonality.

Learning   Those activities that include skill learning sequence,
Sequence   content learning sequence (tonal and rhythm), and pattern
Activities   learning sequence (tonal and rhythm). They take place during the first ten minutes of a class or rehearsal. A tonal register book and a rhythm register book are used by the teacher in learning sequence activities.

Macrobeats   The fundamental beats in a rhythm pattern. In usual duple meter with the measure signature 2/4, quarter notes are the performed or underlying macrobeats. In usual triple meter with the measure signature 6/8, dotted-quarter notes are the performed or underlying macrobeats. In usual triple meter with the measure signature 3/4, dotted-half notes are the performed or underlying macrobeats. In unusual meters with the measure signatures 5/8 and 7/8, the performed or underlying macrobeats are combinations of quarter notes and dotted-quarter notes.

Mean   The average score.

Measure Signature   Traditionally called a time signature or a meter signature. A measure signature, however, indicates neither meter nor time. It indicates only the fractional value of a whole note that will be found in a measure. Because measure signatures are enrhythmic, a measure signature cannot indicate any one meter. Tempo markings and metronome markings indicate tempo, measure signatures do not.

Measurement   The objective analysis of students' music aptitude and music achievement. Measurement provides the objective basis for subjective evaluation.

Melodic Rhythm   The rhythm of the text or the melody in a piece of music. It is superimposed on macrobeats and microbeats.

Memorization   Repeating without the use of notation music that was read or heard, but not necessarily audiated.

Meter   Usual meter is determined by how macrobeats of equal length are divided. There are three types of usual meter. When macrobeats are divided into two microbeats of equal duration, the result is usual duple meter. When macrobeats are divided into three microbeats of equal duration, the result is usual triple meter. When some macrobeats are divided into two microbeats and others are divided into three microbeats, and not all of the microbeats are of equal duration, the result is usual combined meter. Unusual meter is determined by how macrobeats of unequal temporal lengths, some of which may be intact, are grouped. There are four types of unusual meter. They are unusual paired, unusual unpaired, unusual paired intact, and unusual unpaired intact.

Microbeats   The equal divisions of a macrobeat. The following are examples. In usual duple meter with the measure signature 2/4, groups of two eighth-notes are the performed or under-lying microbeats. In usual triple meter with the measure signature 6/8, groups of three eighth-notes are the performed or underlying microbeats, or in usual triple meter with the measure signature 3/4, groups of three quarter-notes are the performed or underlying microbeats. In unusu-al meters with the measure signatures 5/8 and 7/8, groups of two eighth-notes and groups of three eighth-notes are the performed or underlying microbeats.

Movable "do" Syllables   The tonal system in which the placement and position of "do" are dependent on keyality. For example, in major tonality, C is "do" in the keyality of C; D is "do" in the keyality of D; and so on. The ascending chromatic syllables are "do, di, re, ri, mi, fa, fi, so, si, la, li, ti, and do." The descending chromatic syllables are "do, ti, te, la, le, so, se, fa, mi, me, re, ra, and do." In the immovable or fixed "do" system, regardless of keyality, C is always "do." The tonal syllable system that is used in learning sequence activities is movable "do" with a "la" based minor.

Multimetric   Music in which two or more meters are represented.

Multiple Regression   A technique for estimating the relation of a group of factors to a single factor, in contrast to the relation of a single factor to one other factor.

Multitonal   Music in which two or more tonalities are represented.

Music Achievement   Accomplishment in music.

Music Aptitude   The potential to achieve in music.

Music Babble   The "musical" sounds a young child makes before develop-ing an objective sense of tonality and an objective sense of meter. Music babble is to music what speech babble is to language.

Music Learning Theory   The analysis and synthesis of the sequential manner in which we learn when we learn music.

Normal Distribution Data in the form of a bell-shaped curve.

Normal Illusion Consciously or unconsciously hearing sound in audiation that is different from what is or was actually aurally perceived.

Normative Evaluation Comparing a student's music aptitude and music achievement with the music aptitude and music achievement of other students in the same grade or of the same age.

Normative Grading Grading a student by comparing that student's music achievement with the music achievement of other students in the same grade or of the same age.

Norms Frames of reference for interpreting test scores.

Norms-Referenced Test A test that yields a score that is based on normative data.

Notational Audiation The audiation of what is seen in music notation without the aid of physical sound.

Note A symbol that is read or written in music notation and represents what is being audiated.

Omnibus Theory Gestalt theory of the composition of music aptitude.

Ontogeny The development of an individual.

Parallel Test Forms Equivalent forms of the same type of test, usually used for estimating test reliability.

Partial Synthesis A level of discrimination learning. At this level of learning students learn by rote to audiate the tonality of a series of familiar tonal patterns and the meter of a series of familiar rhythm patterns.

Percentile Ranks Scores that are derived from raw scores. Because they have standard meaning, they provide for immediate and clear interpretation. A percentile rank indicates the percent of students who scored at or below the raw-score equivalent.

Phylogeny

The historical development of humans.

Pitch Names

The letter names associated with the sounds of pitches.

Predictive Validity

The correlation between a pretraining test score and a criterion value obtained after a period of instruction.

Preparatory Audiation

Hearing and comprehending music while in the "music babble"stage as a readiness for engaging in audiation. There are three types of preparatory audiation and seven stages of preparatory audiation.

Psychological Construct

An aspect of a theory of the nature of music aptitude and how it might be best tested.

Random Sample

A sample of cases drawn from a population in such a way that every member of the population has an equal chance of being selected.

Raw Score

The number of correct answers on a test.

Recognition

Familiar patterns are recognized, whereas unfamiliar patterns are identified. The ability to identify unfamiliar patterns in inference learning is based on the ability to recognize familiar patterns in discrimination learning.

Readiness

The necessary background to achieve a sequential objective.

Reliability

The degree to which students' scores on a test remain the same when that test is administered to them again after a short period of time.

Reliability Coefficient

A correlation coefficient that represents the relation between two sets of scores on a test, a relation reflecting the stability or consistency (reliability) of the test scores.

Resting Tone

Sometimes referred to as a "scale tone" or a "home tone." A tonal center or centers to which a piece of music gravitates. A resting tone is specified by a movable "do" syllable in the movable "do" system with a "la" based minor. A tonality has a resting tone, whereas a keyality has a tonic.

Rhythm	That which consists of three fundamental parts: macrobeats, microbeats, and melodic rhythm. In audiation, microbeats are superimposed on macrobeats, and melodic rhythm is superimposed on microbeats and macrobeats.
Rhythm Pattern	Two or more durations in a given meter that are audiated sequentially and form a whole.
Rhythm Syllables	Different names that are chanted for different durations in a rhythm pattern. The rhythm syllables that are used in learning sequence activities are based on beat functions rather than on the time-value names of notes.
Rote Learning	Information that students learn as a result of repeating what they are told or by repeating what has been performed for them. The rote learning of skills, content, and patterns takes place at every level of discrimination learning.
Score Distribution	How test results are dispersed from the highest to the lowest score.
Semantic Meaning	The programmatic suggestions of a piece of music that are extrinsic to the music itself.
Sign	Anything that is audiated. For example, the audiation of the singing of tonal syllables and the chanting of rhythm syllables. A sign is audiated, whereas a symbol is read.
Skill Learning Sequence	A curriculum that includes all of the discrimination and inference skills that are taught sequentially to students in conjunction with tonal or rhythm content learning sequence.
Spearman-Brown Prophecy Formula	A technique for estimating the reliability of a full-length test.
Split-Halves Reliability	An estimate of reliability determined by dividing one test into two halves for scoring purposes and using a Spearman-Brown Prophecy Formula.
Stabilized Music Aptitude	Music potential that is no longer affected by environmental factors. A child enters the developmental music aptitude stage at approximately nine years old, and remains there throughout life.

Standard Deviation	A statistic that describes how scores vary around a mean.
Standard Error of a Difference	The extent to which a student's standing is different on two tests.
Standard Error of Measurement	The extent to which a student's obtained score differs from that student's "true" score.
Standard Score	A test score that has consistent meaning and thus is immediately interpretable.
Standardized Test	A test that has standard administrative and scoring procedures. A standardized test may or may not have standard scores.
Statistical Significance	The degree to which observed facts cannot be attributed to chance.
Stratified Sample	A sample of cases drawn from a population in such a way that members of every segment of the population are proportionately represented.
Subtest	One of the tests in a test battery.
Symbol	That which represents a sign. For example, the notation of a pitch or duration or of a tonal pattern or rhythm pattern. A symbol is read, whereas a sign is audiated.
Symbolic Association- reading	A level of discrimination learning. At this level of learning students learn by rote to read familiar tonal patterns and rhythm patterns in familiar or unfamiliar order that they have been taught by rote at the aural/oral and verbal association levels of learning.
Symbolic Association- writing	A level of discrimination learning. At this level of learning students learn by rote to notate familiar tonal patterns and rhythm patterns in familiar or unfamiliar order that they have been taught by rote at the aural/oral and verbal association levels of learning.

Synchronic Audiation	Concern with music that is being heard.
Syntax	The orderly arrangement of pitches and durations that establishes the tonality and meter of a piece of music. Music has syntax but not grammar.
Tempo	1) The speed at which rhythm patterns are performed and 2) The relative lengths of macrobeats within rhythm patterns.
Test-Retest Reliability	An estimate of test reliability determined by administering the same test on two occasions.
Theoretical Mean	The score midway between a chance score and the total possible score on a test.
Theoretical Understanding	The highest level of inference learning. Theoretical understanding includes three subparts: aural/oral, verbal, and symbolic. At this level of learning students learn theoretical information, such as the letter names of the lines and spaces on the staff and the time-value names of notes as they work with familiar and unfamiliar tonal patterns and rhythm patterns in unfamiliar order. At previous levels of learning, "what," "when," and "how" are emphasized. "Why" is emphasized at the theoretical understanding level of learning.
Tonal Pattern	Two, three, four, or five pitches in a given tonality that are audiated sequentially and form a whole. The eight pitches in a diatonic scale comprise at least two tonal patterns.
Tonal Syllables	Different names that are sung for different pitches in a tonal pattern. The tonal syllables that are used in learning sequence activities are based on the movable "do" system with a "la" based minor, not a "do" based minor.
Tonality	That which is determined by the resting tone. If "do" is the resting tone, the tonality is major; if "la" is the resting tone, the tonality is harmonic minor or Aeolian; if "re" is the resting tone, the tonality is Dorian; if "mi" is the resting tone, the tonality is Phrygian; if "fa" is the resting tone, the tonality is Lydian; if "so" is the resting tone, the tonality is

Mixolydian; and if "ti" is the resting tone, the tonality is Locrian. A tonality is always in a keyality but a keyality may not be in a tonality.

Total Test

Two or more subtests in a test battery that are related by their content. Together, they give rise to a total score.

Unusual Meter

Four types of meter in which macrobeats are of unequal length, regardless of whether they are audiated in pairs or more than a pair, whether some of them are intact, or whether they are divided into two or three microbeats of equal length.

Usual Meter

Three types of meter in which macrobeats of equal length are audiated in pairs. The macrobeats are divided into two or three microbeats of equal length or into two and three microbeats of unequal length, depending on the meter.

Validity

The verification of the one or more purposes for which a test is designed.

Validity Coefficient

A correlation coefficient that represents the relation between test scores and criterion values.

Variability

The extent to which test scores deviate from the mean, usually described by a standard deviation.

Verbal Association

A level of discrimination learning. At this level of learning students learn by rote a vocabulary of tonal patterns using tonal syllables and a vocabulary of rhythm patterns using rhythm syllables. The same patterns are taught at the aural/oral and verbal association levels of learning. Proper names of classifications and functions are also learned at the verbal association level of learning.

BIBLIOGRAPHY

Agnew, Marie. "A Comparison of the Auditory Images of Musicians, Psychologists, and Children," *Psychological Monographs*, 31 (1922), 268-278.

Aiello, Rita, ed. *Musical Perceptions*. New York: Oxford University Press, 1994.

Altenmüller, Eckart and Wilfried Gruhn. "Music, the Brain, and Music Learning: Mental Representation and Changing Cortical Activation Patterns Through Learning," *GIML Monograph Series*, 2, 1997, 7-71.

Asmus, Edward P. and Carole S. Harrison. "Characteristics of Motivation for Music and Music Aptitude of Undergraduate Nonmusic Majors," *Journal of Research in Music Education*, 38 (1990), 258-268.

Baddeley, Alan D. "How does acoustic similarity influence short-term memory?," *Quarterly Journal of Experimental Psychology*, 20, (1968), 249-264.

Bamberger, Jeanne. *The Mind Behind the Musical Ear*. Cambridge: Harvard University Press, 1991.

Baxter-Rowe, Patricia. *An Investigation of the Relationship of Rhythm Achievement in African-Derived Music Performance to the Rhythm Aptitude and Overall Rhythm Achievement of Fourth Grade Students*. Diss. Philadelphia: Temple University, 1993.

Bell, William. *An Investigation of the Validity of the Primary Measures of Music Audiation for Use with Learning Disabled Children*. Diss. Philadelphia: Temple University, 1981.

Belczyk, Mark. *Using Developmental Music Aptitude and Timbre Preference Test Results to Predict Performance Achievement Among Beginning Band Students*. Diss. Philadelphia: Temple University, 1992.

Benham, Evelyn. "The Creative Activity: Introspective Experiment in Musical Composition," *British Journal of Psychology*, 20 (1929), 59-65.

Bentley, Arnold. *Musical Ability in Children and Its Measurement*. New York: October House, 1966.

Bentley, Arnold. *Measures of Musical Abilities*. London: Harrap Audio-Visual, 1966.

Bentley, Richard. *A Critical Comparison of Certain Music Tests*. Los Angeles: Diss. University of Southern California, 1956.

Bergan, John. "The Relationship Among Pitch Identification, Imagery for Musical Sounds, and Musical Memory," *Journal of Research in Music Education*, 15 (1967), 99-109.

Bienstock, Sylvia. "A Predictive Study of Musical Achievement," *Journal of Genetic Psychology*, 61 (1942), 135-145.

Bienstock, Sylvia. "Review of Recent Studies on Musical Aptitude," *Journal of Educational Psychology*, 33 (1942), 427-442.

Bingham, Walter Van Dyke. *Aptitudes and Aptitude Testing*. New York: Harper, 1937.

Bixler, John. "Musical Aptitude in the Educable Mentally Retarded Child," *Journal of Music Therapy*, 5 (1968), 41-43.

Bloom, Benjamin. *Stability and Change in Human Characteristics*. New York: John Wiley and Sons, 1964.

Bogen, David. "The Significance of Tonal Memory and Sense of Pitch in Musical Talent," *Psychological Bulletin*, 30 (1933), 599.

Bolton, Beth. *An Investigation of 'Same' and 'Different' as Manifested in the Developmental Music Aptitudes of Students in Kindergarten Through Third Grade.* Diss. Philadelphia: Temple University, 1995.

Bower, Libbie. *A Factor Analysis of Music Tests.* Washington: Catholic University Press, 1945.

Boyle, J. David and Rudolf E. Radocy. *Measurement and Evaluation of Musical Experiences.* New York: Schrimer Books, 1987.

Brenan, Flora. "The Relation Between Musical Capacity and Performance," *Psychological Monographs*, 36 (1927), 190-248.

Briscuso, Joseph. *A Study of Ability in Spontaneous and Prepared Jazz Improvisation Among Students Who Possess Different Levels of Music Aptitude.* Diss. Iowa City: University of Iowa,, 1972.

Brodsky, Warren and Avishai Henik. *Demonstrating Inner Hearing Among Musicians.* Unpublished paper. Beer-Sheva, Israel: Ben-Gurion University of the Negev, Department of Behavioral Sciences.

Brown, Andrew. "The Reliability and Validity of the Seashore Tests of Musical Talent," *Journal of Applied Psychology*, 12 (1928), 468-476.

Brown, Merrill. "The Optimum Length of the Musical Aptitude Profile Subtests,"*Journal of Research in Music Education*, 17 (1969), 240-247.

Bruner, Jerome. *The Process of Education.* Cambridge: Harvard University Press, 1960.

Bruton-Simmonds, I. V. "A Critical Note on the Value of the Seashore Measures of Musical Talents," *Psychologia Africana*, 13 (1969), 50-54.

Bryne, Brian. "Handedness and Musical Ability," *British Journal of Psychology*, 65 (1974), 279-281.

Buck, Percy. *Psychology for Musicians.* London: Oxford University Press, 1961.

Budd, Malcolm. *Music and the Emotions.* London: Routledge and Kegan Paul, 1985.

Buros, Oscar, ed. *Seventh Mental Measurements Yearbook.* Highland Park, New Jersey, Gryphon Press, 1972.

Burt, Cyril. *Psychological Tests of Educable Capacity.* London: Board of Education, 1924.

Burt, Cyril. *The Factors of the Mind.* London: University of London Press, 1940.

Butler, David. *The Musician's Guide to Perception and Cognition.* New York: Schirmer Books, 1992.

Cameron, Edward H. "Effects of Practice in the Discrimination and Singing of Tones," *Psychological Monographs*, 23 (1917), 159-180.

Capurso, Alexander A. "The Effect of an Associative Technique in Teaching Pitch and Interval Discrimination," *Journal of Applied Psychology*, 18 (1934), 811-818.

Carson, Andrew D. "Why has Musical Aptitude Assessment Fallen Flat? And What Can We Do About It?" *Journal of Career Assessment*, (in press).

Cattell, Raymond B. and D. Saunders. "Musical Preferences and Personality Diagnosis,"*Journal of Social Psychology*, 39 (1954), 3-24.

Chadwick, J. Elbert. "Predicting Success in Sight Singing," *Journal of Applied Psychology,* 17 (1933), 671-674.

Chuang, Wuei-Chun Jane. *An Investigation of the Use of the Music Aptitude Profile with Taiwanese Students in Grades Four Through Twelve.* Diss. East Lansing: Michigan State University, 1997.

Clifton, Thomas. *Music as Heard.* New Haven: Yale University Press, 1983.

Clynes, Manfred. *Sentics.* Garden City, New York: Doubleday, 1977.

Colwell, Richard. *The Evaluation of Music Teaching and Learning.* Englewood Cliffs: Prentice Hall, 1970.

Connette, Earle. "The Effect of Practice with Knowledge of Results," *Journal of Educational Psychology,* 32 (1941), 523-532.

Conoley, Jane Close and James C. Impara, eds. *The Twelfth Mental Measurements Yearbook.* Lincoln, Nebraska: The Buros Institute of Mental Measurements: University of Nebraska Press, 1995.

Cooley, John. "A Study of the Relation Between Certain Mental and Personality Traits and Ratings of Musical Ability," *Journal of Research in Music Education,* 9 (1961), 108-117.

Cowell, Henry. "The Process of Musical Creation," *American Journal of Psychology,* 37 (1926), 233-236.

Cox, Catherine. *Genetic Studies of Genius.* Stanford: Stanford University Press, 1926.

Critchley, MacDonald and R. A. Henson, eds. *Music and the Brain.* Springfield, Illinois: Charles C. Thomas, 1977.

Crump-Taggart, Cynthia. "A Validity Study of Audie: A Test of Music Aptitude for 3- and 4-Year-Old Children," *Council for Research in Music Education,*121 (1994), 42-54.

Culver, Florence. *A Study of the Musical Aptitude Profile.* Thesis. Iowa City: University of Iowa, 1965.

Curtis, Cynthia. *A Comparative Analysis of the Musical Aptitude of Normal Children and Mildly Handicapped Children Mainstreamed into Regular Classrooms.* Diss. Nashville: George Peabody College for Teachers of Vanderbilt University, 1981.

Dahlhaus, Carl and Helga de la Motte-Haber. "Systematische Musikwissenschaft: Neues Handbuch der Musikwissenschaft," Laaber: *Akademische Verlagsgesellschaft Athenaion,* 10 (1986), 269-308.

Dashiell, J. F. "Children's Sense of Harmonies in Colors and Tones," *Journal of Experimental Psychology,* 2 (1917), 466-475.

Davies, John Booth. *An Analysis of Factors Involved in Musical Ability, and the Derivation of Tests of Musical Aptitude.* Diss. Durham: University of Durham, 1969.

Davies, John Booth. "New Tests of Musical Aptitude," *British Journal of Psychology,* 62 (1971), 557-565.

Davies, John Booth. *The Psychology of Music.* Stanford: Stanford University Press, 1978.

Deliège, Irène and John Sloboda, eds. *Musical Beginnings.* Oxford: Oxford University Press, 1996.

Deliège, Irène and John Sloboda, eds. *Perception and Cognition of Music.* East Suxxex: Psychology Press, 1997.

DeYarman, Robert. "An Investigation of the Stability of Musical Aptitude Among Primary-Age Children," *Experimental Research in the Psychology of Music: Studies in the Psychology of Music,* 10 (1975), 1-23.

DiBlassio, Richard. *An Experimental Study of the Development of Tonal and Rhythm Capabilities of First Grade Children.* Diss. Philadelphia: Temple University, 1984.

Disserens, Charles M. and Harry A. Fine. *A Psychology of Music.* Cincinnati: College of Music, 1939.

Dittemore, Edgar. "An Investigation of Some Musical Capacities of Elementary School Children," *Experimental Research in the Psychology of Music:Studies in the Psychology of Music,* 6 (1970), 1-44.

Dowling, W. Jay and Dane L. Harwood. *Music Cognition.* New York: Academic Press, 1986.

Doxey, Cynthia and Cheryl Wright. "An Exploratory Study of Children's Music Ability," *Early Childhood Research Quarterly,* 5 (1990), 425-440.

Drake, Raleigh. "Four New Tests of Musical Talent," *Journal of Applied Psychology,* 17 (1933), 136-147.

Drake, Raleigh. *Musical Memory Test.* Bloomington, Illinois: Public School Publishing Company, 1934.

Drake, Raleigh. "Factorial Analysis of Music Tests by the Spearman Tetrad-Difference Technique," *Journal of Musicology,* 1 (1939), 6-16.

Drake, Raleigh. "The Relation of Musical Talent to Intelligence and Success in School," *Journal of Musicology,* 2 (1940), 28-44.

Drake, Raleigh. "The Effect of Ear Training on Musical Talent Scores," *Journal of Musicology,* 4 (1943), 110-112.

Drake, Raleigh. *Drake Musical Aptitude Tests.* Chicago: Science Research Associates, 1954.

Duda, Walter B. *The Prediction of Three Major Dimensions of Teacher Behavior for Student Teachers in Music.* Diss. Urbana, University of Illinois, 1961.

Dunlevy, Eve. "Musical Training and Measured Musical Aptitude," *Journal of Musicology,* 4 (1944), 1-5.

Ebel, Robert L. *Essentials of Educational Measurement.* Englewood Cliffs: Prentice-Hall, 1972.

Eisner, Elliot W. *Cognition and Curriculum.* New York: Longmans, 1982.

Eells, Walter. "Musical Ability of the Native Races of Alaska," *Journal of Applied Psychology,* 17 (1933), 67-71.

Epperson, Gordon. *The Musical Symbol.* Ames: Iowa State University Press, 1967.

Estrella, Stephen. *Effects of Training and Practice on Advanced Measures of Music Audiation Scores.* Diss. Philadelphia: Temple University, 1992.

Farnsworth, Charles. *Short Studies in Musical Psychology.* London: Oxford University Press, 1965.

Farnsworth, Paul. "The Effect of Repetition on Ending Preferences in Melodies,"
      American Journal of Psychology, 37 (1926), 116-122.

Farnsworth, Paul. "The Effects of Nature and Nurture on Musicality," *27th
      Yearbook, National Society for the Study of Education*, 2 (1928), 233-245.

Farnsworth, Paul. "An Historical, Critical, and Experimental Study of the
      Seashore-Kwalwasser Test Battery," *Genetic Psychology
      Monograph*, 9 (1931), 291-393.

Farnsworth, Paul. "Studies in the Psychology of Tone and Music," *Genetic
      Psychology Monographs*, 15 (1934), 1-94.

Farnsworth, Paul. "Ratings in Music, Art, and Abnormality in the First
      Four Grades," *Journal of Psychology*, 6 (1938), 89-94.

Farnsworth, Paul. "Auditory Acuity and Musical Ability in the First Four
      Grades," *Journal of Psychology*, 6 (1938), 95-98.

Farnsworth, Paul. "Data on the Tilson-Gretsch Test for Musical Aptitude,"
      Journal of Musicology, 4 (1945), 99-102.

Farnsworth, Paul. *The Social Psychology of Music*. Ames: Iowa State University
      Press, 1969.

Farrell, John. *A Validity Investigation of the Drake Musical Aptitude Tests*.
      Diss. Iowa City: University of Iowa, 1961.

Faulds, Bruce. *The Perception of Pitch in Music*. Princeton: Educational Testing
      Service, 1959.

Feis, Oswald. *Studien über die Genealogie und Psychologie der Musiker*.
      Wiesbaden: J. F. Bergman, 1910.

Feldman, David Henry and L. T. Goldsmith. *Nature's Gambit: Child Prodigies and
      the Development of Human Potential*. New York: Basic Books, 1986.

Ferguson, Donald N. *The Why of Music*. Minneapolis: University of
      Minnesota Press, 1969.

Flohr, John. "Short-Term Music Instruction and Young Children's
      Developmental Music Aptitude," *Journal of Research in Music
      Education*, 29 (1981), 219-223.

Forsythe, Rosemary. *The Development and Implementation of a Computerized
      Pre-school Measure of Music Audiation*. Diss. Cleveland: Case Western
      University, 1984.

Fosha, Leon. *A Study of the Validity of the Musical Aptitude Profile*. Diss.
      Iowa City: University of Iowa, 1960.

Foss, Roger. *An Investigation of the Effect of the Provision of the 'In Doubt'
      Response on the Validity of the Iowa Tests of Music Literacy*. Diss.
      Iowa City: University of Iowa, 1972.

Fracker, Cutler C. and Virgie M. Howard. "Correlation Between Intelligence and
      Musical Talent," *Psychological Monographs*, 39 (1928), 157-161.

Franklin, Erik. *Tonality as the Basis for the Study of Musical Talent*. Goteborg,
      Sweden: Gumperts Forlag, 1956.

Freeman, Joan. "Musical and Artistic Talent in Children," *Psychology of Music*,
      2 (1974), 5-12.

Friend, Ruby. *An Experimental Investigation of the Seashore Musical Tests with Specific Reference to Their Reliability for Children of Kindergarten Age, and to the Relationship Between the Children and Their Parents in the Performance on These Tests.* Diss. Minneapolis: University of Minnesota,1930.

Froseth, James. "Using MAP Scores in the Instruction of Beginning Students in Instrumental Music," *Journal of Research in Music Education,* 19 (1971), 98-105.

Fullen, David. *An Investigation of the Validity of the Advanced Measures of Music Audiation with Middle and Secondary School Students.* Diss. Philadelphia: Temple University, 1992.

Gardner, Howard. *Frames of Mind.* New York: Basic Books, 1983.

Gaede, Steven E., Oscar A. Parsons, and James H. Bertyera. "Hemispheric Differences in Music Perception: Aptitude vs Experience," *Neuropsycholgia,* 16 (1978), 369-373.

Gallagher, Fulton. *A Study of the Relationship Between the Gordon Musical Aptitude Profile, the Colwell Music Achievement Tests, and the Indiana-Oregon Music Discrimination Test.* Diss. Bloomington: Indiana University, 1971.

Garth, Thomas R. and Sarah Rachel Isbell. "The Musical Talent of Indians," *Music Supervisors Journal,* 15 (1929), 83-87.

Gaston, E. Thayer. *Tests of Musicality.* Lawrence, Kansas: Odell's Instrumental Service, 1957.

Gaw, Esther Allen. "Five Studies of the Music Tests," *Psychological Monographs,* 39 (1928), 145-156.

Geissel, Leonard. *An Investigation of the Comparative Effectiveness of the Musical Aptitude Profile, the Intermediate Measures of Music Audiation, and the Primary Measures of Music Audiation with Fourth Grade Students.* Diss. Philadelphia: Temple University, 1985.

Gfeller, K. E., and C. Lansing. "Musical Perception of Cochlear Implant Users as Measured by the Primary Measures of Music Audiation," *Journal of Music Therapy,* 29 (1992), 18-39

Gibbons, Alicia Clair. "Musical Aptitude Profile Scores in a Noninstitutional, Elderly Population," *Journal of Research in Music Education,* 30 (1982), 23-29.

Gibbons, Alicia Clair. "Item Analysis of the Primary Measures of Music Audiation," *Journal of Music Therapy,* 20 (1983), 201-210.

Gilbert, Gustave. "Aptitude and Training: A Suggested Restandardization of the K-D Music Test Norms," *Journal of Applied Psychology,* 25 (1941), 326-330.

Gilbert, Gustave. "Sex Differences in Musical Aptitude and Training," *Journal of General Psychology,* 26 (1942), 19-33.

Gilbert, J. Allen. "Experiments on the Musical Sensitiveness of School Children," *Studies in the Yale Psychological Laboratory,* 1 (1893), 80-87.

Gilbert, J. Allen. "Researches on School Children and College Students,"*Studies in Psychology.* Iowa City: University of Iowa, 1 (1897), 1-39.

Gordon, Edwin. "A Study to Determine the Effects of Practice and Training on Drake Musical Aptitude Test Scores," *Journal of Research in Music Education,* 4 (1961), 63-68.

Gordon, Edwin. *Musical Aptitude Profile.* Chicago: GIA, 1995, 1988, 1965. 7404 South Mason Avenue, Chicago, Illinois 60638. 800 442 1358 or 708 496 3800.

Gordon, Edwin. *A Three-Year Longitudinal Predictive Validity Study of the Musical Aptitude Profile.* Studies in the Psychology of Music 5. Iowa City: University of Iowa Press, 1967.

Gordon, Edwin. "A Comparison of the Performance of Culturally Disadvantaged Students With That of Culturally Heterogeneous Students on the Musical Aptitude Profile," *Psychology in the Schools,* 15 (1967), 260-268.

Gordon, Edwin. "Implications for the Use of the Musical Aptitude Profile with College and University Freshman Music Students," *Journal of Research in Music Education,* 15 (1967), 32-40.

Gordon, Edwin. "The Contribution of Each Musical Aptitude Profile Subtest to the Overall Validity of the Battery," *Council for Research in Music Education,* 12 (1968), 32-36.

Gordon, Edwin. "A Study of the Efficacy of General Intelligence and Music Aptitude Tests in Predicting Achievement in Music," *Council for Research in Music Education,* 13 (1968), 40-45.

Gordon, Edwin. "The Use of the Musical Aptitude Profile with Exceptional Children," *Journal of Music Therapy,* 5 (1968), 37-40.

Gordon, Edwin. "An Investigation of the Intercorrelation Among Musical Aptitude Profile and Seashore Measures of Music Talents Subtests," *Journal of Research in Music Education,* 17 (1969), 263-271.

Gordon, Edwin E. *Iowa Tests of Music Literacy* Chicago: GIA, 1991, 1970. 7404 South Mason Avenue, Chicago, Illinois 60638. 800 442 1358 or 708 496 3800.

Gordon, Edwin. "Taking Into Account Musical Aptitude Differences Among Beginning Instrumental Music Students," *American Educational Research Journal,* 7 (1970), 41-53.

Gordon, Edwin. "First-Year Results of a Five Year Longitudinal Study of the Musical Achievement of Culturally Disadvantaged Students," *Journal of Research in Music Education,* 18 (1970), 195-213.

Gordon, Edwin. "Taking Into Account Musical Aptitude Differences Among Beginning Instrumental Students," *Experimental Research in the Psychology of Music: Studies in the Psychology of Music,* 6 (1970), 45-64.

Gordon, Edwin, ed. *Experimental Research in the Psychology of Music: Studies in the Psychology of Music.* Volumes 6-10. Iowa City: University of Iowa Press, 1970-75.

Gordon, Edwin. "Second-Year Results of a Five Year Longitudinal Study of the Musical Achievement of Culturally Disadvantaged Students," *Experimental Research in the Psychology of Music: Studies in the Psychology of Music,* 7 (1971), 131-143.

Gordon, Edwin. *The Psychology of Music Teaching.* Englewood Cliffs: Prentice-Hall, 1971.

Gordon, Edwin. "Third-Year Results of a Five Year Longitudinal Study of the Musical Achievement of Culturally Disadvantaged Students," *Experimental Research in the Psychology of Music: Studies in the Psychology of Music,* 8 (1972), 42-60.

Gordon, Edwin. *The Psychology of Music Teaching.* Tokyo: Kawai Gakufu Company, 1973.

Gordon, Edwin E. "Fourth-Year Results of a Five Year Longitudinal Study of the Musical Achievement of Culturally Disadvantaged Students," *Sciences de l'Art Scientific Aesthetics,* 9 (1974), 79-89.

Gordon, Edwin E. "Toward the Development of a Taxonomy of Tonal and Rhythm Patterns: Evidence of Difficulty Level and Growth Rate," *Experimental Research in the Psychology of Music: Studies in the Psychology of Music,* 9 (1974), 39-232.

Gordon, Edwin E. "Fifth-Year and Final Results of a Five-Year Longitudinal Study of the Musical Achievement of Culturally Disadvantaged Students," *Experimental Research in the Psychology of Music: Studies in the Psychology of Music,* 10 (1975), 24-52.

Gordon, Edwin E. *Tonal and Rhythm Patterns: An Objective Analysis.* Albany: State University of New York Press, 1976.

Gordon, Edwin E. *A Factor Analytic Description of Tonal and Rhythm Patterns and Objective Evidence of Pattern Difficulty Level and Growth Rate.* Chicago: GIA, 1978.

Gordon, Edwin E. "Developmental Music Aptitude as Measured by the Primary Measures of Music Audiation," *Psychology of Music,* 7 (1979), 42-49.

Gordon, Edwin E. *Primary Measures of Music Audiation.* Chicago: GIA, 1979. 7404 South Mason Avenue, Chicago, Illinois 60638. 800 442 1358 or 708 496 3800.

Gordon, Edwin E. *Learning Sequences in Music: Skill, Content, and Patterns.* Chicago: GIA, 1997, 1993, 1988, 1984, 1980.

Gordon, Edwin E. "Developmental Music Aptitudes Among Inner-City Primary Grade Children," *Council for Research in Music Education,* 63 (1980), 25-30.

Gordon, Edwin E. "The Assessment of Music Aptitudes of Very Young Children," *The Gifted Child Quarterly,* 24 (1980), 107-111.

Gordon, Edwin E. "Wie Kinder Klänge als Musik wahrnehmen - Eine Längsschnittuntersuchung zur musikalischen Begabung," *Musikpädagogische Forschung,* 2 (1981), 30-63.

Gordon, Edwin E. *The Manifestation of Developmental Music Aptitude in the Audiation of "Same" and "Different" as Sound in Music.* Chicago: GIA, 1981.

Gordon, Edwin E. *Intermediate Measures of Music Audiation.* Chicago: GIA, 1982. 7404 South Mason Avenue, Chicago, Illinois 60638. 800 442 1358 or 708 496 3800.

Gordon, Edwin E. *Instrument Timbre Preference Test.* Chicago: GIA, 1984.
    7404 South Mason Avenue, Chicago, Illinois 60638. 800 442 1358 or
    708 496 3800.
Gordon, Edwin E. "A Longitudinal Predictive Validity Study of the Intermediate
    Measures of Music Audiation," *Council for Research in Music Education,*
    78 (1984), 1-23.
Gordon, Edwin E. *"Research Studies in Audiation: 1," Council for Research in
    Music Education,* 84 (1985), 34-50.
Gordon, Edwin E. *The Nature, Description, Measurement, and Evaluation of
    Music Aptitudes.* Chicago: GIA, 1986.
Gordon, Edwin E. *Musikalische Begabung: Beschaffenheit, Beschreibung,
    Messung, und Bewertung.* trans. Michael Roske. Mainz: Schott, 1986.
Gordon, Edwin E. "The Importance of Being Able to Audiate 'Same' and
    'Different' for Learning Music." *Music Education for the Handicapped,* 2
    (1986), 3-27.
Gordon, Edwin E. "Final Results of a Two-Year Longitudinal Predictive Validity
    Study of the Instrument Timbre Preference Test and the Musical Aptitude
    Profile." *Council for Research in Music Education,* 89 (1986), 8-17.
Gordon, Edwin E. "A Factor Analysis of the Musical Aptitude Profile, the Primary
    Measures of Music Audiation, and the Intermediate Measures of Music
    Audiation," *Council for Research in Music Education,* 87 (1986), 17-25.
Gordon, Edwin E. "The Effects of Instruction Based Upon Music Learning Theory
    on Developmental Music Aptitudes," *Research in Music Education,*
    International Society for Music Education, Trowbridge, Wiltshire, Great
    Britain, 2 (1988),53-57.
Gordon, Edwin E. "Aptitude and Audiation: A Healthy Duet," *Medical Problems of
    Performing Artists,* 3, 1 (March, 1988), 33-35.
Gordon, Edwin E. "Music Aptitudes and Music Achievement," *Ala Breve,* 35, 3,
    (March, 1988), 9, 10, 30.
Gordon, Edwin E. "Musical Child Abuse," *The American Music Teacher,* 37, 5,
    (April/May 1988), 14-16.
Gordon, Edwin E. "Implications for Music Learning," *Music and Child
    Development:* St. Louis, MMB Music, (1989), 325-335.
Gordon, Edwin E. "Audiation, Imitation, and Notation: Musical Thought and
    Thought About Music," *The American Music Teacher,* 38, 3, (April/May
    1989), 15, 16, 17, 59.
Gordon, Edwin E. "Audiation, Music Learning Theory, Music Aptitude, and
    Creativity," *The Proceedings of The Suncoast Music Education Forum on
    Creativity,* Tampa, Florida, (1989), 75-89.
Gordon, Edwin E. "The Nature and Description of Developmental and Stabilized
    Music Aptitudes: Implications for Music Learning," *Music and Child
    Development: Proceedings of the 1987 Denver Conference,* St. Louis,
    MMB Music, (1989), 325-335.
Gordon, Edwin E. *Advanced Measures of Music Audiation.* Chicago: GIA, 1989.
    7404 South Mason Avenue, Chicago, Illinois 60638. 800 442 1358 or 708
    496 3800.

Gordon, Edwin E. *Audie.* Chicago: GIA, 1989. 7404 South Mason Avenue, Chicago, Illinois 60638. 800 442 1358 or 708 496 3800.

Gordon, Edwin E. *Predictive Validity Studies of the Intermediate Measures of Music Audiation and the Instrument Timbre Preference Test.* Chicago: GIA, 1989.

Gordon, Edwin. *The Psychology of Music Teaching.* Shanghai: The Shanghai Music Press, 1989.

Gordon, Edwin E. *A Music Learning Theory for Newborn and Young Children.* Chicago: GIA, 1997, 1990.

Gordon, Edwin E. *Predictive Validity Study of AMMA.* Chicago: GIA, 1990.

Gordon, Edwin E. "Two New Tests of Music Aptitude: Advanced Measures of Music Audiation and Audie," *Measurement and Evaluation,* 10 (Spring 1990), 1-4.

Gordon, Edwin E. "Nowe testy badania zdolnosci muzycznych." *The International Seminar of Researchers and Lectures in the Psychology of Music,* Akademia Muzyczna im. Fryderyka Chopina. Warszawa, Poland, (1990), 300-310.

Gordon, Edwin E. "A Study of the Characteristics of the Instrument Timbre Preference Test," *Council for Research in Music Education,* 110 (1991), 33-51.

Gordon, Edwin E. *The Advanced Measures of Music Audiation and the Instrument Timbre Preference Test: Three Research Studies.* Chicago: GIA, 1991.

Gordon, Edwin E. "A Study of the Characteristics of the Instrument Timbre Preference Test," *Courcil for Research in Music Education,* 110 (1991), 35-51.

Gordon, Edwin E. "Is It Only in Academics that Americans Are Lagging?" *The American Music Teacher,* 37, 5, (December/January 1992-93), 24, 25, 80-83.

Gordon, Edwin E." A Comparison of Scores on the 1971 and 1993 Editions of the Iowa Tests of Music Literacy: Implications for Music Education," *GIML Monograph Series,* 1, 1994, 7-32.

Gordon, Edwin E. "Selecting an Appropriate String Instrument for Study Using the Instrument Timbre Preference Test," *GIML Monograph Series,* 1 1994, 33-47.

Gordon, Edwin E. "The Role of Music Aptitude in Early Childhood Music," *Early Childhood Connections,* 1, 1 & 2, (Winter, 1995), 14-21.

Gordon, Edwin E. "Testing Musical Aptitudes from Preschool Through College," *Psychology of Music Today,* Frederyk Chopin Academy of Music, Warsaw, (1995), 170-176.

Gordon, Edwin E. "Early Childhood Music Education: Life or Death? No, a Matter of Birth and Life," *Early Childhood Connections,* 2, 4, (Fall, 1996), 7-13.

Gordon, Edwin E. *Harmonic Improvisation Readiness Record.* Chicago: GIA, 1996. 7404 South Mason Avenue, Chicago, Illinois 60638. 800 442 1358 or 708 496 3800.

Gordon, Edwin E. "Taking Another Look at the Established Procedure for Scoring the Advanced Measures of Music Audiation," *GIML Monograph Series*, 2, 1997, 72-88.

Gordon, Edwin. *A Music Learning Theory for Newborn and Young Children.* Kraków: Wydawninctwo amiast Korepetycji, 1997.

Gordon, Kate. "Some Tests on the Memorizing of Musical Themes," *Journal of Experimental Psychology*, 2 (1917), 93-99.

Gould, Stephen Jay. *The Mismeasure of Man.* New York: W. W. Norton, 1981.

Gray, Clarence T. and C. Walter Bingham. "A Comparison of Certain Phases of Musical Ability in Colored and White School Pupils," *Journal of Educational Psychology*, 20 (1929), 501-506.

Gross, Bella and Robert H. Seashore. "Psychological Characteristics of Student and Professional Musical Composers," *Journal of Applied Psychology*, 25 (1941), 159-170.

Haecker, V. and Theodor. Ziehen. Über die Erblichkeit der musikalischen Begabung," *Zeitschrift für Psychologie*, 33 (1925), 191-214.

Haecker, V. and Theodor Ziehen. "Beitrag zur Lehre von der Vererbung und Analyse der zeichnerischen und mathematischen Begabung insbesondere mit Bezug auf die Korrelation zur musikalischen Begabung." *Zeitschrift für Psychologie und Physiologie der Sinnesorgane*, 79 (1930), 1-45.

Hargreaves, David J. *The Developmental Psychology of Music.* Cambridge: Cambridge University Press, 1986.

Hargreaves, David J. and Adrian C. North, eds. *The Social Psychology of Music.* New York: Oxford University Press, 1997

Harrington, Charles. "An Investigation of the Primary Level Musical Aptitude Profile for Use with Second and Third Grade Students," *Journal of Research in Music Education*, 17 (1969), 193-201.

Harrison, Carole S. "Predicting Music Theory Grades: The Relative Efficiency of Academic Ability, Music Experience, and Music Aptitude," *Journal of Research in Music Education*, 38 (1990), 124-137.

Harrison, Carole S. "Relationships Between Grades in the Components of Freshman Music Theory and Selected Background Variables," *Journal of Research in Music Education*, 38 (1990), 175-186.

Harrison, Carole S., Edward Asmus, and Richard Serpe. "Effects of Musical Aptitude, Academic Ability, Music Experience, and Motivation on Aural Skills," *Journal of Research in Music Education*, 42 (1994), 131-144.

Hatfield, Warren. *An Investigation of the Diagnostic Validity of MAP with Respect to Instrumental Performance.* Diss. Iowa City: University of Iowa, 1967.

Heinlein, Christian Paul. "A Brief Discussion of the Nature and Function of Melodic Configuration in Tonal Memory with Critical Reference to the Seashore Tonal Memory Test," *Pedagogical Seminary and Journal of Genetic Psychology*, 35 (1928), 45-61.

Heinlein, Christian Paul. "An Experimental Study of the Seashore Consonance Test," *Journal of Experimental Psychology*, 8 (1928), 408-433.

Heinlein, Christian Paul. "A New Method of Studying the Rhythmic Responses of Children," *Journal of Genetic Psychology*, 36 (1929), 205-228.

Heller, Jack. *The Effects of Formal Training on Wing Musical Intelligence Scores.* Diss. Iowa City: University of Iowa, 1962.

Hevner, Kate. "Appreciation of Music and Tests for the Appreciation of Music," *Studies in the Appreciation of Art,"* 4 (1934), 83-151.

Hevner, Kate, John Landsbury, and Robert Seashore. *Oregon Music Discrimination Test.* Chicago: Stoelting, 1936.

Highsmith, James Albert. "Selecting Musical Talent," *Journal of Applied Psychology*, 13 (1929), 486-493.

Hobbs, Christine. "A Comparison of the Music Aptitude, Scholastic Aptitude, and Academic Achievement of Young Children," *Psychology of Music*, 13 (1985), 93-98.

Hodges, Donald A., ed. *Handbook of Music Psychology.* Lawrence, Kansas: National Association for Music Therapy, 1995.

Hoffren, James. *The Construction and Validation of a Test of Expressive Phrasing in Music.* Diss. Urbana: University of Illinois, 1963.

Holahan, John. *The Effects of Four Conditions of 'Same' and 'Different' Instruction on the Developmental Music Aptitudes of Kindergarten Children.* Diss. Philadelphia: Temple University, 1983.

Holahan, John and Selma Thomson. "An Investigation of the Suitability of the Primary Measures of Music Audiation for Use in England," *Psychology of Music*, 9 (1981), 63-68.

Hollingsworth, Leta. "Musical Sensitivity of Children Who Score Above 135 I.Q.," *Journal of Educational Psychology*, 17 (1926), 95-109.

Holmes, James. "Increased Reliabilities, New Keys, and New Norms for a Modified Kwalwasser-Dykema Test of Musical Aptitudes," *Journal of Genetic Psychology*, 85 (1954), 65-73.

Holström, Lars Gunnar. *Musicality and Prognosis.* Studia Scientia Pedagogical Upsaliensia 5. Stockholm: Svenska Bokforlaget, 1963.

Horner, V. *Music Education.* Hawthorne, Victoria: Australian Council for Educational Research, 1965.

Howell, Peter, Ian Cross, and Robert West, eds. *Musical Structure and Cognition.* New York: Academic Press, 1986.

Howes, Frank. *The Borderland of Music and Psychology.* London: Oxford University Press, 1927.

Hufstader, Ronald A. "Predicting Success in Beginning Instrumental Music Through the Use of Selected Tests," *Journal of Research in Music Education*, 22 (1974), 52-57.

Humphreys, Jere. "Precursors of Musical Aptitude Testing: From the Greeks Through the Works of Francis Galton," *Journal of Research in Music Education*, 41 (1993), 315-327.

Jacobs, C. "Psychology of Music: European Studies," *ACTA Psychology*, 1 (1960), 273-296.

Jessup, Linda. *The Comparative Effects of Direct and Indirect Music Teaching Upon the Developmental Music Aptitude and Music Achievement of Early Primary Grade Children.* Diss. Philadelphia: Temple University, 1984.

Johnson, Guy Benton. "Musical Talent and the American Negro," *Music Supervisors Journal,* 81 (1928), 13, 86.

Johnson, Guy Benton. "A Summary of Negro Scores on the Seashore Music Talent Tests," *Journal of Comparative Psychology,* 11 (1931), 383-393.

Juhacz, Andor. "Zur Analyse des musikalischen Wiedererkennens," *Zeitschrift für Psychologie,* 55 (1924), 142-180.

Kane, Maryanne. *The Effects of Teacher Training Upon the Developmental Music Aptitude and Music Achievement of Kindergarten Children.* Diss. Philadelphia: Temple University, 1993.

Karlin, J. E. "Factor Analysis in the Field of Music," *Journal of Musicology,* 3 (1941), 41-52.

Karlin, J. E. "A Factorial Study of Auditory Function," *Psychometrika,* 7 (1942), 251-279.

Karma, Kai. "Musical Aptitude as the Ability to Structure Acoustic Material." *The International Journal of Music Education,* 3 (May, 1984), 27-30.

Karma, Kai. "Components of Auditive Structuring-Towards a Theory of Musical Aptitude," *Council for Research in Music Education,* 82 (1985), 1-13.

Karma, Kai. "Item Difficulty Values in Measuring Components of Music Aptitude," *Council for Research in Music Education,* 89 (1986), 18-31.

Karma, Kai. "Auditory and Visual Temporal Structuring: How Important is Sound to Musical Thinking?" *Psychology of Music,* 22 (1994), 20-30.

Kehrberg, Donald A. "An Investigation of the Relationships Between Musical Aptitude, General Music Achievement, Attitude Toward Music, School Music Participation, School Music Achievement, and Students' Outside-of-School Environment in a Rural Ethnic Community," *Council for Research in Music Education,* 100 (1989), 68-72.

Kemp, Anthony E. *The Musical Temperament.* Oxford: Oxford University Press, 1996.

Kerman, Joseph. *Contemplating Music.* Cambridge: Harvard University Press, 1985.

Koch, Hans and Fridjok Mjøen. "Die Erblichkeit der Musikalität." *Zeitschrift für Psychologie und Physiologie der Sinnesorgane,* 80 (1931), 136-140.

Kovácz, Sandor. "Untersuchungen über das musikalische Gedächtnis," *Zeitschrift für Angewandte Psychologie,* 11 (1916), 113-135.

Kretschmer, Ernst. *The Psychology of Men of Genius.* New York: Harcourt Brace Jovanovich, 1931.

Kwalwasser, Jacob. *Tests of Melodic and Harmonic Sensitivity.* Camden: Victor Talking Machine Company, 1926.

Kwalwasser, Jacob. *Tests and Measurements in Music.* Boston: C. C. Birchard, 1927.

Kwalwasser, Jacob. *Kwalwasser Music Talent Test.* New York: Mills Music, 1953.

Kwalwasser, Jacob. *Exploring the Musical Mind.* New York: Coleman-Ross, 1955.

Kwalwasser, Jacob and Peter Dykema. *Kwalwasser-Dykema Music Tests,* New York: Carl Fischer, 1930.

Lamp, Charles and Noel Keys. "Can Aptitude for Specific Music Instruments be Predicted?" *Journal of Educational Psychology,* 26 (1935), 587-596.

Larson, Delia Louise. "An Experimental Critique of the Seashore Consonance Test," *Psychological Monographs, 38 (1928), 49-81.*

Larson, Ruth Crewdson. *Studies on Seashore's Measures of Musical Talent.* Studies on Aims and Progress of Research 2. Iowa City: University of Iowa, 1930.

Larson, William. *Measurement of Musical Talent for the Prediction of Success in Instrumental Music.* Studies in the Psychology of Music. Iowa City: University of Iowa, 1930.

Lawshe, Charles and Wendell Wood. "Membership in Musical Organizations as a Criterion of Talent," *American Journal of Psychology,* 60 (1947), 250-253.

Lee, Robert. "An Investigation of the Use of the Musical Aptitude Profile with College and University Freshman Music Students," *Journal of Research in Music Education,* 15 (1967), 32-40.

Lehman, Charles. "A Comparative Study of Instrumental Musicians on the Basis of the Otis Intelligence Test, the Kwalwasser-Dykema Music Test, and Minnesota Multiphasic Personality Inventory," *Journal of Educational Research,* 44 (1950), 57-61.

Lehman, Charles. "A Study of Musically Superior and Inferior Subjects as Selected by the Kwalwasser-Dykema Tests," *Journal of Educational Research,* 45 (1952), 517-522.

Lehman, Paul R. *Tests and Measurements in Music.* Englewood Cliffs: Prentice Hall, 1968.

Lehman, Paul R. "The Predictive Measurement of Musical Success," *Journal of Research in Music Education,* 17 (1969), 16-31.

Lenoire, Z. *Measurement of Racial Differences in Certain Mental and Educational Abilities.* Diss. Iowa City: University of Iowa, 1925.

Leopold, P. Musical Savants: *Implications for the Relation Between Music and Language.* Diss. Chicago: University of Illinois, 1997.

Levendusky, Neil. "The Theoretical Relationship Between Item Difficulty and the 'In Doubt' Response in Music Tests,"*Journal of Research in Music Education,* 27 (1979), 163-172.

Lewis, Don H. "The Construction of a Timbre Test," *Psychological Record,* 9 (1939), 117-136.

Lifton, Walter. "The Development of a Music Reaction Test to Measure Affective and Aesthetic Sensitivity," *Journal of Research in Music Education,* 9 (1961), 157-166.

Long, Newell. "A Revision of the University of Oregon Music Discrimination Test," Diss. Bloomington: Indiana University, 1965.

Lowery, Harry. "Cadence and Phrase Tests in Music," *British Journal of Psychology,* 17 (1926), 111-118.

Lowery, Harry. "Music Memory," *British Journal of Psychology,* 19 (1929), 397-404.

Lowery, Harry. "Estimation of Musical Capacity," *Proceedings of the Manchester Library and Philosophical Society,* 6 (1932), 53.

Lowery, Harry. "On the Integrative Theory of Musical Talent," *Journal of Musicology,* 2 (1940), 1-14.

Lowery, Harry. *The Background of Music.* London: Hutchinson, 1952.

Lundin, Robert W. "Preliminary Report on Some New Tests of Musical Ability," *Journal of Applied Psychology,* 28 (1944), 393-396.

Lundin, Robert W. "The Development and Validation of a Set of Musical Ability Tests," *Psychological Monographs,* 63 (1949), 1-20.

Lundin, Robert W. *An Objective Psychology of Music.* New York: Ronald Press, 1967.

Madison, Thurber H. "Interval Discrimination as a Measure of Musical Aptitude" *Archives of Psychology,* (1942), 268.

Mainwaring, James. "Experiments in the Analysis of Cognitive Processes Involved in Musical Ability and in Music Education," *British Journal of Educational Psychology,* 1 (1931), 180-203.

Mainwaring, James. "Tests of Musical Ability," *British Journal of Educational Psychology,* 1 (1931), 313-321.

Mainwaring, James. "The Assessment of Musical Ability," *British Journal of Educational Psychology,* 17 (1947), 83-96.

Mainwaring, James. "Psychological Factors in the Teaching of Music," *British Journal of Educational Psychology,* 21 (1951), 105-121, 199-213.

Malmberg, Constantine F. "The Perception of Consonance and Dissonance," *Iowa Studies in the Psychology of Music,* 7 (1918), 93-133.

Manzer, Charles and Samuel Morowitz. "The Performance of a Group of College Students on the Kwalwasser-Dykema Music Tests," *Journal of Applied Psychology,* 19 (1935), 331-346.

Martin, James. "Aptitude Test Score Changes Following Musical Training," *Journal of Educational Research,* 57 (1964), 440-442.

McAdams, Stephen and Emmanuel Bigand, eds. *Thinking in Sound.* Oxford: Clarendon Press, 1993.

McCarthy, Dorothea. "A Study of the Seashore Measures of Musical Talent," *Journal of Applied Psychology,* 14 (1930), 437-455.

McCrystal, Richard. *A Validity Study of the Advanced Measures of Music Audiation Among Undergraduate College Music Majors.* Diss. Philadelphia: Temple University, 1994.

McGinnis, Esther. "Seashore Measures of Musical Talent Applied to Children of Pre-School Age," *American Journal of Psychology,* 40 (1928), 620-623.

McLeish, John. "The Validation of Seashore's Measures of Musical Talent by Factorial Methods," *British Journal of Psychology, Statistical Section,* 3 (1950), 129-140.

McLeish, John. *The Factor of Musical Cognition in Wing's and Seashore's Tests.* Music Education Research Papers 2. London: Novello, 1968.

McLeish, John and Geoffrey Higgs. "Musical Ability and Mental Subnormality: An Experimental Investigation," *British Journal of Educational Psychology,* 52 (1982), 370-373.

Meyer, Leonard B. *Emotion and Meaning in Music.* Chicago: University of Chicago Press, 1956.

Meyer, Max. "Experimental Studies in the Psychology of Music," *American Journal of Psychology*, 14 (1903), 192-214.

Meyer, Max. "Special Ability Tests as Used in Missouri: Including a Demonstration of a Typical Test," *Psychological Bulletin*, 21 (1924), 114-116.

Miceli, Jennifer Scott. *An Investigation of an Audiation Based High School General Music Curriculum and its Relationship to Music Aptitude, Music Achievement and Student Perception of Learning.* Diss. Rochester: Eastman School of Music, 1998.

Michel, Paul. "Optimum Development of Musical Abilities in the First Years of Life," *Psychology of Music*, 2 (1973), 14-20.

Miller, Leon K. *Musical Savants.* Hillsdale, New Jersey: LEA Associates, 1989.

Miller, Leon K. "Assessment of Musical Aptitude in People with a Handicap," *Mental Retardation*, 29 (1991), 175-185.

Miller, Richard. "Über musikalische Begabung und ihre Beziehung zu sonstigen Anlagen," *Zeitschrift für Psychologie*, 97 (1966), 243-253.

Mitchell, Deborah H. *The Influence of Preschool Musical Development on the Development of Tonal Memory.* Diss. Los Angeles: University of Southern California, 1985.

Mjøen, Jan Alfred and Fridjok Mjøen. "Die Bedeutung der Tonhöhenunterschiedsempfindlickeit für die Musikalität und ihr Verhalten bei der Vererbung." *Hereditas*, 7 (1926), 161-188.

Mohatt, James. *A Study of the Validity of the Iowa Tests of Music Literacy.* Diss. Iowa City: University of Iowa, 1971.

Monroe, Will S. "Tone Perception and Music Interest of Young Children," *Pedagogical Seminary*, 10 (1903), 144-146.

Montesssori, Maria. *The Advanced Montessori Method.* New York: Stokes, 1917.

Moore, Henry. "The Genetic Aspect of Consonance and Dissonance," *Psychological Monographs*, 17 (1914), 1-68.

Moore, Janet L. S. *Rhythm and Movement: An Objective Analysis of Their Association with Music Aptitude.* Diss. Greensboro: University of North Carolina, 1984.

Moore, Ray. "The Relationship of Intelligence to Creativity," *Journal of Research in Music Education*, 14 (1966), 243-253.'

Moorhead, Evelyn and Donald Pond. *Music of Young Children.* Santa Barbara, California: Pilsbury Foundation for Advancement of Music Education, 1978.

More, Grace Van Dyke. "Prognostic Testing in Music on the College Level," *Journal of Educational Research*, 26 (1932), 199-212.

Morrow, Robert. "An Analysis of the Relations Among Tests of Musical, Artistic, and Mechanical Abilities," *Journal of Psychology*, 5 (1938), 253-263.

Mursell, James L. "Measuring Musical Ability and Achievement: A Study of the Correlations of Seashore Test Scores and Other Variables," *Journal of Educational Research*, 26 (1932), 116-126.

Mursell, James L. *The Psychology of Music.* New York: W. W. Norton, 1937.

Mursell, James L. "Intelligence and Musicality," *Education,* 59 (1939), 559-562.
Mursell, James L. *Psychological Testing.* New York: Longmans, Green, 1947.
Nelson, David J, Anthony L. Barresi, and Janet R. Barrett. "Musical Cognition within
    an Analogical Setting: Toward a Cognitive Component of Musical Aptitude
    in Children," *Psychology of Music,* 20 (1992), 70-79.
Nielson, J. T. "A Study in the Seashore Motor-Rhythm Test," *Psychological
    Monographs,* 40 (1930), 74-84.
Nierman, Glenn E. and Michael H. Veak. "Effect of Selected Recruiting Strategies on
    Beginning Instrumentalists' Participation Decisions," *Journal of Research
    in Music Education,* 45 (1997), 380-389.
Norton, Doris. "Interrelationships Among Music Aptitude, IQ, and Auditory
    Conservation," *Journal of Research in Music Education,* 28 (1980),
    207-217.
Noy, Pinchas. "The Development of Musical Ability," *Psychoanalytic Study of
    the Child,* 23 (1968), 332-347.
Obler, Loraine and Deborah Fine, eds. *The Exceptional Brain: Neurophysiology of
    Talent and Special Abilities.* New York: Guilford, 1988.
Ogden, Charles K. and Armstrong Richards. *The Meaning of Music.* New York:
    Harcourt, Brace, 1952.
O'Hagin, Isabel Barbara. *The Effects of a Discovery Approach to Movement
    Instruction on Children's Responses to Musical Stimuli.* Diss. Tuscon:
    University of Arizona, 1997.
Orsmond, G. and L. Miller. "Correlates of Musical Improvisation in Children with
    Dissabilities," *Journal of Music Therapy,* 32 (1995), 152-166.
Ortmann, Otto. "A Dynamograph," *Journal of Experimental Psychology,* 8
    (1925), 160-165.
Ortmann, Otto. "On the Melodic Relativity of Tones," *Psychological
    Monographs,* 35 (1926), 1-47.
Owens, William A. and W. Grimm. "A Note Regarding Exceptional Musical Ability
    in a Low-Grade Imbecile," *Journal of Educational Psychology,* 32 (1941),
    636-637.
Pannenborg, H. J. and W. A. Pannenborg. "Die Psychologie des Musikers,"
    Zeitschrift für Psychologie, 17 (1915), 91-136.
Parker, Olin. "A Study of the Relationship of Aesthetic Sensitivity to Musical Ability,
    Intelligence, and Economic Status," Lawrence: University of Kansas, 1961.
Peacock, Wesley. *A Comparative Study of Musical Talent in Whites and Negroes
    and Its Correlation with Intelligence.* Diss. Atlanta: Emory University,
    1928.
Pear, Tom Hatherly. "The Classification of Observers as 'Musical' and 'Unmusical',"
    British Journal of Psychology, 4 (1911), 89-94.
Peterson, Joseph and Lyle Lanier. "Studies in Comparative Abilities of Whites and
    Negroes, "*Mental Measurements Monographs,* 5 (1929), 31-42.
Pettit, Raymond Charles. *An Investigation of the Construct Validity and Factor
    Structure of the Primary Measures of Music Audiation Through Structural
    Equation Modeling.* Diss. Urbana-Champaign: University of Illinois, 1996.

Phillips, David. "An Investigation of the Relationship Between Musicality and Intelligence," *Psychology of Music,* 4 (1976), 16-31.

Piaget, Jean. *Construction of Reality in the Child.* New York: Basic Books, 1954.

Piaget, Jean. *Origins of Intelligence in Children.* trans. Margaret Cook. New York: W. W. Norton, 1963.

Pinkerton, Frank. "Talent Tests and Their Application to the Public School Instrumental Program," *Journal of Research in Music Education,* 10 (1963), 75-80.

Polakowski, Krzysztof. "The Concepts of Musicality," *Psychologia Wychowawcza,* 12 (1969), 421-433.

Porter, Raymond. *A Study of the Musical Talent of the Chinese Attending Public Schools in Chicago.* Chicago: University of Chicago Press, 1931.

Radocy, Rudolf E. and J. David Boyle. *Psychological Foundations of Musical Behavior.* Springfield, Illinois: Charles C. Thomas, 1979.

Raffman, Diana. *Language, Music and Mind.* Cambridge, Massachusetts: MIT Press, 1993.

Raim, Rolland. *A Comparison of the Musical Aptitude Profile and the Seashore Measures of Musical Talents.* Thesis. Iowa City: University of Iowa, 1965.

Rainbow, Bernarr. *Music in Educational Thought and Practice.* Aberystwyth Dyfed, Wales: Boethius Press, 1990.

Rainbow, Edward. "A Pilot Study to Investigate the Constructs of Musical Aptitude," *Journal of Research in Music Education,* 13 (1965), 3-14.

Redfield, John. *Music: A Science and an Art.* New York: Alfred A. Knopf, 1928.

Révész, Geza. *The Psychology of a Musical Prodigy.* New York: Brace Jovanovich, 1925.

Révész, Geza. *Introduction to the Psychology of Music.* trans. G. I. C. deCourcy. Norman: University of Oklahoma Press, 1954.

Reynolds, Alison. *An Investigation of Processes for Measuring Music Audiation Skills of Kindergarten Students.* Thesis. Philadelphia: Temple University, 1990.

Reynolds, Alison. "A Study of the Relationship Between Peabody Picture Vocabulary Test Scores and Primary Measures of Music Audiation Scores for Kindergarten Students," *Bulletin of Research in Music Education,* 18 (1992), 44-49.

Rhone, Jeffrey. *A Comparison of Sine-Wave and Child Voice Timbre on the Kindergarten Child's Ability to Discriminate Tonal Patterns.* Thesis. West Hartford: Hartt School of Music, 1997.

Ribke, Juliane. *Musikalität als Variable von Intelligenz, Denken und Erleben.* Hamburg: Karl Dieter Wagner, 1979.

Rice, James. "Abbreviated Gordon Musical Aptitude Profile with EMR Children," *American Journal of Mental Deficiency,* 7 (1970), 107-108.

Robinson, Viola and Mary Holmes. *A Comparison of Negroes and Whites in Musical Ability.* Diss. Syracuse: Syracuse University, 1932.

Roby, A. Richard. "A Study in the Correlation of Music Theory Grades with the Seashore Measures of Musical Talents and the Aliferis Music Achievement Test," *Journal of Research in Music Education,* 10 (1962), 137-142.

Rodrigues, Helena. *The Evaluation of the Music Aptitude of Primary Grade Children: The Standardization of the Intermediate Measures of Music Audiation in Lisbon.* Diss. Coimbra, Portugal: Faculdade de Psicologia e de Ciências da Educação, Universidade de Coimbra, 1977.

Romaine, Robert. *A Comparative Study of Iowa Tests of Music Literacy Norms for United States Dependent Students Attending School in Frankfurt, Germany and Norms for Students Who Participated in the Standardization of the Test Battery.* Diss. Iowa City: University of Iowa, 1973.

Ross, Verne "Musical Talents of Indian and Japanese Children," *Journal of Juvenile Research,* 20 (1936), 133-136.

Rowell, Lewis. *Thinking About Music.* Amherst: University of Massachusetts Press, 1983.

Rowntree, John. "A Longitudinal Study of Musical Development," *Psychology of Music,* 1 (1973), 29-32.

Rupp, Hans. "Über die Prüfung musikalischer Fähigkeiten," *Zeitschrift für experimentelle und angewandte Psychologie,* 9 (1911), 1-76.

Ryan, Patricia M. *A Investigation of the Inverse and Criterion-Related Validity of Audie.* Thesis. West Hartford, Hartt School of Music, 1992.

Saetveit, Joseph, Don Lewis, and Carl E. Seashore. *Revision of the Seashore Measures of Musical Talent.* Series on Aims and Progress of Research 65. Iowa City: University of Iowa, 1940.

Sanderson, Helen. "Differences in Musical Ability in Children of Different National and Racial Origins," *Journal of Genetic Psychology,* 42 (1933), 100-120.

Saunders, Thomas Clark and John Holahan. "Computerized Response Procedure to Assess Young Student Reaction Times of Judgments of Sameness and Difference Among Paired Tonal Patterns," *Council for Research in Music Education,* 115 (1993), 31-48.

Schienfeld, Amram. *The New Heredity and You.* London: Chatto and Windus, 1956.

Schleuter, Stanley. "An Investigation of the Interrelation of Personality Traits, Musical Aptitude, and Musical Achievement," *Experimental Research in the Psychology of Music: Studies in the Psychology of Music,* 8 (1972), 90-102.

Schleuter, Stanley. "An Analysis of the Use of the 'In Doubt' Response by University Students on the Musical Aptitude Profile and the Iowa Tests of Music Literacy," *Psychology in the Schools,* 4 (1975), 481-483.

Schleuter, Stanley. "The Development of a College Version of the Musical Aptitude Profile," *Psychology of Music,* 6 (1978), 39-42.

Schleuter, Stanley and Lois Schleuter. "A Predictive Study of an Experimental College Version of the Musical Aptitude Profile with Music Achievement of Non-Music Majors," *Contributions to Music Education,* 6 (1978), 2-8.

Schmidt, Charles and Barbara Lewis. "A Validation Study of the Instrument Timbre Preference Test," *Psychology of Music,* 16 (1988), 143-155.

Schmidt, Charles and Jean Sinor. "An Investigation of the Relationships Among Music Audiation, Musical Creativity, and Cognitive Style," *Journal of Research in Music Education,* 34 (1986), 160-172.

Schoen, Max. "Validity of Tests of Musical Talent," *Journal of Comparative Psychology,* 3 (1923), 101-121.

Schoen, Max. "Tests of Musical Feeling and Musical Understanding," *Journal of Comparative Psychology,* 5 (1925), 31-52.

Schoen, Max. *The Psychology of Music.* New York: Ronald Press, 1940.

Schoenoff, Arthur. *An Investigation of the Comparability of American and German Norms for the Musical Aptitude Profile.* Diss. Iowa City: University of Iowa, 1973.

Schussler, H. "Das unmusikalische Kind." *Zeitschrift für Angewandte Psychologie,* 11 (1916), 136-166.

Sears, Charles. "Studies in Rhythm," *Pedigogical Seminary,* 8 (1901), 3-44.

Sears, Charles. "A Contribution to the Psychology of Rhythm," *American Journal of Psychology,* 13 (1902), 28-61.

Seashore, Carl E. "Hearing and Discriminative Sensibility for Pitch,"*Studies in Psychology.* Iowa City: University of Iowa, 2 (1899), 55-64.

Seashore, Carl E. "Motor Ability, Reaction Time, Rhythm, and Time Sense,"*Studies in Psychology.* Iowa City: University of Iowa, 2 (1899), 64-84.

Seashore, Carl E. "The Measurement of Pitch Discrimination: A Preliminary Report," *Psychological Monographs,* 53 (1910), 21-60.

Seashore, Carl E. *Seashore Measures of Musical Talent.* New York: Columbia Graphophone Company, 1919.

Seashore, Carl E.*The Psychology of Musical Talent.* New York: Silver Burdett, 1919.

Seashore, Carl E. *A Survey of Musical Talent in the Public Schools.* Studies in Child Welfare 1. Iowa City: University of Iowa, 1920.

Seashore, Carl E. "Measures of Musical Talent, A Reply to Dr. Heinlein," *Psychological Review,* 37 (1930), 178-183.

Seashore, Carl E. "Two Types of Attitude Toward the Evaluation of Musical Talent," *Music Educators Journal,* 24 (1937), 14-16.

Seashore, Carl E. *The Psychology of Music.* New York: McGraw-Hill, 1938.

Seashore, Carl E., Don Lewis, and Joseph Saetveit. *Seashore Measures of Musical Talents.* Camden, New Jersey: RCA Manufacturing Company, 1939.

Seashore, Carl E., Don Lewis, and Joseph Saetveit. *Seashore Measures of Musical Talents.* New York: Psychological Corporation, 1957.

Seashore, Carl E. and G. Mount. "Correlations of Factors in Musical Talent and Training," *Psychological Monographs,* 25 (1918), 47-92.

Seashore, Robert H. "Improvability of Pitch Discrimination," *Psychological Bulletin,* 32 (1935), 545.

Sell, Vernon. *The Musical Aptitude of Finnish Students: An Investigative Study in Comparative Music Education.* Diss. Madison: University of Wisconsin, 1976.

Semeonoff, Boris. "A New Approach to the Testing of Musical Ability," *British Journal of Psychology,* 30 (1940), 326-340.

Semeonoff, Boris. "Further Developments in a New Approach to the Testing of Musical Ability, with Special Reference to Groups of Secondary School Children," *British Journal of Psychology,* 31 (1940), 145-161.

Serafine, Mary Louise. *Music as Cognition.* New York: Columbia University Press, 1988.

Sergeant, Desmond and Gillian Thatcher. "Intelligence, Social Status, and MusicalAbilities," *Psychology of Music,* 2 (1947), 32-57.

Shuter-Dyson, Rosamund and Clive Gabriel. *The Psychology of Musical Ability.* London: Methuen, 1981.

Simmons, Christine Hughes. *An Investigation of the Relationships Among Primary-Level Student Performance on Selected Measures of Music Aptitude.* Diss. Nashville: George Peabody College for Teachers of Vanderbilt University, 1981.

Simons, Gene. *Simons Measurements of Music Listening Skills.* Chicago: Stoelting, 1974.

Sloboda, John. *The Musical Mind.* Oxford: Clarendon Press, 1985.

Spearman, Charles. "General Intelligence Objectively Determined and Measured," *American Journal of Psychology,* 15, 2 (1904), 201-293.

Spearman, Charles. *The Abilities of Man, Their Nature and Measurement,* London: Macmillan, 1927.

Squire, R. C. "Genetic Study of Rhythm," *American Journal of Psychology,* 1 (1930), 492-589.

Squires, Paul C. "The Creative Psychology of Carl Maria von Weber," *Character and Personality,* 6 (1938), 203-217.

Squires, Paul C. "The Creative Psychology of Cesar Franck," *Character and Personality,* 7 (1938), 41-49.

Squires, Paul C. "The Creative Psychology of Chopin," *Journal of Musicology,* 2 (1940), 27-37.

Smith, Franklin O. "The Effect of Training in Pitch Discrimination," *Psychological Monographs,* 16 (1914), 67-103.

Smith, Olin W. "Relationship of Rhythm Discrimination to Meter and Rhythm Performance," *Journal of Applied Psychology,* 41 (1957), 365-369.

Stanton, Hazel. "The Inheritance of Specific Musical Capacities," *Psychological Monographs,* 31 (1922), 157-204.

Stanton, Hazel and Wilhelmine Koerth. *Musical Capacity Measures of Children Repeated After Musical Training.* Studies on Aims and Progress of Research 42. Iowa City: University of Iowa, 1933.

Stanmou, Lelouda. *The Effect of Suzuki Instruction and Early Musical Experiences on the Developmental Music Aptitude and Performance Achievement of Beginning Suzuki Students.* Diss. East Lansing: Michigan State University, 1998.

Stanton, Hazel. *Measurement of Musical Talent: The Eastman Experiment.* Studies in the Psychology of Music 2. Iowa City: University of Iowa, 1935.

Streep, Rosalind. "A Comparison of White and Negro Children in Rhythm and Consonance," *Journal of Applied Psychology,* 15 (1931), 53-71.

Stumpf, Carl. "Akustische Versuche mit Pepito Areola," *Zeitschrift für Experimentelle und Angewandte Psychologie,* 2 (1909), 1-11.

Stumpf, Carl. *Die Anfänge der Musik.* Leipzig: Barth, 1911.

Suzuki, Shinichi. *Nurtured by Love.* trans. Waltraud Suzuki. New York: Exposition Press, 1969.

Swadley, Ellis. *A Study of the Correlation Between the Measurements of Musical Talent by C. E. Seashore and the Musical Memory Test by Raleigh M. Drake.* Diss. Muncie, Indiana: Ball State Teachers College, 1948.

Swanwick, Keith. "Musical Cognition and Aesthetic Response," *Bulletin of the British Psychological Society,* 26 (1973), 285-289.

Swanwick, Keith. *Music, Mind, and Education.* London: Routledge, 1988.

Sward, Keith T. "Jewish Musicality in America," *Journal of Applied Psychology,* 17 (1933), 675-712.

Swinchoski, Albert. "A Standardized Music Achievement Test Battery for the Intermediate Grades," *Journal of Research in Music Education,* 13 (1965), 159-168.

Swindell, Warren. *An Investigation of the Adequacy of the Content and Difficulty Levels of the Iowa Tests of Music Literacy.* Diss. Iowa City: University of Iowa, 1970.

Swisher, Walter. *Psychology for the Music Teacher.* Boston: Oliver Ditson, 1927.

Tamaoka, Shindo. "Musical Talent Tests," *Japan Journal of Psychology,* 22 (1952), 309-321.

Tarrell, Vernon. "An Investigation of the Validity of the Musical Aptitude Profile," *Journal of Research in Music Education,* 13 (1965), 195-206.

Taylor, Elizabeth. "A Study in the Prognosis of Musical Talent," *Journal of Experimental Education,* 10 (1941), 1-28.

Taylor, Sam. "Musical Development of Children Aged Seven to Eleven," *Psychology of Music,* 1 (1973), 44-49.

Teplov, Boris M. *Psychologie des Aptitudes Musicales.* Paris: Presses Universitaires de France, 1966.

Thackray, Ruppert. "Rhythmic Abilities and Their Measurement," *Journal of Research in Music Education,* 17 (1969), 144-148.

Thayer, Robert. "The Interrelation of Personality Traits, Musical Achievement, and Different Measures of Musical Aptitude," *Experimental Research in the Psychology of Music: Studies in the Psychology of Music,* 8 (1972), 103-118.

Thorndike, Robert M., Robert C. Thorndike, George K. Cunningham, and Elizabeth Hagen. *Measurement and Evaluation in Psychology and Education.* New York: MacMillan, 1991.

Tighe, Thomas J. and W. J. Dowling. *Psychology and Music: The Understanding of Melody and Rhythm.* Hillsdale, New Jersey: Lawrence Erlbaum Associates, 1993.

Tilson, Lowell. "A Study of the Prognostic Value of the Tilson-Gretsch Test for Musical Aptitude," *Teachers College Journal,* 12 (1941), 110-112.

Valentine, Charles W. *The Experimental Psychology of Beauty.* London: Methuen, 1962.

Vance, Thomas F. and Medora B. Grandprey. "Objective Methods of Ranking Nursery Children on Certain Aspects of Musical Capacity," *Journal of Educational Psychology,* 22 (1931), 577-585.

Vernon, Philip E. "The Personality of the Composer," *Music and Letters,"* 11 (1930), 38-48.

Vernon, Philip E. "Method in Music Psychology," *American Journal of Psychology,* 42 (1930), 127-134.

Vernon, Philip E. "Auditory Perception: The Gestalt Approach," *British Journal of Psychology,* 25 (1934), 123-139.

Vernon, Philip E. "Auditory Perception: The Evolutionary Approach," *British Journal of Psychology,* 25 (1935), 265-281.

Vernon, Philip E. *The Structure of Human Abilities.* New York: John Wiley & Sons, 1950.

Vernon, Philip E. "What is Potential Ability?," *Bulletin of the British Psychological Society,* 21 (1968), 211-219.

Vidor, Martha. *Was ist Musikalität?* Munich: Beck, 1931.

Vispoel, Walter and Don Coffman. "Computerized Adaptive Testing of Music Related Skills," *Council for Research in Music Education* , 112 (1992), 29-49.

Volger, Thelma. "An Investigation to Determine Whether Learning Effects Accrue From Immediate Sequential Administrations of the Six Levels of the Iowa Tests of Music Literacy," *Experimental Research in the Psychology of Music: Studies in the Psychology of Music,* 10 (1975), 98-185.

Vygotsky, Lev S. *Thought and Language.* ed. and trans. Eugenia Haufmann and Gertrude Vakar. Cambridge: MIT Press, 1967.

Vygotsky, Lev S. *Mind in Society.* trans. Michael Cole, Vera John-Steiner, Sylvia Scribner, and Ellen Souberman. Cambridge: Harvard University Press, 1978.

Wagner, Robert. *Untersuchungen zur Entwicklung der Musikalität mit Hilfe eines Musikleistungstests.* Munich: Ernst Reinhardt, 1970.

Watkins, John. *Objective Measurement of Instrumental Performance.* Contributions to Education 860. New York: Teachers College, Columbia University, 1942.

Watkins, John and Stephen Farnum. *The Watkins-Farnum Performance Scale.* New York: Hal Leonard Music, 1954.

Weaver, Sally. *An Investigation of the Relationship Between Preferences for Natural and Synthesized Timbres.* Diss. Philadelphia: Temple University, 1987.

Webber, George H. *The Effectiveness of Musical and Nonmusical Measures as Predictors of Success in Beginning Instrumental Music.* Diss. Austin: University of Texas, 1974.

Whellams, Frederick S. "The Relative Efficiency of Aural-Musical and Non-Musical Tests as Predictors of Achievement in Instrumental Music," *Council for Research in Music Education,* 21 (1970), 15-21.

Whellams, Frederick S. "Has Musicality a Structure?" *Psychology of Music,* 1 (1973), 7-9.

Whipple, Guy M. "Studies in Pitch Discrimination," *American Journal of Psychology,* 14 (1903), 289-309.

Whistler, Harvey and Louis Thorpe. *Musical Aptitude Test.* Los Angeles: California Test Bureau, 1952.

Whitley, Mary. "A Comparison of the Seashore and Kwalwasser-Dykema Music Tests," *Teachers College Record,* 33 (1932), 731-751.

Whitley, Paul. "The Influence of Music on Memory," *Journal of General Psychology,* 10 (1934), 137-151.

Whybrew, William. *Measurement and Evaluation in Music.* Dubuque: Brown, 1962.

Wiener, M. *Effect of Home Practice on Musical Ability as Measured by Five of the Kwalwasser-Dykema Tests.* Diss. New York: City College of New York, 1938.

Williams, Clarence O. "A Critique of Measures of Musical Talent," *Music Supervisors Journal,* 16 (1929), 67, 69, 71, 73, 75, 77, 79, 81, 95.

Williams, David. "A Study of the Internal Validity of the Instrument Timbre Preference Test," *Journal of Research in Music Education,* 44 (1996), 268-277.

Williams, Harold. "An Objective Aid in the Standardization of Verbal Directions," *Pedagogical Seminary and Journal of Genetic Psychology,* 39 (1931), 289-293.

Williams, Harold. "Immediate and Delayed Memory of Pre-School Children for Pitch in Tonal Sequences," *Studies in Child Welfare,* 11 (1935), 85-95.

Williams, Harold, Clement Sievers, and Melvin Hattwick. *The Measurement of Musical Development.* Studies in Child Welfare 7. Iowa City: University of Iowa, 1932.

Williams, Robert. "Effects of Musical Aptitude, Instruction, and Social Status on Attitudes Toward Music," *Journal of Research in Music Education ,* 20 (1972), 362-369.

Wilson, Frank R. and Franz L. Roehmann. eds. *Music and Child Development.* St. Louis, Missouri: MMB Music, 1990.

Wing, Herbert. "A Factorial Study of Music Tests," *British Journal of Psychology,* 31 (1941), 341-355.

Wing, Herbert. "Tests of Musical Ability and Appreciation," *British Journal of Educational Psychology, Monograph Supplement,* 8 (1948), 1-88.

Wing, Herbert. "Some Applications of Test Results to Education in Music," *British Journal of Educational Psychology,* 24 (1954), 161-170.

Wing, Herbert. *Standardized Tests of Musical Intelligence.* Sheffield: City of Sheffield Training College, 1958.

Wing, Herbert. "A Revision of the Wing Musical Aptitude Tests," *Journal of Research in Music Education,* 10 (1962), 39-46.

Wing, Herbert. *Tests of Musical Ability and Appreciation.* Cambridge, England: University Press, 1971.

Wolner, Manuel and W. H. Pyle. "An Experiment in Individual Training in Pitch Deficient Children," *Journal of Educational Psychology,* 24 (1933), 602-608.

Woodruff, Louis. *A Predictive Validity Study of the Primary Measures of Music Audiation.* Diss. Philadelphia: Temple University, 1983.

Woodrow, Herbert. "A Quantitative Study of Rhythm: The Effect of Variations
    in Intensity and Duration," *Archives of Psychology,* 2 (1909), 1-66.
Woodrow, Herbert. "The Reproduction of Temporal Intervals," *Journal of
    Experimental Psychology,* 13 (1930), 473-499.
Woods, Roy C. and Lureata R. Martin. "Testing in Musical Education,"
    Educational and Psychological Measurement, 3 (1943), 29-42.
Wolfe, Dael. *The Discovery of Talent.* Cambridge: Harvard University Press, 1969.
Wright, Frances. "The Correlation Between Achievement and Capacity in Music,"
    Journal of Educational Research, 17 (1928), 50-56.
Wunderlich, Henry. "Theories of Tonality," *Journal of Genetic Psychology,* 37
    (1947), 169-176.
Wyatt, Ruth. "The Improvability of Pitch Discrimination," *Psychological
    Monographs,* 58 (1945), 1-58.
Young, William. "The Role of Music Aptitude, Intelligence, and Academic
    Achievement in Predicting the Music Attainment of Elementary
    Instrumental Students," *Journal of Research in Music Education,* 19
    (1971), 385-398.
Young, William. "A Statistical Comparison of Two Recent Musical Aptitude
    Tests," *Psychology in the Schools,* 19 (1972), 165-169.
Young, William. "Musical Aptitude Profile Norms for Use with College and
    University Nonmusic Majors," *Journal of Research in Music Education,*
    20 (1972), 385-390.
Young, William. "A Longitudinal Comparison of Four Music Achievement and
    Music Aptitude Tests," *Journal of Research in Music Education,* 24 (1976),
    97-109.
Zdzinski, Stephen F. "Relationships Among Parental Involvement, Musical
    Aptitude, and Musical Achievement of Instrumental Music Students,"
    Journal of Research in Music Education, 40 (1992), 114-125.
Zenatti, Arlette. "Etude de l'acculturation musicale chez l'enfant dans une épreuve
    d'identification mélodique," *Journal de Psycholgie,* 70 (1973), 453-464.
Zenatti, Arlette. *Tests Musicaux Pour Jeunes Enfants.* Issy-les-Moulineaux: Editions
    Scientifiques et Psychologiques, 1980.
Zuckerkandl, Victor. *Sound and Symbol.* trans. Willard R. Trask. New York:
    Pantheon Books, 1956.
Zuckerkandl, Victor. *Man the Musician.* trans. Norbert Guterman. Princeton,
    New Jersey: Princeton University Press, 1973.

Appendix - Explanation of Reliability and Validity

Though various types of statistics are used to interpret measurement, such as a mean, a standard deviation, and a percentile rank, the correlation coefficient is fundamental, because it can be used in a variety of ways for determining important qualities of a test. Correlation means relation. A relation between two factors may be positive or negative, or, of course, there may be no relation at all between them.

Consider test scores as factors. If two sets of scores derived from the same test administered twice to the same students, or from single administrations of two different tests, reinforce each other, they demonstrate a positive relation because they indicate that students tend to maintain their relative positions on both tests. That is, in general, students who score high on one test score high on the other, those who score average on one test score average on the other, and those who score low on one test score low on the other. When the relation is negative, high and low-scoring students tend to reverse their positions on the tests. In general, students who score high on one test score low on the other, those who score average on one test score average on the other, and those who score low on one test score high on the other. When sets of scores do not show any relation (a zero correlation), some students may have maintained their relative positions, but the positions of most others will have changed without any clear logical explanation or pattern. In that case, there is no consistency among individual student's scores on both tests, and so students' scores on one test cannot be predicted with accuracy on the basis of their scores on the other.

For a perfect positive relation, the correlation coefficient is +1.00, and for a perfect negative relation, the correlation coefficient is -.1.00. When there are relation tendencies with discrepancies, the correlation index will range from +.01 to +.99 if it is positive (the higher the coefficient, the more positive the relation) or from -.01 to -.99 if it is negative (the higher the coefficient, the more negative the correlation). If there is no relation at all, the correlation will be 0.00. Be sure not to interpret a negative relation as a zero (0.00) correlation.

The correlation between overall music aptitude test scores and general intelligence test scores is approximately +.20, a correlation not much higher than zero. That coefficient simply suggests that, because there is only a modest positive correlation between the two factors, persons with high overall music aptitude may possess almost any degree of general intelligence and persons with low overall music aptitude may possess almost any degree of general intelligence, and, of course, vice versa.

When one interprets a correlation coefficient, however, it is important to remember that the more students differ, in both the characteristics that are being tested as well as in those that may not be, such as age and past achievement, and the greater the range of the test questions in terms of levels of difficulty, the higher one can expect the correlation coefficient to be.

Above all, it is important to understand that if a relation is found between two factors, either positive or negative, it is not necessarily true that a student's standing in relation to one factor is the cause of the student's standing in relation to the other. One or more other factors may be responsible for the relation. For example, it is known that there is a positive correlation between educational achievement and school tax assessment. That fact has led some to believe that it is the advantage of a school district's relative wealth that causes student achievement to be high. That may or may not be true. What is true, however, is that home environmental influences in terms of parental interest in a child's school progress correlates positively with both educational achievement and school tax assessment. Therefore, parental interest rather than financial advantage may be the causative factor, or the cause may be a combination of the two factors or a result of one or more unknown factors.

With regard to music, there is a known positive correlation between a student's membership in a school band and the student's overall academic achievement, and so some music educators automatically assume that if students are band members they will receive high grades in most of their school subjects. That conclusion is not necessarily warranted, however, because the cause of students' outstanding educational achievement may have more to do with the fact that they are by nature highly motivated, and band may be just another activity in which they are participating. It is possible that if the students chose to pursue an activity other than band, their grade-point averages would be just as high. Negative correlations have also been reported between membership in school music ensembles and drug addiction and between membership in school music ensembles and encounters with law enforcement agencies. To draw the causative conclusion that membership in a school music ensemble will prevent students from engaging in substance abuse and from becoming involved in other unlawful pursuits may seem logical, or reasonable, but it cannot be justified simply on the basis of the correlative relations.

The primary function of a correlation coefficient in measurement is to describe test reliability and test validity. When a correlation coefficient is used to describe test reliability, it is called a reliability coefficient, and when a correlation coefficient is used to describe test validity, it is called a validity coefficient.

A test is considered to be reliable when students maintain their relative, but not necessarily their exact, score positions when the same test is administered on different days, typically during adjacent weeks, under the same administrative conditions. The magnitude of the reliability coefficient depends directly on the degree of the relation between the two sets of scores, so that the higher the positive reliability coefficient, the more reliable the test.

Different types of tests may be expected to yield different degrees of reliability. For example, because the content of a music aptitude test has less specificity than that of a music achievement test, a music aptitude test may be expected to be less reliable than a music achievement test, as is a test with many questions usually more reliable than a test with few questions. In general, a satisfactory reliability coefficient for a music achievement or music aptitude test battery (a comprehensive test that includes two or more subtests) is at least +.90 for the composite score (all subtests in the battery combined), at least +.80 for a total score (combinations of related subtests in a battery, such as two tonal subtest scores—melody and harmony—and two rhythm subtest scores—tempo and meter), and at least +.70 for each individual subtest score. That all reliability coefficients are less than perfect (+1.00) indicates that there is no test without some error of measurement. This is true for published tests as well as for teacher-made tests. There is less error of measurement with a well-designed test, however, than there is with a teacher's subjective evaluations that are not based on measurement at all.

The traditional definition of validity is considered to be as follows: "A test is valid if it measures what it purports to measure." Notwithstanding that it is the test author who determines what the test is supposed to measure, this definition may be appropriate for a test of an athlete's speed in running fifty yards, because it is obvious that such a test is measuring what it is supposed to measure, and therefore its validity need not be further investigated. Often it is difficult to prove, however, that a test measures what its author claims it measures. For example, it is not simple to prove that scores on a test of students' achievement in reading music notation, which is based on the students' ability to read a series of short phrases, are related to students' practical achievement in reading the notation of a piece of music. Even in the unlikely event that students' scores on the test and the ratings of their skill in actually reading music literature demonstrates a perfect positive correlation, without further evidence there are no grounds for concluding that the two factors represent the same skill with any more certainty than concluding that because a perfect positive relation is found between students' height and weight, height and weight are not different from each other.

Simply claiming a test is valid rather than validating the purposes for using that test are quite different matters. For example, when it has been demonstrated that students who score high on a music aptitude test before they receive formal music instruction also score high on a validity criterion, such as a music achievement test, after at least a year of formal instruction, it can be assumed that the music aptitude test has longitudinal predictive validity. That is, it will have been demonstrated that the music aptitude test may be used for the purpose of identifying those students with the greatest potential to profit from music instruction. Or if it has been demonstrated that students' scores on various subtests in a music aptitude test battery correlate highly after a year or more of formal instruction with corresponding validity criteria that are indicative of the students' musical strengths and weaknesses in music performance, it can be assumed that the subtests have diagnostic validity, and so the individual subtest scores may be used for the purpose of adapting music instruction to students' individual musical differences.

Normally, one can expect that there will be a higher relation between two sets of scores for the same test than between a set of scores on one test and a set of scores on another, which may, for example, be serving as a validity criterion for the first. Therefore, a reliability coefficient is usually higher than a validity coefficient for a given test. The extent to which the validity coefficient of a test will be lower depends in part on the reliability of the validity criterion itself. A validity criterion with a low reliability tends to reduce the validity of the test under investigation. Also, if the test itself has low reliability, its validity will tend to be reduced even more, and the more alike to one another the students to whom the test and the validity criterion are administered are, the lower the validity of the test for that group of students. It should be clear, then, that tests may be valid for one group of students but not for another. Satisfactory validity coefficients associated with composite scores for a music aptitude or music achievement test battery generally range from +.40 to +.75, the majority being +.50. Validity coefficients for total and subtest scores, because they have fewer questions, can be expected to be lower.

Theoretically, the validity coefficient for a test can be no higher, and is usually lower, than the square root of the reliability coefficient for that test. If a test is not reliable, it cannot be valid. That is, a test with a reliability coefficient of 0.00 must have a validity coefficient of 0.00. The more reliable a test is, the more valid it *may* be. For example, a test with a reliability of +.81 could have, though it is unlikely, validity as high as

+.90, but no higher, and a test with a reliability +.49 could conceivably have validity as high as +.70.

There are numerous ways to compute a correlation coefficient, identified by the symbol "r." The method used in the following example is comparatively simple and may be used with or without a calculator or a computer. Only after you understand how a correlation coefficient is computed should you use a computer to facilitate the computation, however.

The example shown here includes two sets of hypothetical test scores (X and Y) for ten students. As you can see, the first student received a score of 3 on the first test (X) and a score of 3 on the second test (Y), and so on for each student, with the mean (M) for each set of test scores at the bottom of each column. The third column (xd) indicates how each student's score deviates from the average X score, so that, for example, the first student's xd score is 0.0 because the student's X score did not deviate at all from the average X score. The third student's xd score was one point higher than the average X score, and that resulted in a positive (+) xd score +1.0. The sixth student's xd score was one point lower than the average X score, and that resulted in a negative (-) xd score -1.0. The fourth column (yd) indicates how each student's Y score deviates from the average Y score.

When negative scores are added to positive scores in a set of normally distributed scores, the theoretical result, the sum (Σ), is zero. In practice, however, particularly with small groups of students, the result is usually slightly higher than or slightly lower than zero.

The fifth column (xyd) represents each student's xd score multiplied by the student's yd score. (Any score multiplied by zero equals zero, a positive score multiplied by a negative score results in a negative score, and a negative score multiplied by another negative score results in a positive score.) The sixth column (xd^2) includes each student's xd score squared, and the seventh column (yd^2) includes each student's yd score squared.

If the sum for the xyd column is positive, the correlation coefficient will be positive, indicating a positive correlation between the two sets of scores, and if the sum for the xyd column is negative, the correlation coefficient will be negative, indicating a negative correlation between the two sets of scores.

The formula for computing a correlation coefficient using the figures from the example, followed by the actual computation, is given in sequential steps below the figures. A table of squares and square roots might be helpful, particularly if a calculator is not being used.

	X	Y	xd	yd	xyd	xd2	yd2
1.	3	3	0.0	—0.1	0.0	0.0	.01
2.	3	4	0.0	+0.9	0.0	0.0	.81
3.	4	5	+1.0	+1.9	+1.9	1.0	3.61
4.	4	4	+1.0	+0.9	+0.9	1.0	.81
5.	3	3	0.0	—0.1	0.0	0.0	.01
6.	2	1	—1.0	—2.1	+2.1	1.0	4.41
7.	1	2	—2.0	—1.1	+2.2	4.0	1.21
8.	3	3	0.0	—0.1	0.0	0.0	.01
9.	5	4	+2.0	+0.9	+1.8	4.0	.81
10.	2	2	—1.0	—1.11	+1.1	1.0	1.21
	M=3.0	M=3.1	$\sum$0.0	$\sum$0.0	$\sum$+10.0	$\sum$12.0	$\sum$12.9

$$r = \frac{\Sigma xyd}{\sqrt{(\Sigma xd^2)(\Sigma yd^2)}} = \frac{+10.0}{\sqrt{(12.0)(12.9)}} = \frac{+10.0}{\sqrt{154.8}} = \frac{+10.0}{12.4} = +.81$$

RELIABILITY

Correlation may be used for deriving various types of reliability. The three most common types of reliability coefficients are those that are associated with the coefficients of stability, equivalence, and internal consistency. A coefficient of stability, popularly referred to as test-retest reliability, describes the relation between two sets of scores from the same test administered to the same students under the same conditions from three to ten days apart. A coefficient of equivalence, popularly referred to as parallel-forms reliability, describes the relation between two sets of scores from different tests that measure the same factor administered to the same students under the same conditions from three to ten days apart. A coefficient of internal consistency, popularly referred to as split-halves or odds-evens reliability, describes the relation between two sets of scores from the same test, the test having been divided after it was administered and then scored in two parts as if there were two tests in one. In the last case, the test is usually divided into two "equal" parts on the basis of one or more of the following considerations: the number of questions; the content of the questions; the type of learning, either discrimination or inference, associated with the questions; the difficulty of the questions; and the reliability and validity of the questions. The test should not be arbitrarily split into halves or divided in terms of odd-numbered and even-numbered questions if the most realistic internal consistency is to be determined. Some test theorists recommend that an alpha coefficient, which is a theoretical average of all internal consistency coefficients that would be found if a test were split into all possible halves, be used, rather than a coefficient of internal consistency, to determine the reliability of a test.

When the test is divided into halves for scoring purposes, the coefficient of internal consistency yields a reliability estimate for a test half the length of the actual test. The more questions in a test, however, the more reliable the test is likely to be. To solve the problem and thus to obtain an appropriate estimate of the reliability of the actual full-length test, a Spearman-Brown prophecy formula is used. For example, if the correlation coefficient for the half-length test is +.60, using the formula, the corrected-for-length correlation coefficient as it relates to the actual full-length test is predicted to be +.75. That is determined by dividing two times the reliability of the half-length test by one plus the reliability of the half-length test, as shown in the formula below. (If the correlation coefficient has neither a plus nor a minus sign, it is assumed to be positive.) An adaptation of the Spearman-Brown prophecy formula may also be used for estimating the reliability of a test more than twice as long or for a test shorter than half-length.

$$\text{S-B Prophecy Formula } = \frac{2(r)}{1 + r} = \frac{2(.60)}{1 + .60} = \frac{1.20}{1.60} = .75$$

Because of the amount of time it takes to administer the same test twice or to administer two different tests, the coefficient of internal consistency is most widely used to derive test reliability in that only one test administration is necessary. As I will explain presently, when appropriate test statistics are available, a Kuder-Richardson formula may also be used to estimate the reliability of a test that is administered only once. Each type of reliability coefficient should be interpreted in accordance with what it does and does not take into account. Of the three types of reliabilities that might be reported for a given test, internal consistency usually yields the highest coefficient and equivalency the lowest, with the coefficient of stability falling somewhere between the two. Although the differences are usually not great, the coefficient of internal consistency will be highest, because it does not take into account changes in students' physical and psychological well-being from day to day, as do the coefficients of stability and equivalence. The coefficient of equivalence will be lowest, because in addition to the normal physical and psychological changes that occur in students from day to day, it, like the coefficient of internal consistency, takes into account the effect of different questions that pertain to the same subject matter. The coefficient of stability is affected only by the same kinds of changes in students' physical well-being or psychological outlook that affect the coefficient of equivalence. Students' physical and psychological changes from day to day can have a more profound affect on test scores than can differences associated with varied questions that pertain to the same subject matter.

VALIDITY

Objective validity

Correlation may also be used for determining various types of objective validity for a test. Concurrent validity, otherwise known as criterion-related validity, is the most popular; longitudinal predictive validity and diagnostic validity are the two most important types because they bear on practical needs; and congruent validity is least important. All are objective and experimentally derived, and all are usually described in terms of correlation coefficients. In general, published tests are validated objectively.

Concurrent validity describes the relation between scores on a test and a criterion (a validity criterion or criterion measure) that the test is designed to measure. For example, a test that requires students to read small samples of music notation is said to demonstrate concurrent validity if students' scores on that test correlate substantially with the teacher's ratings of their ability to read the notation of actual music. The test is administered and the teacher's ratings are collected closely within a short space of time, or, even better, concurrently. Concurrent validity is also called criterion-related validity, because of the relation of the test scores to the criterion. In the example above, the criterion is the reading of actual music notation.

Concurrent validity can be direct, as I have just described, or indirect, direct validity being, of course, the more important of the two. For example, it would be reasonable to expect that results on a music aptitude test would not show a substantial relation with results on a test of general intelligence. When students who receive high scores on one test do not receive high scores on the other, or when students who receive low scores on one test do not receive low scores on the other, that is an indication that the two tests have little in common. That the correlation between them is close to zero offers indirect evidence that the music aptitude test and the general intelligence test are not measuring the same traits, and that they are measuring what they are designed to measure. It is because indirect concurrent validity and criterion-related validity have opposite meanings that the term *criterion-related validity* often causes confusion when used in place of the term *concurrent validity*.

Congruent validity, a variation of concurrent validity, describes, for example, the relation between scores on a newly developed test and scores on an established test of the same type that has already been shown to be valid. When a substantial correlation is found between scores on the two tests, that leads the author of the new test to claim that the new test is also valid.

Longitudinal predictive validity resembles concurrent validity but differs in one very important way. For example, in concurrent validity, music aptitude test scores and criterion data are obtained within a short time span, but in longitudinal predictive validity, the music aptitude test is administered before instruction takes place and the criterion data are gathered later, in most cases years after instruction began. If there is a high positive correlation between pre-training aptitude test scores and post-training achievement criterion data, the test is said to have longitudinal predictive validity, because music aptitude test scores will have shown themselves to be good indicators of the level of students' future music achievement. Although concurrent validity might, in some cases, be acceptable for the validation of an achievement test, it is rarely acceptable for the validation of an aptitude test, because an aptitude test is designed to measure the potential to achieve, not to measure current achievement.

Unfortunately, some test authors substitute concurrent validity for longitudinal predictive validity when they are attempting to validate an aptitude test, because confirmation of longitudinal predictive validity is more expensive in time and money than is concurrent validity. Concurrent validity is a poor substitute for longitudinal predictive validity because when a test is administered at the same time that criterion data are collected, the resultant correlation coefficient cannot be interpreted to explain causation. When test authors assume that the reason students demonstrate high achievement is because they have high aptitude, these authors are assuming causation from relation. It is just as likely, however, that because students have high achievement, they score high on the music aptitude test. In either case the research may be meaningless, because both the test and the criterion data have been validated as either measures of aptitude or of achievement. When an aptitude test is administered before instruction begins and achievement data are collected only after instruction has been completed, as when conducting an investigation of the longitudinal predictive validity of a test, causation may be inferred from the relation between aptitude test scores and the achievement criteria. Only in a study of that type would it be reasonable to conclude that aptitude caused achievement. Obviously, it would be absurd to claim that achievement, which had not yet taken place, is responsible for students' high and low scores on an aptitude test.

Diagnostic validity is indicative of the relation between subtest scores and criteria that each subtest is designed to measure. For example, for a subtest to have diagnostic validity, scores on a tonal subtest should correlate highly with tonal criteria and lower with rhythm criteria. Similarly, scores on a rhythm subtest should correlate highly with rhythm criteria and lower with tonal criteria. The more specific the content of the subtest, the greater its diagnostic value should be. Depending upon the type of test, aptitude or achievement, and thus the intended use of test results, diagnostic validity may be established either longitudinally or concurrently.

Subjective validity

Subjective validity is very important in teacher-made tests and often in published tests as well. Of the three types of subjective validity—content, construct, and process—content validity seems to be most important to teachers and more so in curriculum-based achievement tests than in aptitude tests.

Whether or not objective validity has been demonstrated for a teacher-made achievement test or a published achievement test, content validity (often called face validity) is of primary importance, because in order for an achievement test to have content validity, the test questions must reflect the types of learning skills, both discrimination and inference, called for in a curriculum. Unless one or more teachers subjectively decide that questions in an achievement test reflect the subject matter associated with the sequential and comprehensive objectives in the curriculum, the test cannot be considered to possess content validity. If in the subjective opinion of teachers an achievement test is lacking in content validity, even the most impressive objective validity becomes irrelevant. Published achievement tests are usually said to have poorer content validity than teacher-made achievement tests, because a teacher-made achievement test is expressly written with the specific types of learning and the sequential and comprehensive objectives of a given curriculum in mind. A published achievement test, through necessity, is more comprehensive and thus not restricted to specific content or types of learning.

Unless an achievement test has content validity, it cannot provide pertinent information for the teacher. It cannot serve adequately as an objective aid for improving instruction and for teaching to students' individual differences. Without content validity, results from an achievement test will not indicate whether students have achieved a sequential objective in a curriculum at a level that will permit the next sequential objective to be undertaken with confidence, or whether previous sequential objectives should be reconsidered.

Construct validity, which is closely related to content validity, is a type of subjective validity that is more pertinent to aptitude tests than to achievement tests. Whereas content validity bears on information and learning skills included in test questions, construct validity deals primarily with how the questions are asked. For example, teachers must decide whether recorded musical examples that students are to listen to are satisfactorily performed, whether instruments that are used to perform the examples are acceptable, whether hearing only one instrument throughout the test is better than hearing two or more, or whether the absence of a subtest of pitch discrimination and the inclusion of a subtest of tonal memory in the test battery is acceptable.

As you have probably deduced, it is difficult to draw a sharp line between content and construct validity. Nonetheless, unless teachers are in agreement with the psychological constructs of a test as well as with the content of the test questions, they will not trust the scores that the test offers.

A last type of subjective validity is called process validity, and it has to do with the clarity of the test directions, with whether the test directions are recorded or are meant to be read aloud by the teacher or by the students themselves, with the length of the test, with the design of the answer sheet, with whether the answer sheet and the test directions complement each other, with the ease of scoring the test, with the appropriateness of the norms, and with whether the test manual includes suggestions for interpreting the test results. While some test authors pay little attention to process validity, most teachers are very concerned with it. Neither objective validity nor content or construct validity will persuade teachers to have faith in a test that they believe is confusing or inadequate.

Indirect information

When a teacher is in doubt about the subjective validity of a test, even one that the teacher has written, there are ways of obtaining preliminary objective evidence that will help to determine the validity of the test. Such evidence, although it is derived from coefficients of internal consistency, intercorrelations, test means, and score distributions, is not, of course, sufficient in itself for determining the quality of a test.

A test that has a high internal consistency demonstrates that the test questions have much in common with one another in terms of content. Although that finding is good, because it indicates that extraneous factors are not dominating the test, it does not take into account whether the specific content that is being measured is what should be measured as indicated by the goals of the test as they are stated by the title.

Intercorrelation coefficients, which are computed as correlation coefficients, should more correctly be called intracorrelation coefficients, because they are indexes of the relations among pairs of subtests in the same test battery. A relatively low intercorrelation coefficient suggests that the two subtests under consideration are measuring different content, as their test titles would seem to suggest. A relatively high intercorrelation coefficient suggests that both subtests are associated with the same content, even though they may have different titles. In that case, it would seem that one, if not both, of the subtests lacks validity.

An intercorrelation coefficient must be interpreted in conjunction with the reliability coefficients of the tests in question. It is important to note that an intercorrelation coefficient will be low if the reliability of one or both of the subtests for which it is computed is low, and so a low intercorrelation coefficient should not automatically be looked upon as preferable. Theoretically, when score distributions are normal, an intercorrelation coefficient cannot be higher, though it is usually much lower, than the square root of the product of the reliabilities of the two subtests. For example, if the reliability of one subtest is .80 and the other is .70, the product (one coefficient multiplied by the other) is .56, the square root of .56 is .75, and so the intercorrelation between the two tests is limited to a coefficient of .75. The theory is based on the same assumptions that are used for estimating the theoretical limit of the validity of a test in terms of its reliability, so that if, for example, a subtest has a reliability of .64, its validity is limited to a coefficient of .80. In general, an intercorrelation coefficient for two subtests, though lower than the reliability of either subtest, is generally found to be higher than the validity coefficient of either subtest.

Should a substantial number of students find a test too easy or too difficult, that is, should most scores fall above or below what in the teacher's opinion ought to be an average score (the mean) for the test, this would indicate that the test probably lacks validity for measuring what the test author intended it to measure. This does not necessarily suggest, however, that it would not be found to be valid for another group of students. If, on the other hand, approximately two-thirds of the students score near a theoretical mean and one-sixth score above and one-sixth score below that point, there is reason to believe that the test has validity.

A score distribution can reveal a great deal about the quality of a test. For example, consider a test that includes 60 questions. Suppose the highest score were 45. That would indicate that even the best students in the class could not answer 25 percent of the questions, presumably the most difficult questions in the test, and that as a result, because the test does not discriminate between superior and above-average students, the content validity of the test should be questioned. Suppose the lowest score were 30. That would indicate that 50 percent of the questions in the test are so easy that they were not challenging even to the poorest students. Thus, there is no way to discriminate between below-average students and poor students. Given those data, the validity of the test would again be suspect. In addition, a test with such a narrow score distribution would practically preclude the possibility of using the test results for adapting instruction to students' individual differences.

The standard error of measurement (SE of M) is of special importance for both music achievement and music aptitude tests. It should be reported in a test manual, because it indicates the extent to which a student's score may be expected to fluctuate on a test. That the magnitude of all reliability coefficients is less than perfect demonstrates that there is error of measurement associated with any test score, be it derived from a teacher-made test or a published test. In a sense, the standard error of measurement relates to the reliability of a single score on a test, not to the entire test itself, but by using the standard error of measurement, a teacher can then determine the range within which a student's "true" score may be found. For example, assume that a test has a reliability of .91 and a standard deviation of 10. According to the formula below, the standard error of measurement would be 3.0, because that is the number derived from multiplying the standard deviation for the test by the square root of the remainder of 1 minus the reliability of the test. Thus, in this case, there is about one chance in three that a student's true score may differ from his or her obtained score by as much as 3.0 points, which is equal to one standard error of measurement, and there is about one chance in twenty that a student's true score may differ from his or her obtained score by as much as 6.0 points, which is equal to two standard errors of measurement.

$$SE \text{ of } M = SD \sqrt{1-r} = \sqrt[10]{1-.91} = \sqrt[10]{.09} = 10(.3) = 3.0$$

Another statistic is helpful in idiographically comparing a student's music aptitudes with one another, aspects of a student's music achievement with one another, and a student's music aptitude with his or her music achievement, and this is the standard error of a difference (SE of D). It is particularly useful in adapting instruction to students' individual musical differences. For example, the standard error of a difference aids a teacher in determining whether a student's scores on two subtests that represent different dimensions of music aptitude are actually different, whether a student's scores on two subtests that represent different dimensions of music achievement are actually different, and whether a student's scores on a music aptitude test when compared to his or her scores on a music achievement test are actually different.

Only under certain conditions, however, can the standard error of a difference be used. First, the scores from both tests being examined must be based on the same type of standard score scale, and second, the standard score scales must be derived from the test results of the same group of students or from highly similar groups of students. Some teacher-made music achievement tests may meet those conditions, as do some published music aptitude tests and music achievement tests, and whether specific published tests meet those conditions may be determined from the test manuals. Published test batteries, both music aptitude and music achievement, that yield standard scores for every subtest are particularly suited for comparing a student's standing in separate but corresponding dimensions of music aptitude and music achievement, because the higher the reliability coefficients and the lower the intercorrelation coefficients for the two subtest scores, total test scores, or composite scores, the greater the reliability of the standard error of a difference associated with the two tests.

The standard error of a difference is determined by computing the square root of the sum of the squared standard error of measurement of one test and the squared standard error of measurement of the other, as shown in the formula and computation below. A difference between a student's score on two subtests or tests may be considered to be a real difference if it is of the same or greater magnitude than the standard error of a difference. Teachers may prefer to consider an observed difference as representative of a real difference only when it is at least the magnitude of two standard errors of a difference. A real difference between two subtest or test scores would, as in the example below, need to be 5.0 or 10.0 points, depending on the teacher's preference.

$$\text{SE of D} = \sqrt{\text{SE of M}^2 + \text{SE of M}^2} = \sqrt{4^2 + 3^2} = \sqrt{16 + 9} = \sqrt{25} = 5.0$$

INDEX